Gooseberry Patch

A Country Store In Your Mailbox℠

For Bees & Me

A bouquet of garden-fresh recipes,
sunny memories, helpful hints, simple
pleasures, herbal beauty potions,
backyard entertaining, and
easy-to-make gifts!

Look for Vickie's & JoAnn's
favorite recipes and hints
sprinkled throughout this book

A Country Store In Your Mailbox℠

Gooseberry Patch
149 Johnson Drive
Department Book
Delaware, OH 43015

1-800-85-GOOSE
1-800-854-6673

Copyright 1995, Gooseberry Patch
0-9632978-5-6
Third Printing, August 1997

How To Subscribe

Would you like to receive
"A Country Store in Your Mailbox"℠?
For a 2-year subscription to our
Gooseberry Patch catalog
simply send $3.00 to:
Gooseberry Patch
149 Johnson Drive, Dept. Book
Delaware, OH 43015

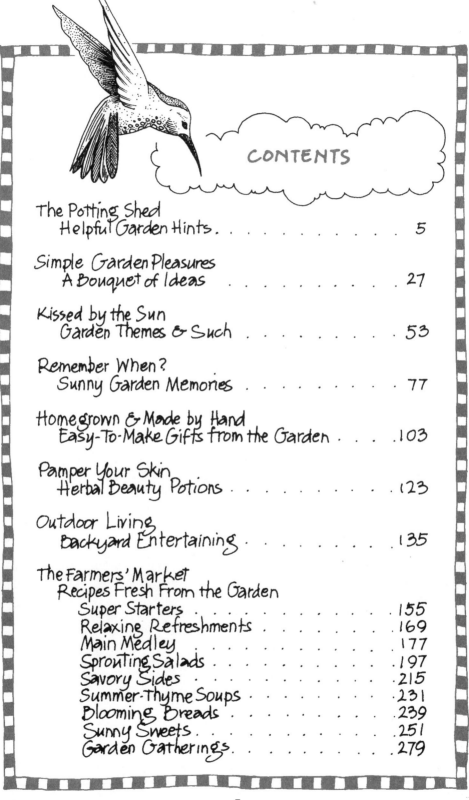

CONTENTS

❧ DEDICATION ❧

To green (and not-so-green) thumbs,
Wishing you a garden filled
with happiness!

❧ APPRECIATION ❧

A very special "Thanks" to everyone
who helped plant the seeds for this book.
From a tiny sprout it's been a joy to
watch grow and grow and grow!

Plant your herb and vegetable garden as close to your back door as possible. Not only will your garden be more convenient to use, but when you see it easily, you are more likely to do the weeding, pruning and harvesting needed to keep it looking good and to notice any insect problems early.

Think about locating your children's wading pool where the draining water will automatically water your vegetables or flowers. You may not have to water your garden at all with strategic pool placement and lots of mulch!

To keep flowers and herbs fresh longer, always cut with a knife instead of scissors; scissors crush the stems and they cannot absorb as much water.

I have a dear friend who does a lot of home canning from her vegetable garden every year. In the heat of summer she does her canning outside near the garden on their camp stove. The kitchen stays cool and the vegetables can't get much fresher from the garden.

At the end of summer, instead of bringing pots of plants inside to preserve the sunshine for winter, walk through the garden picking the best stems of each plant instead. Root the stems in water or fresh potting soil inside to keep the plants from getting leggy and tired looking.

Did you know green peppers freeze beautifully without blanching? When the garden is full of peppers and you can't eat another bite, remove the seeds and chop the extra peppers into medium-size chunks. Slip into a freezer container and they're ready for soups, stews or chili. Take only what you need to use and pop into any dish calling for cooked green pepper. Yum!

Mel Wolk

For those who love to use bittersweet in the fall, here's a little hint. If you cut it before it pops open (while the berries are still yellow), it will stay bright orange for at least a year. Also, if you cut the vines and wind them in wreath form, leaving the leaves on, they make a wonderful wreath. I made one a year ago and hung it in my Barn Bed & Breakfast, and its leaves are still green and the bittersweet berries bright orange. Someone even asked me if it was real!

Sandy Kolb

No need to fill the entire barrel with costly (and heavy) potting soil. After drilling holes in the bottom, fill 1/2 to 1/3 with packing peanuts, cover with landscape cloth and then fill with potting soil and plant your annuals.

Candy Hannigan

In areas with mild winters, hit the trunks of fruit trees with a broomstick to rise the sap. Watch out...you may have a bumper crop of fruit in the spring!

Laurinda & Courtney Dawson

When cutting fresh flowers, place them immediately into a bucket of water you've carried with you. They'll stay fresh longer.

Store gladiolus bulbs in old pantyhose over the winter. Hang them up so air circulates around them.

Jennie Wiseman

In recipes calling for fresh flowers, substitute half the amount if using dried. To dry flowers, gather early in the day, before the sun shines on them. Hang by the stems in a warm, dark area with good air circulation. Individual flowers can be dried differently. Place the clean flowers in a single layer on fine mesh. Let them dry in a warm, dark, dust-free area. Once flowers are dry, store them whole, crumbled or pulverized in airtight glass containers in a cool, dark place.

Tammy Anundson

For sunburn or regular burns, use aloe vera plant or cider vinegar and water. When aloe leaves are broken, they emit a liquid which has remarkable healing qualities.

Plant marigolds in early spring. You don't need a green thumb! They will reward you up until November, they transplant easily and you'll have loads of flowers in many varieties.

To have berries on your bittersweet vines, plant 2 or 3 vines as they cross-pollinate.

The most important thing about gardening is the soil. You can recognize poor soil if it's caked and forms clods, is difficult to cultivate, has lots of weeds, or your plants seem to be susceptible to diseases. Try adding humus (manure, peat, leaf mold). You'll get a better texture.

Mrs. Travis Baker

Remember to NEVER use any flower for food or garnish unless you are sure it is edible; and NEVER use herbs or flowers that have been sprayed.

Tamara Gruber

My husband stretches a piece of old wire fence along my cucumber row as soon as they begin to bloom. They climb the fence, are easy to pick and never get muddy.

Martha Steele

I like a lot of bird feeders in my garden but using birdseed made such a mess and sprouted weeds, so instead I use sunflower seeds. When the seeds fall as the birds eat, I have sunflowers that grow in the flower beds.
Looks so pretty!

Kim Smeets

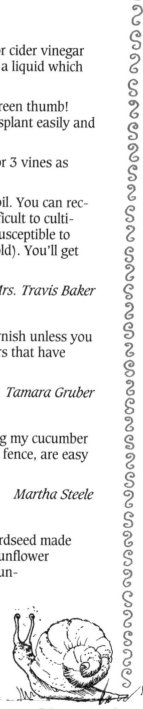

helpful garden hints

Potting Mix

Here's how to make your own potting mix for container gardening:

2 cubic ft. peat moss   1 handful 5-10-10 fertilizer
40 oz. bag perlite   1 handful ground lime
40 oz. bag vermiculite

Mix these ingredients well and make sure mixture is well soaked before adding plants. You will need to water more often when using this "soil," but the results will be well worth the effort.

Katherine Gaughan

Use a child-sized rake for cleaning out underneath shrubs and plants. It works great!

Glenda Lewis

Before you work in your garden, push your fingernails into a bar of soap. After gardening, your nails will clean up quickly with a nail brush.

Nancy Campbell

To control slugs and snail population growth in your vegetable garden, simply spread bran (available at feed stores) around the base of the plants. A natural way to protect your veggies!

Deborah Murray

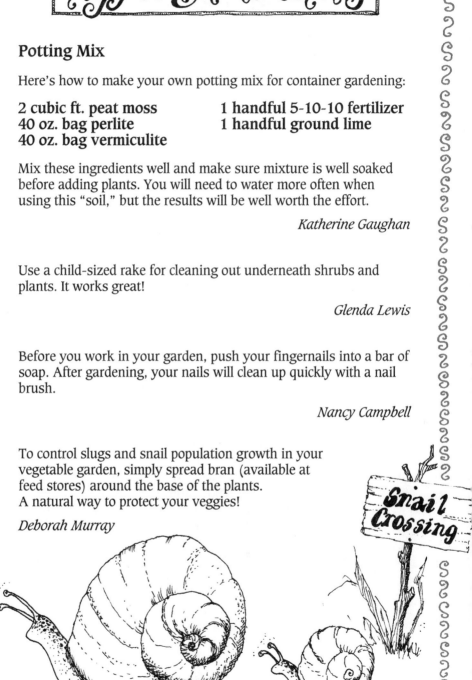

When purchasing plants, resist the temptation to buy the larger ones in full bloom. These plants have already reached their peak. Instead pick the youngest plants, they will have a much longer flowering season than the plants already in full bloom. At least once a week, remove dead and faded blooms from your plants and they will continue to produce more blooms. Your garden also looks neater when you "deadhead."

As a resident of drought-ridden California, I take every measure to conserve water. In the kitchen and bathtub I save the water from the running faucet when waiting for hot water. I keep a plastic bucket nearby and use the "saved" water in my garden. You will be surprised at how much water you collect.

Nancie Gensler

Rid your house of pests naturally this summer by hanging bouquets of dried tomato leaves in all your rooms. Mosquitoes, flies and spiders will exit quickly.

Use a bay leaf in your flour canister to keep out the bugs all year!

Jan Sofranko

To attract butterflies, find out which ones live in your part of the country and the types of plants they like to eat. My pot of parsley on the front steps played host to black swallowtail butterflies. We watched as the tiny (1/4" long) critter grew into a 2" long caterpillar, formed a chrysalis and finally emerged as a beautiful butterfly two weeks later. If possible, take pictures of the whole process to help children remember this exciting nature lesson.

Beverly Botten

Make small brush piles in your yard for the birds and small creatures. Don't worry if this isn't neat looking. All your friends will envy you as towhees, Harris' sparrows and Fox sparrows will be visiting your yard.

Jo Ann Bodkin

A favorite of both butterflies and hummingbirds is the Mexican sunflower. It blooms in August with a bright orange and red color. They grow to about 3 to 4 feet tall. The stems feel like velvet and the flowers are about 1 to 2 inches wide. They are an annual, but you can collect the seeds for use the next year.

Barb Agne
Gooseberry Patch

To enjoy fresh blooms during winter months, try forcing branches. Gather branches and cut the ends on a slant. Immediately place them in tepid water. Keep the water clean and high, and place the vases in a cool location (about 60 degrees). As a rule, branches that bear small flowers may be cut early, but those bearing larger blooms should not be cut until the buds are plump and well developed. It may take from a week to a month for the branches to blossom, but it's well worth it.

When forcing hyacinths, add a little charcoal to the water to sweeten it and keep it from smelling "swampy."

Ildiko Mulligan

Crush freshly dried catnip and sew inside tiny pouches for your favorite kitty!

When pests strike, mix 1 tablespoon of dishwashing detergent with 1 cup of cooking oil. Then mix 1 to 1 1/2 teaspoons of the detergent/oil mixture with each cup of water. The detergent causes the oil to emulsify in the water. It can be sprayed on plants every 10 days with a pump sprayer. For larger volume use 3 tablespoons of concentrated detergent/oil solution to 1 quart of water; or 12 tablespoons (approximately 1/3 cup) of detergent/oil solution to 1 gallon of water. Add one tablespoon baking soda per gallon to maintain alkaline pH. Besides aphids and whiteflies, the mixture works against spider mites and beet army worms (don't they sound dreadful?). It has been used successfully on eggplant, carrots, lettuce, celery, watermelon, peppers and cucumbers. It tends to burn the leaves of squash, cauliflower and red cabbage.

From the U.S. Department of Agriculture
Christel Zuber Fishburn

When cutting daylilies for bouquets, be sure to remove the individual pollen-covered stamens. The pollen can stain your lace doilies and linens.

Glenda Nations

A good way to save seeds for next year's planting is to leave them in the hot sun for several days to dry thoroughly. Then put in a plastic bag, seal tightly and slip in freezer until next spring. This does away with insects and disease.

When planting a tree or shrub, remember this tip on fertilizing. Put an ounce of fertilizer in a plastic bag, punch holes in the bag, then bury it in a hole 6 to 12 inches from a shrub and six inches deep. It will keep fertilizing for several seasons.

I've heard that ferns will grow beautifully if you punch two or three holes in the soil and pour 1/2 teaspoon of castor oil in each hole.

Mary Dechamplain

helpful garden hints

Cut off the bottom of a large plastic trash can. Fill with garden and yard clippings, kitchen peels and leftovers; keep covered. After a period of time, empty from the bottom and work into the soil as fertilizer.

Barbara Rose McCaffrey

If you select a container that may possibly need to be moved, lighten the load with a simple trick. If the planter is large and filling it completely with soil would cause the container to be too heavy, fill the container half full with used aluminum soda pop cans, or leftover styrofoam packing "peanuts." The top half of the container should be filled with potting soil. Happy planting!

Jeannine English

Buy your sunflower seeds early. There are so many varieties and they sell out fast!

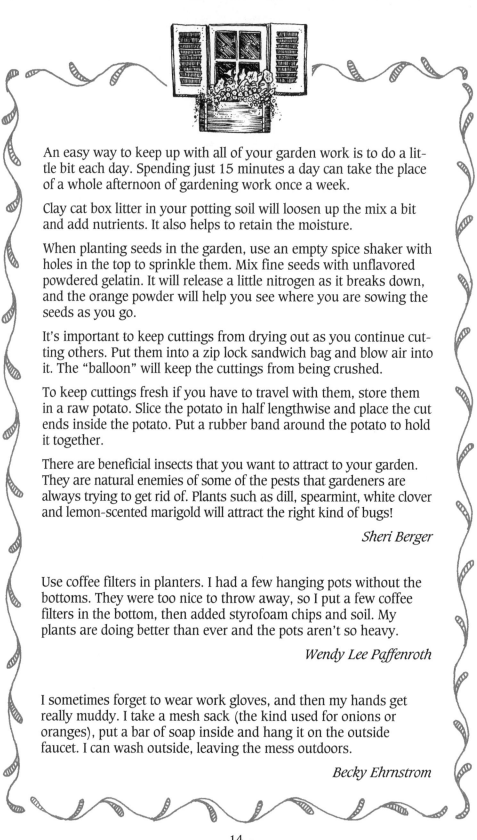

An easy way to keep up with all of your garden work is to do a little bit each day. Spending just 15 minutes a day can take the place of a whole afternoon of gardening work once a week.

Clay cat box litter in your potting soil will loosen up the mix a bit and add nutrients. It also helps to retain the moisture.

When planting seeds in the garden, use an empty spice shaker with holes in the top to sprinkle them. Mix fine seeds with unflavored powdered gelatin. It will release a little nitrogen as it breaks down, and the orange powder will help you see where you are sowing the seeds as you go.

It's important to keep cuttings from drying out as you continue cutting others. Put them into a zip lock sandwich bag and blow air into it. The "balloon" will keep the cuttings from being crushed.

To keep cuttings fresh if you have to travel with them, store them in a raw potato. Slice the potato in half lengthwise and place the cut ends inside the potato. Put a rubber band around the potato to hold it together.

There are beneficial insects that you want to attract to your garden. They are natural enemies of some of the pests that gardeners are always trying to get rid of. Plants such as dill, spearmint, white clover and lemon-scented marigold will attract the right kind of bugs!

Sheri Berger

Use coffee filters in planters. I had a few hanging pots without the bottoms. They were too nice to throw away, so I put a few coffee filters in the bottom, then added styrofoam chips and soil. My plants are doing better than ever and the pots aren't so heavy.

Wendy Lee Paffenroth

I sometimes forget to wear work gloves, and then my hands get really muddy. I take a mesh sack (the kind used for onions or oranges), put a bar of soap inside and hang it on the outside faucet. I can wash outside, leaving the mess outdoors.

Becky Ehrnstrom

helpful garden hints

To remove earwigs from an area, take several sections of your newspaper and roll them up, securing tightly with rubber bands. Lay roll on its side in the targeted area overnight. The next morning, simply pick up the newspaper "trap" and discard. Earwigs like tight, dark areas to hide, and during the night they will have crawled into the newspaper "trap" for shelter.

Robin Kato

To grow a new rose bush, cut a stem with a full bloom rose on it. Stick the stem into the ground. Leave a few of the leaves at the top, with the bloom. Water the ground thoroughly and put a clear glass jar over it and anchor to the ground. Keep soil watered around jar every day until frost. Don't remove glass jar until next spring. You will then have a new rose bush growing.

Kathryn Pedrazzoli

May is a great month to paint outdoor furniture.

To give your plants an "extra" boost, add 1 teaspoon of epsom salt and 1 teaspoon of fish emulsion plant fertilizer to your brand of plant fertilizer, then stand back and watch the results!

Cindy Hull

The worst enemies of successful seed storage are humidity and heat. Most varieties will keep until the next season. Buy your parsley, lettuce and onions fresh each year. Zip lock freezer bags or sealed jars are ideal for storing. Keep your seeds in your coolest room or the refrigerator.

Peggy Gerch

Instead of using boards or bark for pathways in your garden, use sharp gravel. It deters slugs and snails...it hurts their little "feet!"

For the less blood thirsty slugbusters among us, take a margarine container (or other plastic container with a lid) and cut one inch "doors" around the rim. Put the lid upside down on the ground in a likely slug or snail area, and put a pinch of yeast, a bit of lettuce and commercial slug and snail bait in the center. Push the container securely back onto the lid, so the "doors" are level with the soil. You might put a rock on top to keep the wind from blowing the trap away. Rebait every month or so, unless your containers are full (ugh!), or just throw them away without opening and make new traps.

Ever have trouble figuring out what fertilizer to use? Those three numbers on the front of the bag refer to nitrogen, phosphorus and potassium, and they are always in that order. Generally speaking, nitrogen is thought to improve leaf development, phosphorus is for flower and seed growth and potassium promotes healthy root growth and allows the other two nutrients to work. So if your flowers aren't blooming very well, try a fertilizer with a high middle number.

If you want to start seeds indoors, set your flats on a table and hang lights on "S" hooks with light chains from the ceiling in a warm basement or other room. The lights must be no more than 3 to 6 inches from the top of the flat (or the plants, when they start growing), so be sure to make your light set-up adjustable. Plain old

florescent shop lights work best for starting seeds, full spectrum or "grow lights" are just for growing blooming plants indoors, and are very expensive.

Your neighbors will think you are crazy, but those blinking Christmas tree lights will deter porcupines, deer and other critters. String them around in trees or berry bushes.

Plant bulbs about three times their diameter deep, measuring from the "shoulder" (where the bulb starts to flare out) of the bulb. If your soil is wet, dig down a couple of inches deeper and put about an inch of builder's sand (coarse, sharp sand available at sand and gravel companies) at the bottom of the hole. Add the recommended amount of bulb food and/or bone meal, cover with an inch of dirt to keep the fertilizer from damaging the bulb, then plant the bulb...pointed end up. If you're not sure which end of the bulb should be up, plant it on its side.

When planting your flowers, always try to plant in groups of odd numbers, usually 3 or 5. Most plants in the wild naturally grow in odd numbers. Try to avoid planting flowers in a row...they look stilted except in vegetable or very formal gardens.

If you have problems with cats in your garden beds, sprinkle ground citrus peels and cayenne pepper on the soil.

Spring-flowering bulbs (tulips, narcissus, crocus, etc.) should be planted in the fall about a month before your first frost. Choose your bulbs the way you would an onion at the grocery...they should be firm, with no bruised spots. Larger bulbs with more "noses" will produce more and larger flowers. Try to get bulbs that have been stored in a cool area during sale.

Cathy Brown

Herbal Carpet Freshener

Combine 1 cup baking soda, 1 cup corn starch and 30 drops of your favorite essential oil. Allow to dry. Shake freshener onto rugs, allow to sit for 30 minutes and then vacuum. For flea problems: add 30 drops of oil of rosemary and/or oil of pennyroyal, and brush into carpet. Caution: test on a small area of your carpet first!

Jacqueline Lash Idler

Used coffee grounds sprinkled around the garden will keep the snails away and green bell pepper strips scattered around the garden and yard will keep the ants away.

Kimberley Bercaw

When I cut fresh flowers from my garden, instead of those fancy expensive flower preservers, I use a homemade one that contains three items found in every home. I fill my vase with water (8 oz.), add approximately 1/2 teaspoon of regular household bleach and a teaspoon of sugar (sugar cubes work great). My flowers tend to last 2 to 3 weeks this way, sometimes even longer. Use double bleach if you keep your vase of flowers in direct sunlight.

Robin Insco

With increasing awareness of protecting the environment, many gardeners are turning to the benefits of composting. Most know the basics...no fats, grease, animal products, just plant-type material; keep compost evenly moist (not drenched), aerated, and turn it frequently. Composting can be a lengthy process, but a simple step can speed up the process. Simply put proper composting material in blender or food processor and grind for a few seconds. Breaking the material into much smaller particles will greatly speed up the composting process. Only well composted material should be used in the garden, because material that still needs to decompose will take energy out of the soil for the composting process, and thus rob plants of nutrients.

Therese Gribbins

helpful garden hints

When trimming shrubs, lay a plastic tarp under the bushes to catch the clippings. Upon completion, just roll up the tarp and funnel the trimmings into the yard waste can. This procedure saves clean up time and back bending pick-up work. An added bonus is that the decorative bark doesn't get thrown away with the clippings.

Carol Suehiro

I have found two ways to plant mint so that it does not take over my entire herb garden. For rather large areas of mint I use black plastic landscape edging. I follow the instructions for placing this in the ground, except that I dig deep enough to put it all the way into the ground. This way I can cover it with soil and mulch and it does not have to show at all. For containing mint in small spaces, I cut the bottom out of a thin plastic pot, place the mint in the pot and bury the whole pot in the ground.

Donna Crawford

A pot of basil, set on the back porch, keeps flies away from the screen door.

Mary Garramone

Plant peppers between tomato plants and you won't have tomato worms or blight.

Delores Berg

To grow really big pumpkins, pinch off all but one or two healthy pumpkins. Pumpkins, as well as other plants, can be fed and encouraged to grow larger with "manure tea." To make manure tea, fill a 5-gallon pail one-fourth full with manure. Fill the pail to the top with water. Stir the mixture every couple of days, and let it "brew" for about 2 weeks.

Tori Jones

When transplanting, try using a pizza carton. The cardboard keeps your work area clean and contains the soil.

Water deeply once or twice a week to encourage stronger roots and help sustain the plant in dry periods.

Pick herbs often to promote bushier plants.

Jacqueline Lash Idler

Whiteflies are tiny sucking insects that feed and lay eggs on the undersides of leaves. Hang a yellow cord coated with mineral oil in the infested area. Whiteflies are attracted to yellow, and will get caught in the oil.

Slugs hide during the day, but at night they like to feed on plant leaves. Sink a shallow container, half-full with beer into the ground. Slugs slither in and drown.

Companion planting, or planting certain plants near others, is effective in keeping certain pests away. When planted with tomatoes, mint repels tomato hornworm; with radish, flea beetles; and with cabbage, white cabbage butterfly. Horseradish keeps away potato bugs; garlic and nasturtiums will keep aphids at bay; and marigolds repel tomato hornworm, nematodes and whiteflies.

Mold will grow on plants if they do not have time to dry out properly. Watering in the early morning will help discourage this problem.

Marsha Jones

My husband is a horticulturist and has this tip for increasing the growth and output of your tomato plants. Buy tomato plants that are about 1 foot tall or grow them to this height in a seed pot. When transplanting them in the garden, first dig a hole about the length of the plant, then cut all but the top cluster of leaves from the stem. Place the plant into the hole and bury it to within 2 inches of the top leaves. This will increase your root structure and therefore help each plant to produce more tomatoes.

Laura Hodges

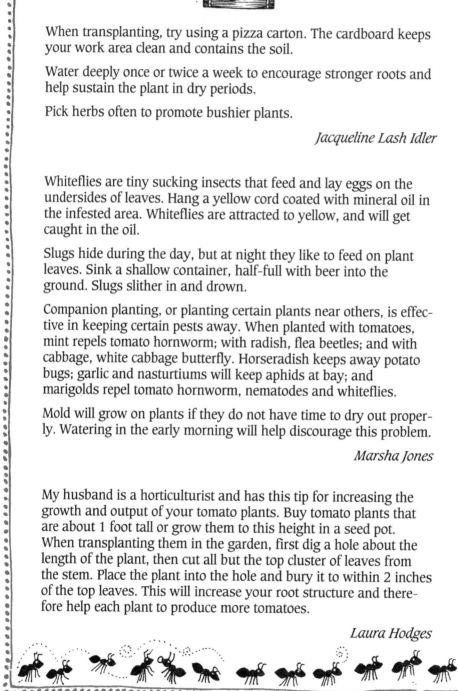

helpful garden hints

A general rule of thumb for cooking vegetables covered or uncovered, is that vegetables that grow underground should be cooked covered; while those that grow above ground should be cooked uncovered. Cook vegetables with a minimum of water.

To prevent discoloration when grating raw potatoes, grate directly into a bowl of ice water.

Add grated raw potato to soup or stew that is too salty. It works wonders!

Many vegetables can be freshened by soaking in cold water. To crisp celery, carrots or lettuce, wrap in a damp towel or place in a plastic bag and refrigerate for an hour.

Apples speed ripening of peaches, pears, tomatoes, and avocados when stored together in a brown bag. Set in a warm, dark place and punch a few holes in the bag for ventilation.

Tap a watermelon with your thumb and middle finger. If you hear a deep, low "plunk" the watermelon is ripe.

Cranberries freeze nicely in a plastic bag. Use in recipes without thawing.

If you have a small amount of honey that has solidified, place the jar in hot water until the honey melts.

Bits of jelly or jam can be melted in a small pan over low heat to make a good sauce for waffles, puddings, or ice cream. This also makes a nice glaze.

Amy Schueddig

Weeding after a rain is the best time, the roots are looser.

Spray your compost pile with a cola to speed the decaying process.

Shelley McHugh

*Pick a bunch of daisies
and give them to
someone you love.*

During the year, save all your citrus peels. Tear into large chunks and dry on paper towels. Sprinkle with orange or tangerine oil and add to your potpourri.

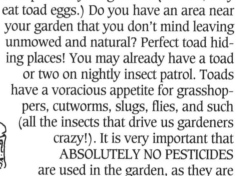

What eats thousands of insects a year and is the best friend an organic gardener can have? Toads, of course! Are you lucky enough to have a pond in your garden? (No fish, they eat toad eggs.) Do you have an area near your garden that you don't mind leaving unmowed and natural? Perfect toad hiding places! You may already have a toad or two on nightly insect patrol. Toads have a voracious appetite for grasshoppers, cutworms, slugs, flies, and such (all the insects that drive us gardeners crazy!). It is very important that ABSOLUTELY NO PESTICIDES are used in the garden, as they are easily absorbed through the toad's skin. There are many books available on amphibians and backyard ponds. It is well worth the effort to attract and keep these insect eating machines.

A shallow birdbath kept clean and filled with fresh water everyday is an essential part of your "bird garden." Dripping or trickly water has a special appeal and will attract species you ordinarily might not see.

Linda Lee

To ripen your fruit that is still firm (plums, peaches, pears, apricots, nectarines), place in a paper bag closed up, or a covered bowl at room temperature. In a few days they will be ripe and juicy. Once ripe, place in refrigerator.

Janice Ertola

When planting green pepper plants in your garden, drop 2 or 3 matches in the hole before you put the green pepper plant in. The sulfur in the matches makes the plants produce more peppers.

Karen Antonides

When staking tomato plants or other vegetable plants, use strips of old nylon stockings/pantyhose to tie the plants to the stake. The nylons will stretch as the plant grows.

When planting small bulbs, such as grape hyacinth, use an apple corer to dig the holes. It is the perfect size for small bulbs.

Instead of throwing your egg shells away, rinse them, crumble them up and put them outside for the birds to eat. The birds love to eat them, and the shells add strength to the eggs that the birds lay.

Carla Huchzermeier

In the spring stick some lint from your dryer in a tree for the nests of birds. Also if you have bathed your dog and brushed out its winter coat, the birds will use this fluffy dog hair to line their nests. Just make sure it's clean dog hair.

Pat Akers

Flowers can be a natural pest control at the same time they make your garden more beautiful and a pleasure to work in. For example, daisies, black-eyed Susans and yarrow attract beneficial insects to their pollen and nectar. Then these good insects stick around to feast on aphids, caterpillar eggs and spider mites.

Sandy Bessingpas

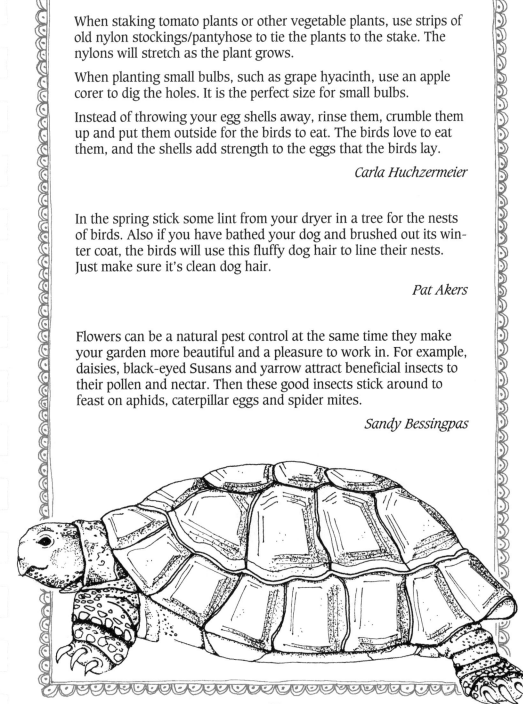

You can dry herbs on drying racks made by stapling mesh screens to a wood frame, or use oven racks. Always line the metal with cheesecloth, just as you would if using a food dehydrator.

A quick once-over with a stiff bristle brush or aluminum foil will remove caked-on soil from garden tools. You may wish to scrape the tool with a putty knife before brushing.

On rainy days be sure to dry metal tools with a piece of old towel before storing.

A 5-gallon bucket filled with oily sand is excellent to store shovels, pitch forks, hoes and spades. Otherwise, coat item with a thin film of oil, using an old rag, before putting away.

Keep a stone or file handy to maintain a relatively sharp blade on shovels, forks, and hoes.

Annually put a few drops of machine oil on the bolts and springs of tools before using.

Theresa Burkeland

Use spring-type clothespins to train vines and climbing plants.

Marion Pfeifer

I have enjoyed developing a perennial bed over the years and have found it helpful to draw a "floor plan" of where everything has been planted. With this plan sheet I include the color and type of perennial that I have planted. Even when markers are placed by the plant, they tend to get lost or destroyed; so each year when plants begin to sprout I know which ones are flowers and which are not. I have mistakenly pulled out sprouting plants without knowing what they were. This plan makes for easy identification in future years. Also, if something doesn't come up the following year, I know what to replace.

To make gardening easier, I keep everything in a long, large basket. Gardening tools, gloves, seeds, markers, and string are all in one handy spot. The basket has a handle and can be carried to the garden with me.

Sandy Wisneski

helpful garden hints

Use lunch-size snack cups from gelatins and puddings for starting seeds. Punch small holes in base of each cup for drainage and line up cups in large flats from a garden center.

Julie Carwile

When I clean out the fireplace, I spread the ashes over my garden and compost pile. Thanks to the ashes, insects don't chew on my garden plants.

A sprinkle of equal parts flour, dry mustard and cayenne pepper on my garden plants discourages hungry chipmunks and rabbits from munching on my vegetables.

To plant tiny seeds such as lettuce and carrots, I start with a can (soup can will work fine) half full of fine, dry soil. I then put in the seeds and shake the can to mix the seeds with the soil. Then, I slowly pour the seed/soil mix along the rows. The seeds won't blow away and they are evenly spaced.

Pat Habiger

To make a natural flea rinse, steep 1 teaspoon of rosemary for each cup of boiling water. Cool, then pour in a spray bottle. During the summer I keep my bottle by the mudroom door to spray my schnauzer before she goes outside.

Mary Murray

Go browsing at your garden store and plan, plan, plan! Before you buy, stop and give some thought to color combinations, height of plants, and planting so your garden will have color all summer long.

Herbal/Spice Mothballs for the Closet

1 oz. coarsely ground cloves   1 oz. cinnamon
1 oz. dried lemon peels   1 oz. dried lavender flowers

Mix above herbs and spices. Fill pretty fabric bags with mixture and place in closets or drawers. A fragrant alternative to mothballs.

Judy Hand

After I dry my flowers, I spray them with hairspray or shaping spray to keep the particles from falling off.

Sherry Hawkes

My daughter had given me a big, beautiful gerber daisy for Mother's Day. To my dismay, within a few weeks it was eaten down to the ground by little gray sow bugs, or cellar bugs as some people call them. I tried relocating it to four different areas with no luck. The roots appeared to be infested with this pest. Not wanting to apply a pesticide, I decided to experiment. I took about 1/2 to 1 teaspoon of my husband's hottest pepper sauce and added it to about 3/4 cup of water. As I applied this mixture to the base of the plant, the little pests actually raced to the top of the soil and moved to cooler territory! I've done this about every other day or so and my plant is big and gorgeous once again.

Candace Faw

Basil, marigolds and borage all help keep your garden pest-free and organic. Borage also has pretty blue and pink flowers which attract bees and aid in the pollination process.

Mary Bellizzi

Paint the handles of your garden tools a bright color like yellow, they are easier to find if misplaced in heavy foliage or tall grass.

Phyllis Peters

Simple Garden Pleasures

A Bouquet of ideas

Not a slight change in the season or a holiday goes by that I do not decorate my fireplace mantel accordingly. It is the first thing you see as you walk in and the results are beautiful! Always, my white lights are left on it. Summertime brings dried hydrangeas, bird nests, old fishing paraphernalia and baskets with a few seashells added in. Autumn includes grapevines, bittersweet, Japanese lanterns and pumpkins. Winter is full of pine boughs, snowmen and candles, candles, candles! Spring arrives with my chalkware bunnies, old birdhouses and a watering can. Let your imagination go wild! Of course there is always room for specific holiday items and treasures made by little hands, that have been saved over the years.

I'm always on the search for old bird nests (especially the small, feathery soft ones) and old birdhouses. I have them all over the house. Not only does this bring a little of the outdoors and nature inside, but you really marvel and appreciate the work and the wonder of nature when you see these close up. As a special Mother's Day gift this year, my two kids gave me a heart-shaped nest, nestled in between 3 branches. They had found it during the winter (when we find all of them) and wrapped it up for a special occasion! Any old birdhouse I see at any sale, I quickly grab! I have replicas of churches, houses, barns and a chicken! They are amazing. I have them in my kitchen, dining and living rooms, in the garden, on my porch and even atop my clothesline pole! They are so homey and unique.

Set a chair out in your garden... just sit, listen, look and smell!

I think that any country garden comes to life when surrounded, even on one side, by a white picket fence with climbing roses and posts topped with birdhouses. Set a tall post on one end of your garden with a purple martin house. It adds just the perfect country touch!

Did you know that if you put several drops of food coloring in your vase before putting in cut Queen Anne's lace, the color will come up through the stem and color the lace? Pink is prettiest!

Grab all the old watering cans you come across. They look beautiful next to the garden, next to the arbor; and even in your kitchen, nestled among your plants.

Deb Damari-Tull

When your garden is in full bloom, take a snapshot. Then, in the fall or spring when it is time to put in the new bulbs or plants, you can refer to the snapshot to see where to add the new plants.

Hanging baskets have a variety of uses! Strawberries can trail over the edge of a hanging basket without letting the berries rot on the ground; birds are discouraged from eating ripe berries; and picking couldn't be easier. How about an herb hanging basket? Plant several types of smaller herbs together in a hanging basket near the kitchen (or above the kitchen window!) and enjoy not just the convenience of a close-at-hand herb garden for cooking, but the relaxing scents of herbs closer to "nose" level. Try hanging an herbal basket in the bathroom, if there is adequate light (most herbs like lots of sun). Don't forget vegetables for hanging baskets. Hang that cherry tomato! Fresh cherry tomatoes in the winter from a hanging basket are such a treat. Grow different varieties of lettuce in a hanging basket...beautiful and tasty. Mix up your vegetables. Lettuce, radish, baby carrots and a small marigold plant makes a fun combination. Use your imagination. Remember that hanging baskets require lots of water, fertilizer and sunshine. A watering wand is most handy for watering hanging gardens.

"Welcome To My Garden" reads the old, red barnwood sign barely visible through the lush growth of yellow trumpet honeysuckle vine that covers the entire trunk and branches of a sycamore tree, that died four springs ago. The tree stands just outside my kitchen window, and when it died I couldn't bear to have it cut down. Instead I decided to find another use for it. Thus it became the lofty perch for a white birdhouse, with a red roof, made by my father. All the dead branches were trimmed off except for five, which became the resting places for my feathered visitors. The ground around the base of the tree was tilled, and a beautiful perennial flower garden was planted, edged with river rock. The once dead tree became the focal point of a colorful flower garden, where honeysuckle vines grace its bare branches; and larkspur, miniature hollyhocks, and creeping phlox abound at its feet.

Martha Haught

To brighten up a narrow kitchen or bathroom windowsill I use old glass baby doll bottles, miniature perfume bottles and old glass dairy creamers that I have found at the flea market and garage sales. I like to put individual pansies in them. Violets and other short stemmed flowers also work well.

Susan Koronowski

I save all my flower and vegetable seed packets, and put them in a little old basket on my Hoosier cabinet for the summer. They are so colorful and pretty (especially my favorites, the morning glory packets). I cannot bear to throw them away and they make such a pretty summertime decoration! I don't buy seeds for their brand names or necessarily performance, but how beautiful the packet is!

Deb Damari-Tull

As a novice to the art of growing herbs, I found that following a long winter I had forgotten where and what had been planted in my garden the previous year. By taking small pieces of broken old slate, painting the name of the herb on it, and spraying it with an acrylic sealer, the situation was remedied, as each piece was placed at the base of the herb. The next spring there was no problem with identification and the slate made a nice addition and appearance to my herb garden.

Kim Stahl

Save any flower garden catalogs you get through the mail, even though you may not be planning to send an order. They are great for future referral, when you do want to plan a flower bed. They usually list the name, color, size, sun/shade requirements and growth habit of plants you may be interested in. These catalogs sometimes also include examples of professionally planned gardens. Many of the plants shown can be found at a large nursery or garden center.

Peg Buckingham

When sending a letter or card, slip in a scented herb such as lavender, peppermint or pineapple-mint. It's a nice touch!

My husband and I made a winding path in our yard, using old broken cement from our garage floor. We busted up big chunks of the floor, then dug out a path. It is in the shape of a long "S." We laid the cement pieces, filled the dirt back in and swept the path. Later we planted thyme and flowers in some of the gaps between the stones. It's gorgeous!

Natalie Morrissette

Make a fairy teapot that is sure to delight every little girl (or the one inside of all us grown up little girls)...a rosehip is the teapot, a thorn for a spout and a small twig handle. An acorn cup and saucer complete the set!

Jeannine English

Nothing smells better than a bouquet of fresh sweet onions, garlic, and sweet basil. When we go to the farmers' market and put these things in the trunk of the car to take home, the ride home is delightful.

Margaret Riley

Pine-filled sachets make lovely mementos of a trip to the mountains!

Put a scented geranium in a pot by your back door. When you brush by it, it will release a delightful scent.

Mix a little corn syrup with loose birdseed, and mold with cookie cutters. Add a string then let dry. Hang from the branches of trees or bushes.

Laurinda & Courtney Dawson

When cutting back your lavender plants, either after harvesting the blossoms or just reshaping the plant, put your cuttings somewhere in your yard (I put mine in my fence line). The pretty raspberry colored house finch that likes to nest in my backyard each year wove his nest mostly out of my discarded lavender branch! Maybe he liked the smell or was smart enough to realize that lavender has anti-insect properties. Whatever the case, I enjoyed seeing one of my favorite herbs used in such an industrious way.

After harvesting a bumper crop of herb bunches (several thyme varieties, basil, oregano and numerous herb blossoms), I was at a loss as to where to dry them in my house. Since I have a nice window to the north in my dining room, I decided to remove the fabric valance and hang the rubber-banded bunches with re-bent paper clips on the small round rod. I had so many compliments on my "new window treatment" that I decided to re-arrange them into a pleasing balance and leave them there (that was two years ago!). Since dried herbs and flowers do become brittle, I change them each year with new favorites.

Lynn Peterson

Terra cotta pots and saucers can do more in the garden than hold flowers and herbs. A large saucer (14" to 16") set on the ground in a perennial bed makes a lovely, well-used birdbath if it is kept filled with fresh water near a large shrub or tree for a quick escape if a cat comes prowling. If pots are placed around the patio and each one holds a votive candle, they look lovely for an evening gathering. Lined with foil they make good serving pieces for everything from hors d'oeuvres to dessert.

Sheila Mohler

Paint smooth, round, flat-top rocks with the names of what you've planted in your garden...vegetables, herbs, flowers.

What sweeter bouquet could a mother receive than a bunch of dandelions clutched in the hands of a little child?

Nancy Campbell

A charming way to bring "country" to your garden and to keep your favorite gardener organized, is to mount a mailbox to a wood post and place it in your garden. The "garden box" is a handy catch-all for gardening supplies...gloves, tools, etc. The box is easy to paint and is cute with watermelons, sunflowers or pumpkins adorning its sides. A grapevine wreath mounted to the wood post adds charm to your country garden as well.

Michele Donovan

In the fall, before we have our first frost, bring in your beautiful geraniums. Set them near a window or in the basement. Cut them back and you will have geraniums for the spring. Everyone will envy you having colorful flowers all through the winter.

Sharon Hall
Gooseberry Patch

Hang an old antique ladder from the ceiling of a potting room or tall garage and hang your baskets, herbs and everlasting flowers from the rungs for a country touch.

Jan Sofranko

Got spring fever?
Take a day off!

I keep a little notebook and pen in my gardening basket along with my gloves and trowel. As soon as I plant seeds, or plants, or harvest some veggies, or have a great idea for next year, I quickly jot it down. This has been a tremendous help!

We use an old ice cream bucket that has a lid and a wire handle and fits nicely under the sink for our compost "stuff." It's amazing how quickly it's filled when we add our egg shells, peelings, tea leaves and coffee grounds. After the kitchen is cleaned at night, we take the bucket to the garden compost pile and add to our collection. For me this is a fun job because the garden looks so pretty in the moonlight, when the crickets and the whippoorwill are singing in full serenade!

I love to save seeds and found a great way to share them is with new neighbors, or in a letter that will brighten someone's day!

Cathrin Owens

Extend or offer a touch of "welcome home" to your family or guests when they come to visit by adding some personal touches. For example, wreaths tied with cheery bows; baskets full of flowers or potted plants; a comfy rocker to pass the time resting in; or a set of wicker furniture with fat cushions you can sink down into. Around the porch, place benches, "Welcome" signs, and wind chimes to make magic in the air.

Constance Cascino

My favorite wrap is plain brown paper bag! Fold down the top, punch two holes side by side (with some distance in between), then thread raffia though the holes. Tie in a bow in the front with an herb bundle in the middle. Simple, but very attractive.

Of all the different varieties of flowers that I've grown, sweet peas seem to elicit the most response when given away. It seems that each person I've given them to always relates a special memory associated with sweet peas. Try it...you'll be delighted with the stories you hear!

Sue Carbaugh

a Bouquet of ideas

Old tool boxes make great containers for indoor or outdoor plants. Make sure that you put in saucers for drainage. You can repaint the tool boxes or leave as is for a rustic look.

Susan Koronowski

"Fool-em" pumpkin pie is my new summertime treat. With a garden full of zucchini squash, I just substitute equal amounts of peeled, seeded, cooked, pureed zucchini for pumpkin in any pumpkin pie recipe. Add a little food coloring to get a pleasing orange color. Neither of my teenage sons will eat zucchini, but they sure love my fresh "pumpkin" pie! So far they still don't know my secret ingredient!

Renee Smith

I heard a neighbor was in the hospital and coming home soon. I wanted to cheer her up with a little something, so I went into my herb garden and dug up a small patch of spearmint. I placed it in a small pot, wrapped it in cellophane, and attached a tiny sign reading, "We hope you'll be back in mint condition very soon!" She laughed and that made me feel good too!

If you don't have a lot of space, grow miniature pumpkins. We tried to see who could grow the smallest! We had enough to decorate the house and share with friends.

Experiment with natural dyes (bring to a boil) for hard-boiled eggs at Easter time...yellow (onion skins), purple (beets), aqua (red cabbage), red (red onions). Save the colored egg shells and add directly to the garden. The pretty colors looks like confetti.

Lisa Sett

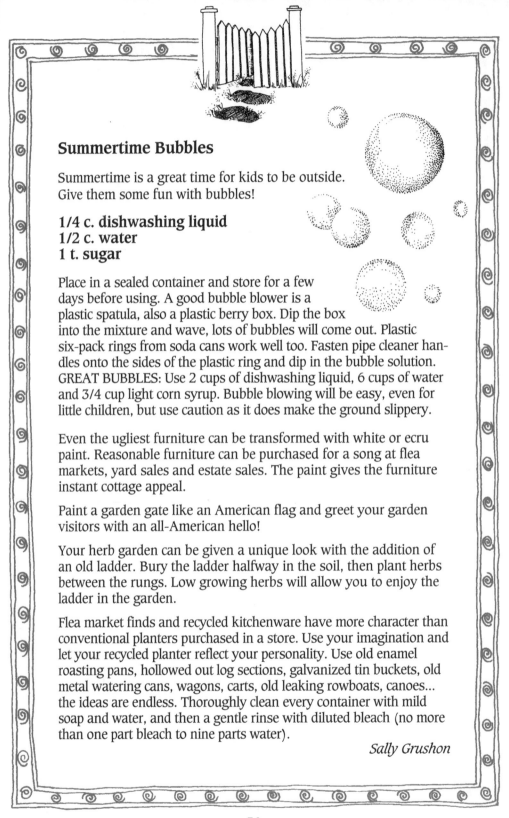

Summertime Bubbles

Summertime is a great time for kids to be outside.
Give them some fun with bubbles!

1/4 c. dishwashing liquid
1/2 c. water
1 t. sugar

Place in a sealed container and store for a few
days before using. A good bubble blower is a
plastic spatula, also a plastic berry box. Dip the box
into the mixture and wave, lots of bubbles will come out. Plastic
six-pack rings from soda cans work well too. Fasten pipe cleaner handles onto the sides of the plastic ring and dip in the bubble solution.
GREAT BUBBLES: Use 2 cups of dishwashing liquid, 6 cups of water
and 3/4 cup light corn syrup. Bubble blowing will be easy, even for
little children, but use caution as it does make the ground slippery.

Even the ugliest furniture can be transformed with white or ecru
paint. Reasonable furniture can be purchased for a song at flea
markets, yard sales and estate sales. The paint gives the furniture
instant cottage appeal.

Paint a garden gate like an American flag and greet your garden
visitors with an all-American hello!

Your herb garden can be given a unique look with the addition of
an old ladder. Bury the ladder halfway in the soil, then plant herbs
between the rungs. Low growing herbs will allow you to enjoy the
ladder in the garden.

Flea market finds and recycled kitchenware have more character than
conventional planters purchased in a store. Use your imagination and
let your recycled planter reflect your personality. Use old enamel
roasting pans, hollowed out log sections, galvanized tin buckets, old
metal watering cans, wagons, carts, old leaking rowboats, canoes...
the ideas are endless. Thoroughly clean every container with mild
soap and water, and then a gentle rinse with diluted bleach (no more
than one part bleach to nine parts water).

Sally Grushon

a Bouquet of ideas

I have a cement goose on my front porch and it is the "hit" of the neighborhood. Everyone checks to see what outfit she is wearing. Storing the clothes was a problem, so I put each outfit in a plastic, gallon-size zip lock bag. I put a cord and hooks on a pegboard and then, with clothes pins, pinned each outfit up so I could see them. Makes changing outfits a lot easier.

Sally Grushon

Heap flower pots into a wood or metal wheelbarrow, or an old red wagon. These make your garden portable, as you might wish to move plants from one spot to another from time to time. You can paint these with the change of the season too!

Coffee or teapots, hanging wire baskets, enamel colanders, colorful tin cans, antique milk bottles and canning jars all make great containers for plants and cuttings.

Let your imagination run wild as you go from room to room looking for unusual containers for your house plants. Old hat boxes, wooden crates, wicker picnic baskets, the seat of an old chair, colorful old pottery bowls and crocks all make lovely containers. Have fun with your plants!

Use a hat stand or peg rack to display an assortment of hanging plants.

Kristen Eddy

Turn a watering can or birdhouse into a country lamp. Just purchase a lamp conversion kit, drill a hole for the cord, and install. It's easy and your friends will rave.

37

In the Spring, when local hardware and drug stores have seeds on sale at ten for a dollar, I stock up and include a package with letters, birthday cards, Mother's Day cards, get-well cards and keep-in-touch notes that I mail to friends. I usually get a mix of easy-to-grow varieties...sunflowers, zinnias, marigolds, morning glories, etc. So even my "black-thumbed" friends can experience lovely flowers in their yards.

One of the best ways of making an inviting entrance to your country home (and making a relaxing retreat) is to add a rocking chair to your front porch. Position a huge pot of flowers (or lots of staggered sizes of pots) near your chair, hang some more flowers (fragrant of course), and you have the perfect place to retreat for a quiet minute and say "welcome" to visitors.

When shopping at garage sales, keep your eyes open for lightly loved teacups with saucers, sugar bowls and creamers, and beautiful old porcelain serving pieces, selling for very little. Small cracks and chips will only add character when the container is planted with a tiny blooming violet and given to a friend.

Nifty ideas for plant containers:

1. Old wagons...plant directly in the wagon or load up with lots of pots of colorful flowers.
2. Old or new barrel halves...plant a whole vegetable garden or fill with extra loose, sandy soil for the carrots that can't possibly grow in your native clay. How about a blueberry or raspberry bush in a barrel? How about lots of flowers and a small birdbath in the middle? Plant tallest plants in the middle, medium-size plants around the edge, and smaller, trailing plants around the sides. Drill holes in the sides and plant a strawberry barrel. Seal the inside and plant a waterlily for a small water garden.
3. Let the kids plant inside their old shoes for a "Grouch Garden," or small, plastic wading pools are great for a small veggie garden.
4. Large tin cans...the lovely enamel ones with pictures of tomatoes and olives are great.
5. Buckets, watering cans...poke in drainage holes.

The list is endless. It's fun to use your imagination!

Mel Wolk

a Bouquet of ideas

Want an unusual container for a hanging basket? Try a colander!
An old-fashioned metal colander with handles can be used as is or
painted with enamel in bright colors for an unusual hanging basket.
Or how about a bright plastic colander garden? Line the colander
with moss or paper towel to keep soil from spilling. Since water
drains freely in a colander, make sure to water often and hang over
a sink or place on the ground until excess dripping stops. These baskets are especially nice to use over a kitchen sink or hanging from
a tree branch.

When working in the garden sunshine, try wearing a sunbonnet
instead of the traditional straw hat. They're lots of fun and I think
a bonnet is much prettier than most hats.

Mel Wolk

*If you have an
outbuilding or shed, you can create
instant country charm with a coat of paint, wreath
on the door, windowbox filled with geraniums
and a bench to sit a spell.*

I have a couple of bound carpet samples (used in carpet show-rooms) that I use as "sit upons" (a cushion or pillow one "sits upon" on the ground or the floor) when I'm doing serious weeding in my garden. They can be obtained inexpensively (or sometimes free) and wear well. Saves wear and tear on the knees and the rear! This term was originally coined during a Girl Scout meeting where the girls were lacing together two squares of oil cloth with news-paper inside as a cushion. The girls would "sit upon" these during camp activities.

A wall or free-standing fountain in the garden offers a relaxing atmosphere for reading or dreaming. It also encourages the birds to swim and bathe, and their melodic chirps make quite a symphony for your own "Secret Garden!"

There is a small garden-themed gift shop in our area that sponsors an annual Sunflower Growing Contest. They provide the seeds, and at the end of summer (sometime around Labor Day), participants harvest the sunflowers and bring them to the shop for judging. There are prizes given for the largest sunflower heads. This would be a wonderful neighborhood event! Announce the date the contest begins, supply some seeds (or let the neighbors choose their own) and everyone gets busy planting. Plan a block party or all-neigh-borhood potluck to celebrate the season's end. The sunflowers wouldn't even need to be harvested. Plan a neighborhood walk where everyone sees everyone else's garden. Home-made ribbons for prizes could be given, with ribbons or stickers for all partici-pants! When the heads mature, save the seeds for next year (if you can beat the jays to them!).

Peg Ackerman

I have an antique teapot that had been my great aunt's. It is black with a small gold fleur-de-lis design. Every summer I like to cut Queen Anne's lace, daisies, or black-eyed Susans and arrange them as a small bouquet in the teapot. I get to enjoy some of sum-mer's flowers and my aunt's teapot. CAUTION: A white powder drops from the Queen Anne's lace which can mar the finish on polished wood furniture.

Barbara Encababian

Let some of your cucumbers get oversized. Cut them in half and have a child hollow them out. They make fun boats for the little ones. I remember floating one in grandma's chicken trough on hot summer days.

On one Halloween I used my toddler's bib overalls to create a scarecrow. He was adorable. My son enjoyed playing with the junior scarecrow, it was just his size. Wouldn't a pint-size scarecrow look sweet in a small garden?

Look through an antique shop for containers for your "porch garden." Paint and stencil an old wash tub with legs, fill with annuals and vining plants. Set potted plants down inside old wooden boxes. Give an ash bucket a fresh coat of black paint and fill with red geraniums.

Donna Olmstead

Try at least one new plant each year. It could be a flower, herb, or vegetable. This year we tried lilac peppers, strawflowers, and scented geraniums. We have enjoyed all of them.

Mary Ann Nemecek

One way to preserve basil for your winter cooking is to freeze it. Wash your basil and spin in a lettuce spinner, being gentle as basil will bruise easily. Measure the amount you will need in your recipes, put in a zip lock plastic bag and freeze. When you are ready to use it, you will have the amount you need all ready. Do not thaw, just add to recipe frozen. This is a great way to have pesto that will take you back to the days of summer.

I always send a sprig of rosemary in a note to a friend to let them know they are remembered. "Rosemary for Friendship and Remembrance."

Elizabeth Timmins
Gooseberry Patch Artisan

Old friendships are the dearest.

Grate all the yellow peel from firm lemons using the small holes of a cheese grater. Pack the grated peel into small, plastic containers and freeze. It keeps well up to a year. When your recipe calls for fresh lemon peel, just "chip" off the correct amount.

Mary Dyer

I love to arrange fresh cuttings from my herb garden. One easy and charming way is to tie a crocheted doily (available at sewing and craft stores, or grandmother's attic) over a glass or jar. The openings in the doily hold the cuttings in place. I often place the arrangement in a window, where a breeze will scent the room with herbal fragrance.

Deborah Mooney

My friend has a darling house in the country. She has dedicated a whole side of her house to birdhouses of every shape, size and color. It is an attractive eye catcher!

Teresa Labat

How to Preserve Children: Take one large grassy field; 1/2 dozen children, all sizes; three small dogs; and one narrow strip of brook, pebbly if possible. Mix the children with the dogs and empty them into the field, stirring continually. Sprinkle with field flowers, pour brook gently over pebbles, cover all with a deep blue sky and bake in a hot sun. When the children are well browned they may be removed. Will be found ready for setting away to cool in the bath tub.

Decide where your flower bed will be the summer or fall prior to planting it. Then collect newspapers and spread them around your bed, with five or six sheets together making sure they overlap, and cover with mulch. By the following spring your newspaper will decompose and also enrich your soil. All the grass and weeds have died plus you have recycled old newspapers to help the environment. Then at this point all you need to do is plant your flowers. This works very well, but, remember to use newspaper with only black print. Do not use the colored advertisements which have dyes in them.

Charlotte Crockett

a Bouquet of ideas

My husband made a heart-shaped metal form. We poured cement and now have markers and stepping stones all over our garden. Messages and tiny handprints can be added before cement dries completely.

Have your child write his or her name on the side of a pumpkin while it is still small. Have an adult go over it with a knife, being careful not to break it from the vine. As the pumpkin grows larger, so will their name.

Eugenia Abril

When a pumpkin is very small, gently place it inside a 1/2 gallon milk carton. Gently ease the carton over the pumpkin. As your pumpkin grows, it will fill the shape of the carton and turn out square.

Tori Jones

Great gift ideas for the gardener are birdhouses, tools, watering cans, garden books, journals, gift certificates to garden catalogs and stores, subscription to a favorite gardening magazine, weathervanes, wind chimes and signs.

Since most of us don't drink enough water, the following is a refreshing idea to help your family towards their 8 glasses of water each day. In my garden I grow peppermint and spearmint. I put a few washed mint leaves in a pretty water container in the refrigerator. It gives the water a refreshing, crisp taste.

Patricia Milton

To introduce flowers into your family's meals, start off slowly by placing a few pansy blossoms or rose petals on top of your salad. Then if they are willing to try them again, add edible flowers to your menu. Consult a good herb book on what flowers are edible.

Jeanne Calkins

Don't throw away those old tennis shoes...plant in them! First cut out a small opening in the front (if your big toe hasn't already done so), loosen the laces and add soil. Fill with hens and chicks, including the toe hole in the front. Try getting an old pair from each family member, and group them by the back door. Kids love them.

Remember, plants can be a great way to camouflage an eyesore. Try covering the side of your garage with lattice work or trellis netting. Plant hollyhocks, morning glories and nasturtiums, or any vining plant. You'll love the results. Jack-be-little and baby boo pumpkins work well too.

Katherine Gaughan

When your dill is at its fragrant best, snip off a handful and put it in a small container of water in your kitchen. Smells good and looks pretty. Put it in an old jar, little crock, old tin cup, or pretty mug.

Sara Walker

Spruce up a plain fence or garage back by painting a garden on it...no matter what the season you'll have a great view!

Maria Vaz Duarte

a Bouquet of ideas

For a "taste" of gardening in our wardrobe closet, my daughter made the girls in our family simple pullover-style jumpers using a vegetable, floral and seed packet patterned fabric. We each wear a knit shirt in a different coordinating color.

Judy Vaccaro

I raise my own herbs and scented geraniums. I routinely pinch off some of the straggly growth from certain plants to keep the plant bushy and to keep the plant more compact, but instead of throwing these clippings away, I let them dry and then crumble them and vacuum them up in my vacuum cleaner. Then every time I vacuum, it scents the room with whatever fragrance of plant I used. Lemon geranium leaves smell wonderful, so does lavender. The scent lasts until you change the bag.

Lois Hagen

An old garden gate can make a perfect display for hanging knick-knacks. Purchase wooden shaker pegs from a hardware store, drill holes at random and insert pegs. You may want to paint the gate and pegs white or barn red to make it uniform color. Hang dried flowers, small baskets, and wooden items...so clever!

Laura Hodges

Times being as they are, everyone is trying to eat a little lighter especially in the summer. Substitute applesauce for vegetable oil in your favorite recipes. This will cut back the fat and it tastes great!

Jennifer Bieniek

Take photos of your garden at the peak of each season. When you sit down to plan next year's garden, it's easy to see the areas you need to concentrate on.

Old deacon's or church benches make attractive garden benches. Old cream cans can become country treasures. They can be sponge painted, stenciled, or even painted in a solid color (I chose barn red). They look great on decks or patios (and don't forget the raffia bow for extra measure!).

Michelle Urdahl

After a full day of working in the garden with my sons, we always have a huge water fight. We relax after that (dripping wet, of course!) with a snack and admire our work.

In times past, a pot of basil on a lady's balcony told her suitor that she was interested in receiving him.

Denise Green

Use panels of a picket fence, painted white to put on the walls around your room; or sand them, paint any color, and make a picket fence headboard. Can be decorated with handpainted flowers or vines of artificial flowers.

Janice Ertola

On a cross beam in my home between kitchen and dining area I have a garden whimsey. I have grapevines arranged over the whole beam and the vines are decorated with small birdhouses, nests, birds and rosehips.

Shirley Behm

A great fall birthday gift...give a variety of spring bulbs that will keep giving for years to come.

A spring fundraiser idea is to have everyone bring a perennial from their garden (one ready to divide) or a plant from the store. All present are free to make a donation for the plants they choose to take home.

Carol Jones

a Bouquet of ideas

My husband and I like to take old wooden ladders and use them both indoors and out for decorating. Inside, a 3-foot section is vertically bracketed to the bathroom wall for towels. Outside they are bracketed to the house and garage lengthwise for holding flowers, decoys, and other collectibles. One is hung so that the flowers show through the bathroom window. The brackets themselves hold tin pails filled with plants and grapevine wreaths. Both ladders outside have gardens of hollyhocks, nasturtiums, and phlox underneath them. The overall effect is really a great, cottage garden look.

Deb Reinke

Need a perfect gift for a gardener? Try a simple set of wind chimes! Nothing is more peaceful and soothing than listening to a fresh breeze tickle the musical notes of wind chimes, as you plant, tend or just "sit a spell" in your garden.

Kim Estes

When sewing, save all thread scraps and scatter on the lawn in early spring. It's fun to see it in the birds' nests.

Shelly McHugh

For a really good conversation piece for your flower garden, take an old iron bed (head or foot or both). Should you use both, set it up as you would a bed. In the middle, plant your flowers, using the center of the head or foot boards for a trellis. At the four posts, plant your tallest flowers, such as hollyhocks. The posts will service as supports for the flowers. This is a really good eye catcher. I call it, "Sherry's Flower Bed."

I find that using an old-fashioned bedspring for a trellis in my flower garden works very well for my sweet peas or any type of climbing plant.

Sherry Hawkes

When we built our home in the woods, we wanted to keep the rustic country look and do something for the environment. For two months before we moved in, I stopped by a concrete dumping area every day and collected discarded concrete. After we had about 150 pieces, we set them in the dirt to form a winding path through the trees from the street to our house.

Candy Hannigan

Find an old wagon and put it in a special place to greet visitors. Each season, paint it a different color and stencil a greeting, proverb, or welcoming message on the side of it like Welcome Friends, Spring Has Sprung, Friends are the Flowers in my Garden, Friendship's Garden, Summer's Bounty, Autumn's Harvest or Merry Christmas. Fill it with an assortment of colorful flowers of the season, and invite visitors to pick a flower as a reminder of their visit to your home.

Wednesday Szollosi

My husband is a real do-it-yourselfer and this year he turned our yard into a "construction zone." Even though it was well orga-nized, it wasn't the most aesthetic view. So I extended our veggie garden by planting two rows of sunflowers in front of the building materials (leaving enough room to give access to the materials). The front row of flowers was a small variety for bouquets, the back row was the tall, mammoth flowers for the birds! Not only did the sunflowers hide the construction zone, it gave us the most beauti-ful view, many bouquets, food for the birds, and lots of smiles.

Edith Beck

Stenciling adds a creative and charming country look to objects not only inside, but outside of your home. Using leftover outdoor paint and inexpensive stencil patterns, decorate the mailbox, flower boxes, around door and window frames, and even the porch steps! You can add little personal touches to the gate on the picket fence, a collection of terra cotta flowerpots, and even accent a bird or dog house. When you decorate any of these items, the outside of your home will become unique and attractive.

Cathryn Galicia

I belong to an herb society and each spring we have "Herbs Galore," an annual fundraiser promoting herbs and gardening. For our booth I made apple-sauce and cinnamon nutmeg cut-outs using a sunflower cookie cutter. In the center, while the mixture was still wet, I pushed in whole cloves (cut or "bite" the stem close to the head). It makes it look like there are seeds in the middle, just like real sunflowers! After they were dry, I glued (E6000) dark steel wire and greenery to the back; great for a garden theme Christmas tree.

Shari Kritikakos

My mother and I correspond back and forth, and we always close our letters with: P.S. My "thyme" with you is a pleasure. I like to include a sprig of garden thyme and lemon thyme between the pages.

Susan Mroz

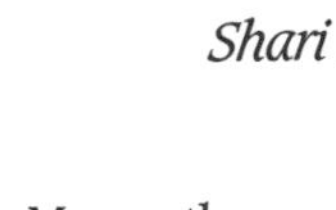

While the wind is howling outside, spend some time browsing through seed catalogs and planning your spring garden.

I freeze zucchini for future baking projects. Just grate (I use my food processor) and put into freezer bags in premeasured quantities. When ready to use, thaw partially in large bowl until just slightly icy. Retain all liquid and mix baking ingredients.

While trimming my herbs, I always save any clippings. These savory tidbits can be used in herb butters, vinegars, mixed to use in teas or seasoning blends to be used in cooking and baking. I have even used them to mix up a batch of herbal insect repellent instead of using mothballs. They are also delightful dried in bundles and hung from old hooks in the ceiling of my kitchen...all my friends tell me how good my house smells!

Judy Hand

One way that I share my herbs is by buying boxes, usually used for long stemmed roses, from a local florist for $2.00 a piece. I tie up different bundles of herbs with jute. On each bundle I attach a card with the herb's name written in calligraphy. I punch a hole in the card, run the jute through the hole and tie, letting the card hang down from the bundle to identify each herb. I fill each box with beautiful tissue paper and place as many different bundles of herbs as I can inside. I tie the boxes with antique lace, ribbon or bits of fabric. What a fragrance when the box is opened! Because the bundles are tied with jute, they are ready to hang up in a kitchen to use.

Judy Gidley

Apricots, growing inside a small-mouthed bottle, will eventually be an intriguing gift. The bottle is eased over a new bloom and secured with electrician's tape. When the fruit is full-grown, remove the bottle from the tree and fill it with brandy. Or, for an even more unusual gift, try growing a cucumber or squash in a bottle.

Grace Meletta

Old clothes-drying racks found at flea markets are great for drying herbs and everlastings.

I sometimes have extra snippets of herbs left over after harvesting and pruning. I use some of the strong herbs such as rosemary and mint to freshen up my car. I put them in the ashtray. In the summer, the heat makes my car smell wonderful.

I live in Kentucky where rosemary usually does not survive the winter. I put my rosemary plants in pots for the cold season. Sometimes I decorate them like little Christmas trees. They look nice on the mantel.

Mary Ann Riehl

Try drying your leafy green herbs in the refrigerator to preserve flavor and color. Harvest as usual, rinse and pat dry. Put the leaves (and/or stems) in a brown paper bag. They will dry in three or four weeks.

To keep herbs fresh, put them in bunches in a jar filled with a bit of water, cover loosely with plastic wrap and store in the refrigerator. They stay fresh for about 2 weeks. You can also store smaller sprigs in paper towels (sealed in plastic bags) in the refrigerator.

Sheri Berger

If you ever find yourself with extra garlic, try this: Peel the cloves, cover them with olive oil, add a splash of vinegar, and refrigerate in a tightly covered jar. The garlic lasts for months and the oil is great to cook with.

Cindy Noborikawa

It's easy to dry herbs using your microwave! Wash and pat semi-dry with paper towels, pull off leaves. Place on several layers of paper towels, cover with additional paper towel. Microwave on full power for 30 seconds, let stand 10 minutes. Herbs should be brittle. If not, microwave a few seconds longer. Store in an airtight container. Check for moisture the following day. If moisture is present, microwave again for a few more seconds. STORE IN AN AIRTIGHT CONTAINER IN A COOL, DARK PLACE. To get maximum flavor of dried herbs, soak them 20 to 40 minutes in some liquid to be used in recipe (broth, water, wine, oil, sauce or lemon juice). When fresh herbs are used in recipe, use twice the amount as you would use for dried herbs (1 tablespoon fresh herbs equals 1 teaspoon dried). The finer you mince fresh herbs, the more flavor you'll get. Mince herbs with scissors for speed, or chop with French cook's knife. For freshest flavor, add herbs to soups or stews during the last 45 minutes of cooking time; or save half to stir in 10 minutes before the dish is done.

Here are some tips if you want to freeze your herbs. Wash herbs and pat dry with paper towel. If you are freezing basil, mint, oregano, or sage, remove the leaves from the stems and discard the stems. Place herbs in a plastic freezer bag, seal tightly, label and date. For best quality, use within one year. Fresh basil will discolor, so before freezing place leaves in boiling water for 2 seconds, rinse immediately in cold water, pat dry and freeze as directed above. When seasoning with fresh herbs, a simple guide is to use 1 tablespoon fresh herbs for every 4 servings of meat, veggies or fish. Add more or less to taste.

Mary McCullough

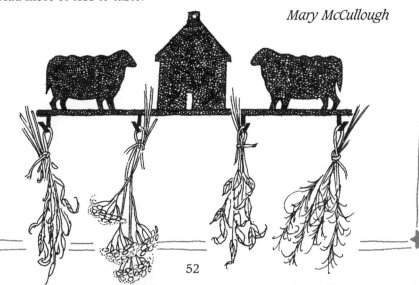

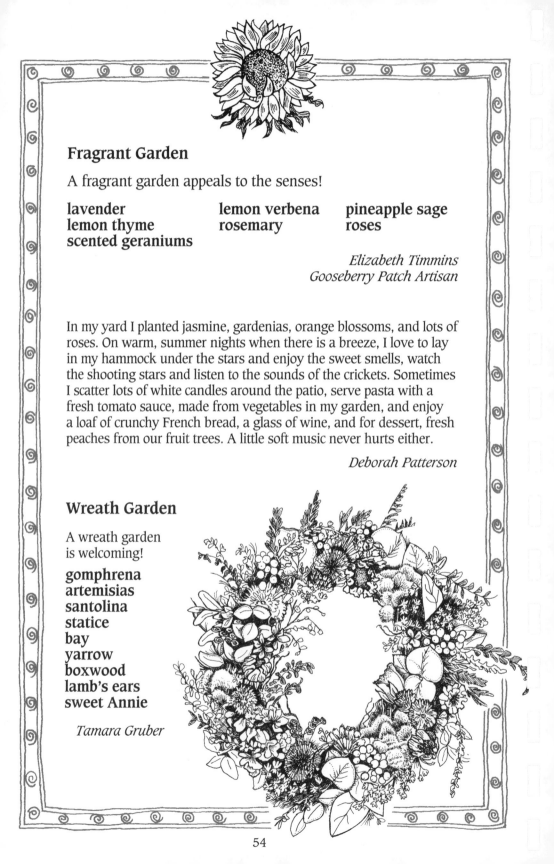

Fragrant Garden

A fragrant garden appeals to the senses!

lavender   **lemon verbena**   **pineapple sage**
lemon thyme   **rosemary**   **roses**
scented geraniums

Elizabeth Timmins
Gooseberry Patch Artisan

In my yard I planted jasmine, gardenias, orange blossoms, and lots of roses. On warm, summer nights when there is a breeze, I love to lay in my hammock under the stars and enjoy the sweet smells, watch the shooting stars and listen to the sounds of the crickets. Sometimes I scatter lots of white candles around the patio, serve pasta with a fresh tomato sauce, made from vegetables in my garden, and enjoy a loaf of crunchy French bread, a glass of wine, and for dessert, fresh peaches from our fruit trees. A little soft music never hurts either.

Deborah Patterson

Wreath Garden

A wreath garden
is welcoming!

gomphrena
artemisias
santolina
statice
bay
yarrow
boxwood
lamb's ears
sweet Annie

Tamara Gruber

Garden Themes & Such

Moonlight Gardens

Here are some plants that will shimmer in the moonlight and add a lovely contrast to the darker foliage in your garden.

aloe	lamb's ears
silver sage	silver tansy
silver thyme	southernwood
wormwood	yarrow
apple mint	lavender
carnation	nutmeg geranium
clary sage	oregano
dwarf sage	pineapple mint
germander	rosemary
grey santolina	silver king artemisia
horehound	silver queen artemisia

Jan Sofranko

White flowers planted in a garden create an especially dramatic effect in the moonlight. The moonlight reflects off the flower petals and makes a beautiful silvery light which is very magical and romantic. Plant a white flower garden in a spot where you can really enjoy the evening, near a porch or entrance to the house. The following are some white flowers I have planted in my garden...night blooming jasmine, cosmos, nicotiana, stock, roses, veronica, impatiens, alyssium and azalea. Also, both jasmine and nicotiana emit their wonderful perfume in the moonlight.

Nancie Gensler

*To own a bit of ground, to scratch it with a hoe,
to plant seeds, and watch the renewal of life...
this is the commonest delight of the race,
the most satisfactory thing a man can do.*
Charles Dudley Warner

Butterfly Garden

Butterflies need you and you need them. Our houses and highways are spreading over the land, so there are fewer places where butterflies can find the flowers they need for food. Your garden will give the butterflies a place to come and drink the sweet nectar that flowers make. These beautiful insects will pay you back with a color show that can't be beaten! On a sunny day plant the following:

white alyssum	phloxes (all kinds)
pink & white rock cress	polianthes (single)
candytuft	primrose (single)
catnip	pincushion flowers
cornflowers	sea hollies
cosmos	sweet rocket (hesperis)
white daisies	sweet William
French marigolds (single)	pink valerian
goldenrod	petunias (single)

Jan Sofranko

The secret to attracting butterflies is to give them what they like to eat and drink! They also prefer direct sunlight and heat. If you live in a windy area, plant your garden in a spot protected from exposed areas, including lots of wind. Put your garden next to a building or evergreen hedge. Also when butterflies aren't searching for food, they like to rest on sun-warmed stones or boards. They also get thirsty. Fill a shallow pan with water and place it slightly in the ground in your garden. Flowers that provide food are zinnia, globe amaranth, marigold, cosmos, butterfly weed, lavender, purple coneflower, butterfly bush, yarrow, and the New England aster. Encourage the butterflies to stay where their young can feed too. The caterpillars will nibble their way through milkweed, clover, nettle, Queen Anne's lace, wild lupine, and goldenrod. They also like garden plants such as carrots, dill, parsley, nasturtium, and violets. Tucking in some of these plants will encourage the butterflies to stay.

Mary Murray

To develop a butterfly garden, use large splashes of color in your design. Butterflies at first are attracted to color. Plant in groups, because for butterflies, groups are easier to locate than isolated plants. Many butterflies seem to like purple, yellow, orange and red flowers. Also, plant single rather than double type flowers, the nectar is more accessible. Sun is also very important to the life of these plants. Your first choice for a butterfly garden should be the shrub buddleia davidii (butterfly bush). The following flowers have been a success for me: cosmos (bright lights), lantana, purple coneflower, verbena and zinnia.

Theresa Manley

Bee Garden

Buzzing with activity...
a bumblebee garden
is delightful!

hyssop
catnip
bee balm
lavender
lemon thyme
pineapple mint
lemon balm

Elizabeth Timmins
Gooseberry Patch
Artisan

Shakespeare Garden *(non-poisonous)*

These plants are all mentioned in William Shakespeare's writings and were popular in Elizabethan England.

parsley	columbine	Johnny jump-ups
rosemary	dyer's broom	lavender
strawberry	flax	lemon balm
bay	wormwood	marjoram
burnet	pink rose	mint
calendula	savory	mustard
carnation	thyme	myrtle
chamomile	hyssop	

Jan Sofranko

Wildflower Garden

Many of my flower beds were started by gathering plants and wildflowers from the fields and woods near my home. Wild ginger, violets, wild geraniums, daylilies, daisies, brown-eyed Susans, irises, bee balm, yarrow, and Queen Anne's lace are just a few of the "country cousins" who are growing happily beside their "cultivated" neighbors in my perennial borders. Not only are these lovely ladies easy on your budget, but they're indigenous to your area and they grow readily in your garden. Enjoy your gathering walks, taking along a shovel, plastic bags with handles, a good wildflower identification book, and a friend. Be aware of the land owners if the "weeds" are not growing on your property. I have never been refused permission, but have certainly gotten some odd looks. Enjoy!

Diann Fox

Everlasting Garden

Everlastings are flowers that can be easily air-dried without losing their color or form. Most of these flowers are dry and papery to the touch even when they're blooming. You can grow them easily from seed after the last frost, and you'll have blooms by mid-summer. If you're like me and can't wait that long, start them inside 6 weeks before the first frost or buy bedding plants at a local nursery.

A good variety of everlastings that are easy to grow are strawflower, statice, blue salvia, nigella, globe amaranth, cockscomb, and baby's breath. Timing is crucial to the drying process. Pick the blooms after the morning dew has evaporated, and when they are fully open and at their best. Bunch together with a rubberband, and hang them up to dry immediately in a dry location, maybe your attic or a spare room. For flowers that don't dry well, but are beautiful (rose, pansy, peony, zinnia, dahlia, lily) use silica gel. Fill a cookie tin with the silica gel and gently place the flowers in. Cover them with more silica gel, carefully spooning in on the petals. Check the tin every 2 days until the petals feel dry and papery.

Mary
Murray

Kids' Gardens

Kids love gardening and here are some fun ideas to get them started!

If you have never planted a Sunflower House, you are in for a treat! You will need an area 5'x6' (can be enlarged or made smaller depending on the area you are working with). This area should receive full sun most of the day. Mark the area to be planted with small stakes and string. Clear out any weeds or growing matter. If you are doing this on the lawn, clear the area just inside the string. This is where you will plant your seeds. The lawn can serve as your "carpet." Buy 1 or 2 packs of sunflower seeds (Grey Stripe or Mammoth, they need to be tall), and 1 or 2 packs of morning glory seeds. According to package, space and plant your sunflower seeds. Leave an 18 to 24 inch area unplanted for your "door." Mark the location of each seed with a twig, stone, or plant marker so you will know where to expect your sunflowers. They should sprout in 7 to 10 days. They will need a lot of water! Soak your morning glory seeds overnight. Plant them, according to the package directions, in between the sunflower seeds. As the sunflower heads begin to form, gently weave a ceiling with string, back and forth from one side to the other. The morning glories will climb up the sunflowers and wind their way across the "ceiling." A special place for the kids to play in!

My 8 year old son loves to help plan the annual spring garden. When he sees the seed displays, he gets so enthusiastic! This year, when I couldn't decide on the type of sunflowers I wanted to plant, he suggested that I get a package of each kind, and pour them all into a bucket. "Just mix them up, Mom, and sprinkle them in the dirt! Then you'll have a surprise garden!"

Peg Ackerman

I like to involve my kids in the joys of gardening, and have found many ways to make it fun for them. Plant something fun, like popcorn! Try growing gourds, when dried they will make great birdhouses. My children always have their favorite seed packets in their Easter baskets, and most importantly, they have never been picky eaters...if they grow it, they'll eat it!

Lisa Sett

I gave my children a special area of their own for planting. My daughter decided to plant many different varieties of flowers, all in her favorite color...pink! The different shades of pink made a beautiful garden.

Lisa Sett

My husband is an avid rose grower. This year he planted a new type of garden with his grandchildren, Adam, 'Manda and Brian. It's a candy garden and what fun it's been. Each of them planted 3 jelly beans. The first "harvest" took about a week...and 3 Disney suckers grew. The children were so excited! Every day they check the garden, but it only grows about once a week. I think it's funny that never once have jelly beans sprouted!

Pat Eveland

Hummingbird Garden

For a hummingbird garden (a butterfly garden is a perfect companion) use tubular, brightly colored flowers. Fragrance is not important to them to locate food, because they rely on sight. Hummingbirds prefer single flowers to doubles. Like butterflies, hummingbirds require a continuous supply of nectar, so plant flowers that bloom over a long season. I have had success with salvia, lobelia, monarda (bee balm) and trumpet vine.

Theresa Manley

To make hummingbird nectar, mix 1 part white granulated sugar to 4 parts of water. First boil the water; then add the sugar, stirring to dissolve thoroughly. Let solution cool. Store unused solution in the refrigerator.

Cheryl Ewer

"Nibbler's Garden"

1. **Find a sunny spot**
2. **Find a special child**
3. **Plant edible flowers together**
4. **When your harvest comes in, nibble wherever you please!**

Be careful not to plant any poisonous flowers in your garden where children roam and play. Let your children know that they are to nibble only the flowers from the "Nibbler's Garden." You may want to create sugared flowers, flower jam and flower salads together, for a garden tea party.

Kristen Eddy

Dyer's Garden

Here are some plants that you can make dyes from for 100% natural fibers, like cotton and wool.

agrimony	goldenrod	onion
ajuga	hibiscus	elecampane
birch	hollyhock	marigold
blackberry	hyssop	elder
bloodroot	indigo (wild)	lily-of-the-valley
coltsfoot	lady's mantle	dandelion
cornflower	larkspur	

Jan Sofranko

Friendship Garden

If you don't have a friendship garden, now is the time to start one. Fill with plants received from friends, or plants that have been traded with friends. Your friendship garden will be a constant reminder of those you love.

Mary Ann Nemecek

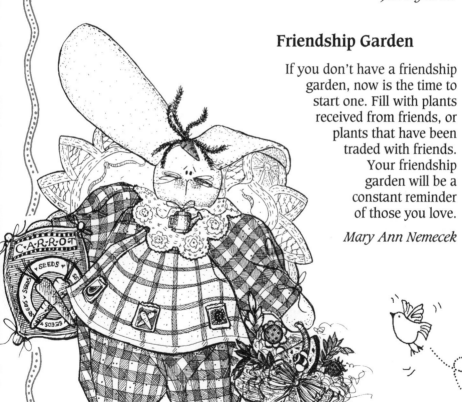

Insect Repellent Garden

Repel those little critters naturally!

rosemary	borage	sage
santolina	catnip	savory
southernwood	chamomile	tansy
tarragon	chervil	thyme
basil	chives	garlic
bay	dill	horseradish
bergamot	yarrow	lavender
lemon balm	mint	oregano
lovage	marjoram	pennyroyal
wormwood		

Jan Sofranko

Indoor Garden

Bring the garden indoors. Old watering cans, twig plant stands and furniture, birdhouses, topiaries, cement yard animals (rabbits, pigs, ducks, cats, whatever), flower drying racks and rustic garden signs look wonderful combined with country furnishings. Use them as accents all around the house. Fill all kinds of outdoor pots with colorful seasonal flowers such as primula, primrose, impatiens or forget-me-nots. Put them near a sunny window and don't forget to water regularly. When the plants begin to fade, transfer them outside and plant in your garden.

Nancie Gensler

Old-Fashioned Flower Garden

Plant a garden with old-fashioned flowers only...hollyhocks, old roses, foxglove, delphiniums, cosmos, lupine, etc. Then surround or line the back of the garden with a simple, white picket fence. Just like grandma's house!

Deb Damari-Tull

Water Garden

After raising five robust children and using our small backyard (40'x 30') as a play yard for 20 years, we spent a whole summer removing all the sod and grass. My husband built two water gardens and raised beds for herbs, perennials, annuals and brick walkways. Our ponds are complete with waterlillies, grasses, frogs, snails and goldfish. We hauled mountain rock and stone to encircle our water gardens, strategically located outside of our screened porch where we sip mint iced tea, while listening to the babbling water and croaking frogs.

Nancy Hutchins

Salad Garden

Salad...fresh from the garden!

burnet	parsley	Johnny jump-ups
lovage	chives	pansies
dill	borage	calendula
nasturtiums		

Kitchen Garden

A snip of this and a snip of that right by your kitchen door!

basil	rosemary	marjoram
dill	parsley	savory
tarragon	sage	oregano
thyme	chives	

Edible Flower Garden

A simple recipe becomes a beautiful creation with edible flowers!

all culinary herbs	scented geraniums
bachelor's button	snapdragon
begonia	tulip
calendula (petals)	viola
cornflower	violet
dandelion (petals)	
fuchsia	
gladiola	
hibiscus	
hollyhock	
honeysuckle	
Johnny jump-up	
nasturtium	
pansy	
rose (petals)	

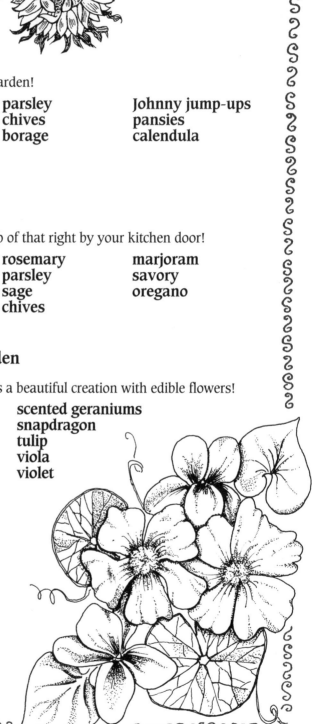

Bible Garden

These plants have meaning and significance in the Bible.

costmary
rue
sage
Our Lady's bedstraw
thyme

rosemary
hyssop
lavender
chamomile

Herbs for Low Borders & Edging

These herbs are great for edging flower beds and walkways!

boxwood
dwarf or bush basil
dwarf sage
Lady's mantle
hyssop

chamomile
dwarf rosemary
thyme
lamb's ears
lavender

Tea Garden

What could be more soothing than a cup of tea...remember Peter Rabbit?

lemon balm
chamomile
catnip
sage
bee balm
mint (apple mint,
    pineapple mint,
    peppermint,
    orange mint)

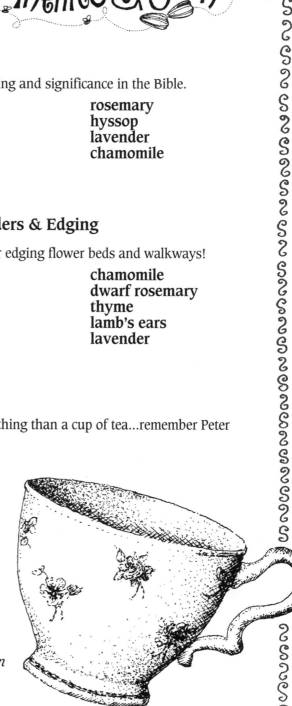

Elizabeth Timmins
Gooseberry Patch Artisan

Herb Gardens

Herbs are fun and easy to grow, and will give you hours of joy! It was customary, in days of old, for the woman of the house to look after the herb garden. She decided which herbs were to be grown and where to plant them. It was her job to weed the beds, harvest the crop, dry them, add them to her cooking, make wines and simple medicine. Her dried herbs and flowers were used for potpourri, strewing and sachets to keep her house smelling sweet. Gardens were planted near the door to the keeping room where the drying and preparation were done. Today culinary gardens are also planted near the kitchen for easy access.

There are several factors to consider when deciding where best to locate your garden. Many herbs have their origin in the warmer climate. You want to reproduce, as nearly as possible, the conditions of their native habitat. Six to eight hours of sun a day is required to develop the essential oils which give the plants their fragrance and flavor. Even plants that require partial shade need up to four hours of sun.

Herbs need protection from wind as this does more damage than low temperatures. A protected corner, near a wall or hedge or a natural slope, can provide good shelter. Once the garden is established, the larger herbs will provide protection for the smaller ones.

Ideally, herbs like a lightly enriched open soil; a soil that is coarse enough to contain air and fine enough to retain some water and with sufficient nutrients to encourage growth. Excessive feeding may result in too lush a plant with little strength of scent or flavor. Raised beds are ideal for herb gardens.

Any size garden can be a joy whether it's a very large, formal garden or a window box of your favorite herbs. Your garden may be an herb and vegetable garden, a tea garden, a Bible garden, a culinary garden, a cosmetic garden, a wreath garden or whatever is your fancy. If this is your first herb garden, a small garden with a few herbs that you have become familiar with is better than trying to take care of a large garden. Each plant is steeped in history and legend and has many uses. You will become fascinated as you get to know each of your herbs.

Garden Themes & Such

Make your herb garden a special place. Stand outside and visualize your garden. Maybe you see a round garden, a garden against a wall or house, a ladder garden where the plants are planted between the rungs, or between the spokes of an old wagon wheel, a raised bed or a garden in a half barrel. Whichever you decide upon, remember that accessibility is important. Flat stones placed in your garden work well. If yours is a large garden, you will need to make paths through your plants. These can be crushed stone, brick, woodchips, sand, whichever will look best.

No herb garden seems complete without a sundial, the most traditional herb garden ornament. The beeskep was also found in many herb gardens. Honey was one of the reasons for growing herbs, as the finest honey came from the herb garden bees. If you choose a rye beeskep it must be brought in during bad weather, or you may wish to build a shelter for it. Bird baths are excellent in herb gardens and the birds coming to your bath will make a healthier and more cheerful garden. Add benches, a whimsical statuary, and whatever you feel good about to your garden. Have fun!

Garden markers are a must, not only for you but for those who will visit your garden. There are great markers to be found in herb shops, country stores or garden centers. You may also be creative and make your own. Pieces of slate, bricks, wooden spoons, pieces of barn board, whatever you can paint or write on can be a marker. I was lucky and a friend gave me a pile of slate. I painted the names of my gardens on the larger pieces and the smaller pieces were used for the individual herbs. Always on the garden signs I would draw a picture or write a verse. A tea cup and saucer for my tea garden, or a Bible verse for my Bible garden. My tea garden also has a little table set with teapot and little bunnies among the chamomile. Be creative and make your garden fun!

So now you have an idea of the size and location where you want your garden. Gather some good herb books, get out pen and paper and start drawing. Visiting other herb gardens is a great way to get inspired and people who love herbs are always happy to show you their gardens. Check size, color, and texture of each plant to place them in the best location.

Elizabeth Timmins
Gooseberry Patch Artisan

69

The most delightful and satisfying plants I know to grow are herbs and edible flowers. Prepare your soil and your herb beds, or if space is a problem grow your herbs in pots. There are culinary herbs that can be grown and harvested for use in the kitchen. There are herbs to grow, harvest and dry for wreath making and for use in decorating your home. Herbs make our gardens beautiful. They attract birds and butterflies and honey bees. They delight our senses, appealing not only to our sense of sight, taste and smell; but also our sense of touch. They will reward you in great measure for a very small investment of time and toil. Herbs and edible flowers may have their own private plot or happily share their space with other plants.

Tamara Gruber

Herbs That Are Fun To Grow

Borage, the herb of courage, was smuggled into the drink of prospective suitors to give them courage to propose marriage. Finely chopped young leaves mixed with cream cheese make a nice tea sandwich. The leaves have a cucumber-like flavor. Can be added to salads or add leaves and flowers to fruit salad. The pretty blue star-like flowers can be candied and used for accents on cakes or ice cream. Add a crushed leaf to your favorite summer drink. Dry the leaves for a winter tea.

Lavender, the herb of devotion and undying love. I always think of those pretty bottles of lavender scented water I bought at the five and dime store for my mom. Lavender has always been associated with washing and in olden days lavender was added to the rinse water for a clean fresh scent, or newly washed clothes were spread to dry over lavender bushes. Victorian ladies made lavender wands and placed them among their fine linens. Try putting a sprig of lavender under a hat to drive away a headache.

Peppermint spreads like crazy and in the spring you can make lots of little plants to share. Just pull up a piece of your plant along with the root. It comes up easy, so this is a fun way to prune your plant. Put in little pots and give away. They are sure to grow. I often have first and second graders to my garden for an herb picnic and they love to go home with an herb of their own. I tell them that the way the peppermint plant spreads is like love...the more we share our love with others, the more it grows...you can't stop it!

Parsley. The symbol of strength and vigor, parsley is a popular kitchen herb. It's a hardy biennial, often grown as an annual. Italian parsley leaves are flat while French parsley leaves are curly. It does best grown in rich soil with full sun. While it can be grown from seed, it takes about 4 weeks to germinate and is sometimes more reliable when grown from small plants. Garnish your summertime dishes with parsley, a rich source of vitamins and minerals. Especially good in potatoes and rice.

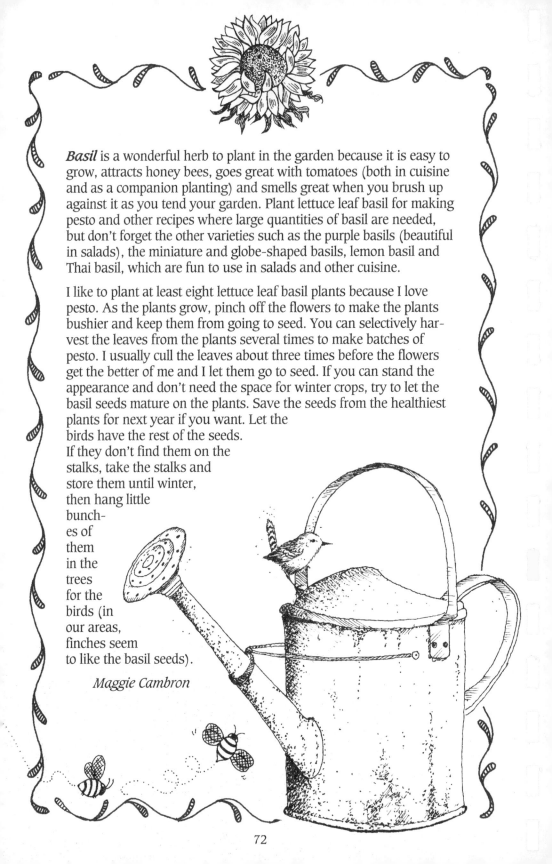

Basil is a wonderful herb to plant in the garden because it is easy to grow, attracts honey bees, goes great with tomatoes (both in cuisine and as a companion planting) and smells great when you brush up against it as you tend your garden. Plant lettuce leaf basil for making pesto and other recipes where large quantities of basil are needed, but don't forget the other varieties such as the purple basils (beautiful in salads), the miniature and globe-shaped basils, lemon basil and Thai basil, which are fun to use in salads and other cuisine.

I like to plant at least eight lettuce leaf basil plants because I love pesto. As the plants grow, pinch off the flowers to make the plants bushier and keep them from going to seed. You can selectively harvest the leaves from the plants several times to make batches of pesto. I usually cull the leaves about three times before the flowers get the better of me and I let them go to seed. If you can stand the appearance and don't need the space for winter crops, try to let the basil seeds mature on the plants. Save the seeds from the healthiest plants for next year if you want. Let the birds have the rest of the seeds. If they don't find them on the stalks, take the stalks and store them until winter, then hang little bunch- es of them in the trees for the birds (in our areas, finches seem to like the basil seeds).

Maggie Cambron

Garden Themes & Such

Basil, "maketh a man merry and glad." To the Romans it was a symbol of love. To the people of India, it is a holy herb. Basil was once used as a strewing herb on floors to keep them sweet and clean and for chasing away witches, flies and headaches.

Chives taste wonderful cut up and sprinkled over baked potatoes. But have you tried them in your scrambled eggs, potato salad, macaroni salad and your fresh green salads? Yummy! I also use the blossoms...the lovely pinks and lavender adds color to a wild-flower and herb bouquet. The scent is pleasing too. Blossoms can be cut and dried upside down (about 2 to 3 weeks) and then used in dried flower arrangements or tucked into wreaths.

Rosemary means "dew of the sea." Rosemary is the herb of friendship and remembrance, and is considered the herb of Christmas, weddings and funerals. It is said that where rosemary flourishes, the woman rules. Rosemary tea with honey will lift the spirits. A strong infusion makes a fine rinse for dark hair. Dried twigs and leaves thrown on the coals of a wood stove or fireplace make a natural incense, and in days of old was used this way to clear the air in a sick room. For weddings, rosemary was either gilded or dipped in scented water and carried in the bride's wreath. I always include rosemary in the bride's and groom's flowers when preparing them for a wedding...may they always remember this day and be the best of friends.

Elizabeth Timmins
Gooseberry Patch Artisan

Thyme. There are several varieties of thyme... lemon, creeping, and common. A perennial herb, it's a favorite of bees! It only grows 6 to 10 inches high and has pink or violet flowers in the early fall. It grows in dry, sandy soil in full sun. If you plant thyme between rocks in your garden path, everytime you pass by you'll delight in its heavenly fragrance. It's best to start with tiny plants as seeds are slow to germinate. Thyme is used in poultry stuffings, and as a seasoning for chicken and pot roast.

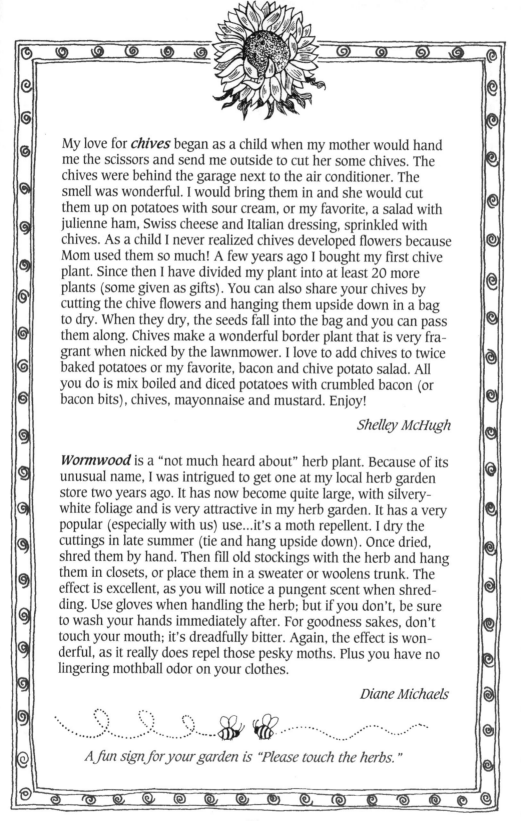

My love for *chives* began as a child when my mother would hand me the scissors and send me outside to cut her some chives. The chives were behind the garage next to the air conditioner. The smell was wonderful. I would bring them in and she would cut them up on potatoes with sour cream, or my favorite, a salad with julienne ham, Swiss cheese and Italian dressing, sprinkled with chives. As a child I never realized chives developed flowers because Mom used them so much! A few years ago I bought my first chive plant. Since then I have divided my plant into at least 20 more plants (some given as gifts). You can also share your chives by cutting the chive flowers and hanging them upside down in a bag to dry. When they dry, the seeds fall into the bag and you can pass them along. Chives make a wonderful border plant that is very fragrant when nicked by the lawnmower. I love to add chives to twice baked potatoes or my favorite, bacon and chive potato salad. All you do is mix boiled and diced potatoes with crumbled bacon (or bacon bits), chives, mayonnaise and mustard. Enjoy!

Shelley McHugh

Wormwood is a "not much heard about" herb plant. Because of its unusual name, I was intrigued to get one at my local herb garden store two years ago. It has now become quite large, with silvery-white foliage and is very attractive in my herb garden. It has a very popular (especially with us) use...it's a moth repellent. I dry the cuttings in late summer (tie and hang upside down). Once dried, shred them by hand. Then fill old stockings with the herb and hang them in closets, or place them in a sweater or woolens trunk. The effect is excellent, as you will notice a pungent scent when shredding. Use gloves when handling the herb; but if you don't, be sure to wash your hands immediately after. For goodness sakes, don't touch your mouth; it's dreadfully bitter. Again, the effect is wonderful, as it really does repel those pesky moths. Plus you have no lingering mothball odor on your clothes.

Diane Michaels

A fun sign for your garden is "Please touch the herbs."

Pennyroyal is a great repellent for mosquitoes. Hang baskets of it on the porch or patio, rub fresh leaves on your arms or legs to keep flies, bees, mosquitoes, wasps and chiggers far away. Be sure not to use it near the eyes. It's even helpful for your pet! Bathe man's best friend weekly with a rinse made from 2 cups of fresh peppermint or pennyroyal that has been simmered in a quart of boiling water. Boil for 30 minutes. Let cool and add this mixture to at least 1 gallon of warm bath water. Sponge on your pet or put him directly in the bath water. Again, be sure to keep the water away from your pet's eyes. The herbs may irritate them.

Mary Murray

Spearmint is one of my favorite herbs. It's easy to grow and spreads everywhere! Take leaves and use in ice molds, throw a stem in when you brew your sun tea. Ah, such a minty taste! I have even frozen some in a resealable plastic sandwich bag, and put it in when I make hot tea in the teapot in winter. It smells and tastes so good. Or try drying some leaves. Keep them in a jar, and around Christmas time add to the potpourri pot or into a dry potpourri sachet. My children aren't always thrilled with the mint. When our son was little he asked me, "Why do you always float a weed in with the iced tea?" Oh yes, a few sprigs of leaves looks nice on the top of a chocolate cake (or vanilla if you prefer) with a few fresh strawberries. It makes a great garnish. It's also good when someone has a cold. Put it in a pot of hot water (where no one can reach it) and let the minty steam fill the air.

Wendy Lee Paffenroth

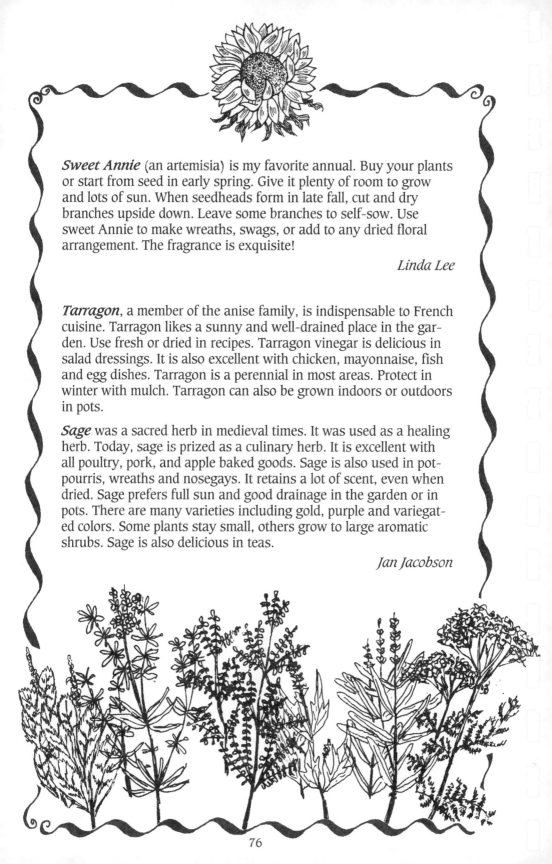

Sweet Annie (an artemisia) is my favorite annual. Buy your plants or start from seed in early spring. Give it plenty of room to grow and lots of sun. When seedheads form in late fall, cut and dry branches upside down. Leave some branches to self-sow. Use sweet Annie to make wreaths, swags, or add to any dried floral arrangement. The fragrance is exquisite!

Linda Lee

Tarragon, a member of the anise family, is indispensable to French cuisine. Tarragon likes a sunny and well-drained place in the garden. Use fresh or dried in recipes. Tarragon vinegar is delicious in salad dressings. It is also excellent with chicken, mayonnaise, fish and egg dishes. Tarragon is a perennial in most areas. Protect in winter with mulch. Tarragon can also be grown indoors or outdoors in pots.

Sage was a sacred herb in medieval times. It was used as a healing herb. Today, sage is prized as a culinary herb. It is excellent with all poultry, pork, and apple baked goods. Sage is also used in potpourris, wreaths and nosegays. It retains a lot of scent, even when dried. Sage prefers full sun and good drainage in the garden or in pots. There are many varieties including gold, purple and variegated colors. Some plants stay small, others grow to large aromatic shrubs. Sage is also delicious in teas.

Jan Jacobson

Summer Shade

It could have been just yesterday
The way memories are remade
That I claimed the canvas hammock
Hanging in the summer's shade.

In Grandma's wide back yard
With fruit ripening on the trees
I was young but had my dreams
And could do just as I pleased.

On days with clouds I'd see images
Or gaze dreamily at the blue
Pushing myself back and forth
I could linger the whole day through...

And might have done just that
If it weren't for fresh lemonade
Topped with just a sprig of mint
Served at a table in the shade.

It could have been just yesterday
But many a year has gone
But when I think of summer...
These memories linger on.

Starrlette L. Howard

Flowers and hearts have always played an important part in the relationship between my daughter and me. Beginning with the times as a toddler when she picked tiny bouquets of wildflowers and presented them to me.

The time as a young child when she entered a Mother's Day contest at a local flower shop, and won, because she drew the mother she saw...a slender, stick figure, when actually I never was! Her prize...a magnificent pot of azaleas.

The wonderful gardens of zinnias, one of our favorite flowers, that she grew herself, as she herself grew.

The many pictures of flowers and hearts she drew and colored, always with a smiley face in the suns.

The beautiful heart-shaped twig basket she put together for a graduation gift, when I finally graduated from college. Each flower and plant carefully chosen for its significant, sentimental reason.

The meaningful, thoughtful flowers she and her family sent when my father died suddenly.

The flowers she now grows in her garden, which she generously shares with her family, friends and church.

Through the years our relationship has been like a garden. Planted tenderly, fertilized, watered and nurtured. Occasionally a weed has grown, which needs to be plucked out, strengthening the flowers already blooming there.

Today we share and treasure the bountiful harvest of that very special garden. From my heart I can tell you that my daughter is a wonderful woman, wife, mother and friend. I only hope that when I grow up, I can be just like she is today!

The fragrance of certain flowers evoke memories of important occasions in my past. Geraniums were Mother's Day in Sunday school, lilacs from our 8th grade graduation, nasturtiums from grandmother's home.

My son was the kind of child who complained bitterly when asked to carry out the garbage, but always picked me a flower on his way back!

Nancy Campbell

Many years ago, before I had children, I worked in an office that looked out onto a vacant lot. Summer was always hard because I wanted to be outside working in the flowers, not inside at a desk. One year, I planted a single sunflower in that vacant lot and talked the maintenance people into mowing around it. All summer, from my desk inside, I watched that sunflower grow. I watched it bloom and the birds pull the seeds out for food in the fall. I finally watched it wither up and die with the first frost. That year, I did not miss summer at all.

Mel Wolk

When I was young, I loved picture books. Among my favorites was one handed down to me by my sister. It was so old and used that the binding was taped and the corners worn, but its beautiful illustrations were one of my first inspirations to be an artist. It had a number of familiar stories in it like Cinderella and Rumpelstiltskin, but my favorite story was about where fireflies come from.

Once upon a time there was a young childless couple who lived in China. They prayed nightly to the lady of the moon to send them a child to love, and one night she sent them her own daughter in the form of a beautiful baby girl. When they found the child on their doorstep, the infant spoke to them. "I am Princess Moonbeam. My mother, hearing your prayers, has sent me to bring you happiness." Eighteen years filled with joy and love passed, and the day finally came for the princess to return to her real mother. Her Earth parents were sad, though they had always known she was only lent to them. She kissed them goodbye, disappearing in a path of moonbeams, but the tears that fell from her eyes turned silver, grew wings and flew into the night. More and more appeared until the night was filled with them. Her parents knew she had left these fireflies behind to remind them of her love for always.

Laurie Micarelli

Sunny Garden Memories

During the summer, my sisters and I would pick clover and tie the flowers together to make a chain and then wear them as bracelets and necklaces. We also picked yellow buttercup flowers and held them to each other's neck. If the yellow appeared on our neck from the reflection, it meant that we liked butter! How simple and refreshing those days were...little girls romping and playing in the grass.

Carolyn Ritz Lemon

I have numerous gardening memories of my grandmother, who lived very frugally in a small mobile home much of her life, and who shared great wisdom in her love for God, family, and the things of the earth. There were always flowers in bloom (it seemed) at Grandma's doorstep, and she never failed to point out their beauty with exclamations like, "Isn't that the most glorious shade of blue you've ever seen?!" She had a certain "snap" that made life seem simple and pure, much like the cleansing of the soul when the "weeds of life" are pulled out by the roots. And I remember the great sunflowers that would tower over me, almost scary to a small child as they waved in the breeze. Yet it was those same sunflowers, out of which I picked the seeds, that taught me to care for God's creatures. And this child took great delight in throwing those seeds on the patio, running inside, and watching the birds feast before my eyes! For me, the lessons of the garden from my grandmother produced growth far beyond what comes out of the soil.

Heather Hood

We loved picking rhubarb in the summer. After wearing a big rhubarb leaf as a sunhat, we ate the stem. Our mouths puckered and our teeth danced but the fresh, tart taste was a shivery thrill!

Joyce Steeby

*Look up
at those billowy, white clouds in the sky...
what shapes do you see?*

My grandfather could grow anything, even in this hot Texas weather. After my grandmother passed away, he made his home with us for 10 years, until he joined her. All that time, he still planted a huge garden, tended fruit trees, and took care of all of the flower beds. Of course, plants that grew for him did not flourish for us after he was gone, for he truly had a "green thumb" and a closeness to the earth. I can see him picking fresh cherry tomatoes, wiping them off, and popping them into his mouth. And, of course, I had to do the same, and warm, tomatoey juice would squirt into my mouth. He grew flower beds full of what he called "pinks." They had a delicious fragrance and were so pretty. I can still see the rows and rows of zinnias...all colors. He had been a farmer, and I think he was totally in touch with the plants and the earth.

One of my favorite memories is my mother purchasing bushels of black-eyed peas, peaches, corn or green beans. We spent several summer afternoons shelling, peeling, or whatever was necessary to get these ready to freeze or can. At about 3:00 we would take a break for some cold watermelon. Such simple pleasures are life's best. Mother would make preserves from the peaches of our three peach trees, and that taste just can't be found anymore. In early spring, a favorite family Sunday dinner was a garden smorgasbord...fresh green beans with new potatoes, green onions, new leaf lettuce salad, corn-on-the-cob, boiled squash sweetened with sugar, fried okra, sliced tomatoes, and cornbread. With all that delicious goodness, who needs meat?

Barbara Loe

These were the rules of my grandmother's garden:

1. Organize gardening supplies
2. Talk to husband
3. Reorganize gardening supplies
4. Talk to husband
5. Forget whole gardening thing
6. Talk to self!

She kept these rules on a card with her salad recipes. She was a very jolly and humorous lady!

Ronda Rivers-Stone

Sunny Garden Memories

As a child, our neighbor's wild pansy field was open for children to pick flowers. What a joy to seek the long stems, with a handful of tiny yellow blooms. I swiftly ran home to place them in a little glass bottle. I would deliver the vase of colorful pansies to an elderly neighbor. Each day until the pansies stopped blooming, I walked amid the field and gathered lovely gifts for free. The repetition of this carefree task was a childhood delight creating lasting memories. I learned the beauty of sharing, and the joy of giving, which I carried over into my adult life. May I pass it on to another generation.

Phyllis Peters

We would walk up past the barn to the truck patch, choose a warmed-by-the-sun tomato, walk over to our cousin's house, slice it onto a soft piece of white bread (one slice of the tomato covered the bread), sprinkle sugar on it, and enjoy it to the fullest ...like only a kid could!

Joy Kinnear

For years my boys, now 33 and 27, would bring me a bouquet of lilacs for Mother's Day. Every time I smell a lilac tree it brings back pleasant memories. They were the nicest flowers I ever received.

Jackie Samo

I am an avid nature-loving person, and treasure my garden. I can't recall the exact words, but there is an old saying, "You are never so close to God as you are when on your knees in a garden." I grew up in Pennsylvania with its wildflower meadows. I envision my grandmother in the 30's. She always wore large pocketed aprons. She gathered flower seed in these pockets. When she traveled the large farm, with its meadows, hillsides and woods, she scattered this seed about. Each spring as we children walked her paths we would remark, "Grandmother was here." Her yard was always a carpet of blossoms. She even hollowed out a large, black log and filled it with bright asters. She created such beauty, and enjoyed sharing with others many seeds and starts.

As a child of the depression, I made my very own toys and fun. My younger sister and cousins would join me. From the time school let out we would play outdoors, except for meals. In the spring the woods were ablaze with white dogwood. We figured out all by ourselves where to hide (usually a tree arbor, thicket or bush). Scouring the meadows and woods daily, we would spend hours searching for wildflower plants...no one ever showed us where to look, or told us their names; it was instinct. We would stain pussy willows with colored chalk, and set Queen Anne's lace in water colored with food coloring (or mother's wash day bluing), resulting in beautifully colored flowers. Skunk cabbage, violets, pussy willows and other countless flowers grew in our glorious meadow, where we made hollyhock dolls and saw faces in the pansies. When we tore apart the bleeding heart we imagined we could see two rabbits or two earrings. We often asked each other, "Do you like butter?" Then holding a dandelion bloom under each other's chins, we would search for that yellow glow meaning yes, we did like butter. Swinging from wild grape vines we shrieked wildly, imitating Tarzan of the Apes. We chewed on sweet grasses and sipped the drops of honey liquid from the honeysuckle. Every blackberry, elderberry, strawberry, gooseberry and blueberry patch was known to us, and we kept it a well-guarded secret. We also knew where to find black cherries, beech, hickories and the wild plum thickets. The sweet-scented crabapple blooms made wonderful wreaths, strung on a string between two sticks implanted on the ground. We played house and store, and begged posters of movie queens from the merchants. Picnics were often held on large boulders where my mother played as a girl. My aunt would treat us to cold watermelon, placed in the well to cool. She had a huge grape arbor over a structure of sorts. We would sit at a table there to eat meals and sip lemonade, when we were lucky enough to be asked.

Mrs. Travis Baker

When I was little, I used to get "butterfly kisses," a delicate and soft whispering of one's eyelashes onto a chin, nose or ear. These create the most delightful giggle from a child.

Susan Mroz

I grew up on the farm and beside our 1/2 acre garden was a wild onion patch. Lo and behold our milk cows got out and raided the garden and the wild onion patch. Boy, from the looks of things those cows had fun and the result of their raid was oniony tasting milk. We couldn't have the milk picked up by the Meadow Gold Company, a dairy in Decatur, Illinois at that time. Mother took all this in good nature and the laughter quickly spread through our family; then in a short while, throughout our farming community. We used the oniony tasting milk in meatloaf, potato soup, onion bread and onion butter. We were even giving the milk away. This lasted nearly two weeks. Meanwhile the fence was mended, talk in town died down and life went on as usual, but our family still talks about our garden memory.

Jennifer Overfield

My mother-in-law was a successful gardener and the food harvested helped to feed her seven children. A Michigan native, she always yearned for winter to end so spring plowing and planting could begin. She kept the garden paths free of weeds and the produce matured to supreme quality. When we visited the folks, my mother-in-law always asked, "Would you like something from the garden?" She would fill a basket with juicy sweet corn, red ripe tomatoes, cucumbers, green beans, and lettuce for our family to take home. The gift of food was most welcome, as a young mother I had little time to spend hours in the garden. What I learned most from my husband's mother was the attitude of giving to others. I later found the joy of sharing one's garden is a simple practice of giving of yourself with love, which had been sown with the seeds and hoed around each plant. Happiness is achieved through gardening, I'm convinced.

My grandmother had a large side porch off the kitchen of her colonial home. Occasionally she would entertain with an afternoon tea for a group of lady friends and invite me to assist with serving the tea and cookies. She allowed me to pick small bouquets of flowers from the yard to decorate each card table. The rich butter cookies were baked in a cookstove oven. The screened-in porch provided a view of nature with every type of flower growing nearby for a colorful background of beauty. The roses growing on the white painted arbor with a simple bench nearby was my fav-orite spot after the tea. Grandpa made the bench and it became my world of imagination...once it was a horse, another time a car. Still another time the bench was a train that took me to a far distant land. Once the wooden seat was a pretend bus taking my family on vacation. Grandma's side porch was a pleasant, cool spot for an afternoon nap. What wonderful memories can be formed all due to a lov-ing grandma, an afternoon tea party and guests who find time for a child.

Phyllis Peters

The smell of fresh-cut grass brings back a flood of childhood memories.

86

Sunny Garden Memories

It was a beautiful spring day, and I had all the windows open airing out the house from a long winter. My daughter had gone outdoors to play with her cousin and was out for just a short time when I heard Charlie, the old man across the street, yelling "Oh no, oh no!" I immediately ran out and was stopped short as I spotted my daughter with a huge bouquet of tulips. With tears in her eyes she said, "I picked these for you Mommy." How could I scold her? Needless to say Charlie never got over losing his tulips so early in the season and I have a 28 year old daughter who even today will not pick flowers until she gets permission!

Margaret Riley

As a child living with my grandparents, I remember my grandfather planting and caring for his vegetable garden and my grandmother caring for her rose and peony garden. She had one particular rose bush that grew on a trellis made of pipes (my grandfather grew up on a farm in Italy and this, he told me, was an easy way to make "support" for the flowers). When I was 18, my grandmother developed Alzheimer's. She still tried to perform her chores, but within the year her Alzheimer's advanced and she died. The rose bush didn't bloom very well that year, as much as I tried pruning it. The following year, in March, I came home from nursing school and saw a rose in full bloom on the very same rose bush (my grandmother had died in March). Every year since, when I go home in March, I go to the back door, look out in the yard and see a single rose in bloom on the rose bush (still growing on the pipe trellis). To me, it's Grandmom's way of telling me she is still with me and that she and Grandpop are okay wherever they are.

Theresa Manley

My father's pride and joy was his wildflower garden...a huge square in the middle of the backyard, chocked full of a multitude of wildflowers too numerous to mention. You never knew what you might discover on your treks around this spectacular kaleidoscope of color. The range went from magnificent poppies to simple bachelor's buttons...each one a unique contribution to Dad's simple, understated, yet somehow poetic, little bit of heaven on earth.

My father passed away and as we sat planning his funeral, we just knew that on his casket must rest a spray of wildflowers. Impossible in the dead of winter in Ohio, you say? Prayers truly are answered when one has a little bit of faith. What a tribute to Dad, in death, to see such a display of beauty, a reflection of the essence of who he really was. Simple, unassuming and full of a generous, giving spirit. As we left the grave site on that cold, snowy morning, I, along with other family members, selected a few of the flowers to take with us. I carefully dried mine and they are now fittingly displayed in an old mason jar that belonged to his mother, my grandmother. On top I have put a small doily crocheted by grandma and tied it with a ribbon. In addition, I keep a small vase on my kitchen windowsill and make sure it always contains a flower in memory of my father. Both items hold a special place in our house and in our hearts. Not only do they serve as a memorial of sorts to a man we loved very much, they also remind us daily of a lesson he taught us, "I shall pass through this world but once. Any good that I can do, or any kindness that I can show another human being, let me do it now and not defer it. For I shall not pass this way again." What greater legacy could a father give a child than this wondrous gift of love?

Margaret Wilson

When I was growing up, we had a large honeysuckle bush right by our front gate. The smell of those little blossoms was great. We would pull the flower off very carefully and then sip the nectar from the base of the flower. However, the most wonderful thing by far was sitting at dusk by the gate to watch the little hummingbirds sip the nectar from the blooms. I could sit and watch them for hours. Someday I want to have a front gate with a honeysuckle bush of my own, so I can again sit at dusk to watch the tiny hummingbirds.

Renee Smith

One of my favorite childhood books was "The Secret Garden" by Frances H. Burnett. It is the story of Mary Lennox, an orphaned girl who is sent to live in England. I was so taken with the story of English moors, castles with secret passages and lush green gardens that I vowed one day to have a "Mary Lennox" garden of my very own. Now I'm all grown up with a little girl of my own, but the dream has never died. We are now sharing the pleasure of reading together "The Secret Garden" and planning our own secret garden just for the two of us in our own backyard!

Carol Bull
Gooseberry Patch

Mary, Mary, quite contrary,
How does your garden grow?
With silver bells,
and cockleshells,
And pretty maids
all in a row.

Anonymous

Honeysuckle has a sweet fragrance that always brings to mind fresh laundry hanging out to dry in the breeze. As a young newlywed, I was thrilled to discover a patch of healthy honeysuckle vines growing happily on our just-purchased property. Our new home had suffered from years of neglect, so it was a miracle that the rambling vines had survived over the years. How fortunate I was to have honeysuckle growing on the back fence right beside my clothesline! In those early years of marriage, finances were tight and a clothes dryer would have seriously stretched our budget much too far. Line drying the laundry came more out of necessity than personal choice. Mother Nature rewarded me generously in the early spring months right on through the year until the first hard freeze, with an abundance of honeysuckle blossoms. Hanging laundry out to dry was a pleasure rather than a chore. Even when the budget allowed a fancy new dryer to lessen my work load, I still enjoyed regular trips to the old clothesline to dry all our bed linens. Mother Nature provided many years of sweet dreams because of those line-dried linens, which had spent the day soaking up the sunshine and honeysuckle breezes. To this day, the scent of honeysuckle conjures up happy memories of hanging laundry out to dry, the good old-fashioned way.

I owe my love of gardening to my maternal great-grandmother. I was privileged to know her for 14 short years. Having spent a great deal of my summer vacations from school on her small farm, I couldn't help but develop a love and respect for the soil and what could be coaxed from it. Grandmama had a beautiful cottage garden that grew right off her farmhouse front porch. The garden had a unique centerpiece...a century-old sycamore tree. Around that old tree, she grew every flower imaginable. Grandmama wasn't a fussy type of gardener and was just as happy calling the flowers by her pet names as knowing their correct scientific names. The garden was never barren, not even in winter. No matter how cold it got outside, there were always happy, smiling, pansy faces in the garden to admire...and sometimes pick if Grandmama's back was turned!

Jeannine English

90

Sunny Garden Memories

Summer was the time of year when the garden really came to life. Not only were the colors of every hue there to be enjoyed, but also sweet smells. Grandmama had a fondness for sweet peas and their perfume. Is it any wonder that sweet peas are to this day one of my favorite cut flowers to bring indoors to enjoy? In Grandmama's house, you were not only treated to the perfume of all the cut flowers she had sitting around in every room, but also the pleasant aromas coming from her kitchen. She was an excellent cook in addition to being an avid gardener. Naturally, she grew her own fruit trees and the bounty was transformed into peach pies cooling on the windowsills or fresh plum jelly resting in a jelly cupboard...awaiting introduction to farm-fresh butter and hot homemade biscuits. Grandmama's cottage garden was a favorite visiting spot for all sorts of creeping and crawling things...even snakes, which I had a great fear of. She always calmed my fears by reminding me everything was put on this earth for a reason.

Jeannine English

Here's just a fond memory of growing up in the country in the 40's. For a few years we lived in a very small town in Washington. I have lovely memories of taking a book and a blanket and, walking into the woods, finding a big log to lean against. I'd read for awhile, listen for awhile, and enjoy the wild bleeding hearts, trillium, and the lily of the valley. My favorite wild plant was the small blackberries that my brother and I would pick so my mother could make a wonderful pie. How tasty it was with a glass of milk. The blackberries were also a favorite of the local bears, and we always had to be alert to their presence. I remember seeing two cubs and found out later that mother was around too! She must have realized I was not a threat. Yes, those were the days.

Constance Cascino

My favorite garden memory is of my wedding reception. The food was arranged on tables in the gazebo. There was a lovely brook and bridge nearby that was perfect for pictures. Chairs for guests were arranged beneath several weeping willows and other trees, which provided a cool spot for eating and visiting. It was a gorgeous June day. The only decorations needed were a few bows around the gazebo.

As we were wandering around to different areas of the gardens for pictures, a woman approached us with a small child. The mother said they had been walking in the gardens and that her little girl had seen us and wanted to see the bride. Her sparkling eyes were full of wonder as she silently took in my dress and wedding finery. I bent down to say "hello," and suddenly she ran over and grabbed me around the knees with a big hug. I returned the hug and looked into a face filled with the joy of childhood. She acted as if I were a fairy princess; for that moment in time I was. What a wonderful memory to add to my already overflowing heart! I never knew the little girl's name, but I know I'll never forget her.

Cheryl Berry

Picking blackberries was a happy pastime for my brother and I in the month of July. Long, hot afternoons were spent picking the juicy berries after we had waited patiently for the white flowers to turn first from green berries then to juicy blackberries. The vines grew profusely on our farm and surrounding farms in rural North Carolina. When mother had canned enough for blackberry sonkers (a southern treat) and filled jar after jar with jam and jelly, she let us start selling to a local cannery. We filled their empty cans for 5 cents each and thought we were rich. Sometimes we made $3.00 for an afternoon's picking. I still remember the briars and chigger bites!

My grandmother lived with us when I was a teenager. I can picture her now as she gathered apples from under the old apple trees on our farm and carried them in her long apron. She peeled and sliced them into small pieces and dried them on a screen in the sun. After drying, they were stored for the winter to be cooked with spices and sugar into wonderful fried apple pies.

Annabelle Whitaker

Sunny Garden Memories

The best memories I have as a child are being able to walk barefoot to the garden, helping Mom water, and also smelling the fresh dirt as we dug potatoes. We would pull radishes and onions, rinse them in the ice-cold water from the windmill, and eat them fresh. Zinnias and marigolds made colorful bouquets and helped keep bugs away from the garden.

Pat Habiger

My parents taught us how to garden. As children, we didn't realize what they were teaching us would be something that would last a lifetime. All seven of us kids would be out with mom and dad in the garden through the wet spring plantings, the hot and humid summer weedings, and the bountiful harvests. We listened to the same old "dadisms" year after year. None of us ever thought we would utter those same things in OUR gardens. Well, one day it happened...while out garden planting with my husband, I uttered a "dadism!" "Those seeds will grow in a crooked row just as well as a straight row!" I just had to laugh. I guess all those little seeds of wisdom dad had planted all those years ago grew after all.

Janet Mallory

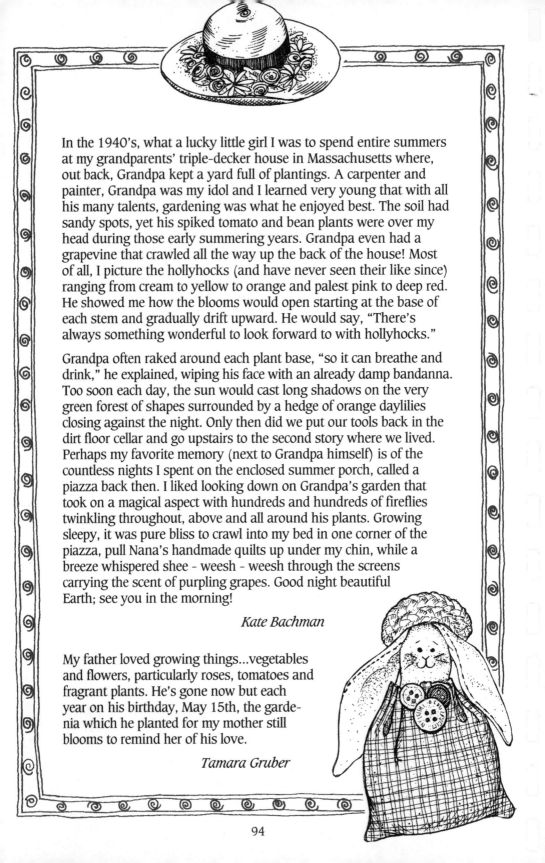

In the 1940's, what a lucky little girl I was to spend entire summers at my grandparents' triple-decker house in Massachusetts where, out back, Grandpa kept a yard full of plantings. A carpenter and painter, Grandpa was my idol and I learned very young that with all his many talents, gardening was what he enjoyed best. The soil had sandy spots, yet his spiked tomato and bean plants were over my head during those early summering years. Grandpa even had a grapevine that crawled all the way up the back of the house! Most of all, I picture the hollyhocks (and have never seen their like since) ranging from cream to yellow to orange and palest pink to deep red. He showed me how the blooms would open starting at the base of each stem and gradually drift upward. He would say, "There's always something wonderful to look forward to with hollyhocks."

Grandpa often raked around each plant base, "so it can breathe and drink," he explained, wiping his face with an already damp bandanna. Too soon each day, the sun would cast long shadows on the very green forest of shapes surrounded by a hedge of orange daylilies closing against the night. Only then did we put our tools back in the dirt floor cellar and go upstairs to the second story where we lived. Perhaps my favorite memory (next to Grandpa himself) is of the countless nights I spent on the enclosed summer porch, called a piazza back then. I liked looking down on Grandpa's garden that took on a magical aspect with hundreds and hundreds of fireflies twinkling throughout, above and all around his plants. Growing sleepy, it was pure bliss to crawl into my bed in one corner of the piazza, pull Nana's handmade quilts up under my chin, while a breeze whispered shee - weesh - weesh through the screens carrying the scent of purpling grapes. Good night beautiful Earth; see you in the morning!

Kate Bachman

My father loved growing things...vegetables and flowers, particularly roses, tomatoes and fragrant plants. He's gone now but each year on his birthday, May 15th, the gardenia which he planted for my mother still blooms to remind her of his love.

Tamara Gruber

Sunny Garden Memories

I lost my kitty, Dypsy, in March and buried her in my rock garden. She has a tombstone and a little sleeping cat birdbath on top of her grave. The chipmunks and ground squirrels busily run across and drink from her birdbath; and her favorite flowers (oriental poppies) are in full bloom.

Judith "JJ" Jamison

My mind's eye holds a wealth of happy summer memories from childhood years visiting my aunt and uncle who lived in the country. Yes, I'm the "city" cousin. When growing up, my cousins would tease me about being from the city. I fondly remember the old swimming creek, stilts made from strong young trees, riding the mule, playing in the hay loft, going to the out-house (Sears catalog and all!), the smell of the smokehouse, the coolness of the earthen pan-try, Sunday dinner, and most of all, the strawberry rows in the garden. Many of the flowers from the country are now in my yard and hold many special memories for me. These memories are only a small part of the whole picture...showing family love in the country (city cousin included!).

Brenda Hessel

I cannot look at daffodils without remembering how I learned to ride a bike. My mother grew such beautiful ones along the side of the house. My father, ever optimistic that one did not really need training wheels, put me on my new bike (a red Schwinn, boy's model...I wanted the red bike, even if it was for a boy) and shoved me off. A few seconds later, I careened out of control, through my mother's daffodil patch, and into the side of the house. Dad quickly reassessed his opinion of training wheels. By the way, my children, now thirty-some years later, have all learned to ride a bike on that little red Schwinn. With training wheels I may add, and far away from my daffodil patches!

Mary Redlin

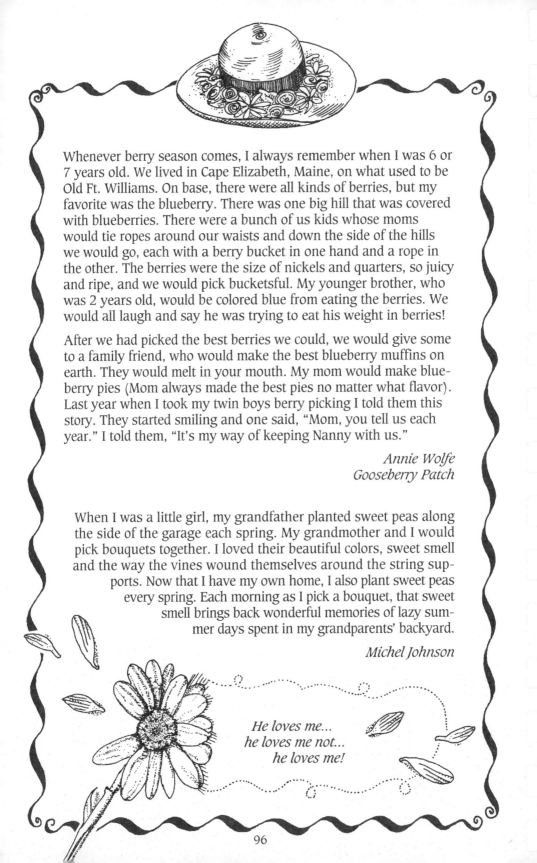

Whenever berry season comes, I always remember when I was 6 or 7 years old. We lived in Cape Elizabeth, Maine, on what used to be Old Ft. Williams. On base, there were all kinds of berries, but my favorite was the blueberry. There was one big hill that was covered with blueberries. There were a bunch of us kids whose moms would tie ropes around our waists and down the side of the hills we would go, each with a berry bucket in one hand and a rope in the other. The berries were the size of nickels and quarters, so juicy and ripe, and we would pick bucketsful. My younger brother, who was 2 years old, would be colored blue from eating the berries. We would all laugh and say he was trying to eat his weight in berries!

After we had picked the best berries we could, we would give some to a family friend, who would make the best blueberry muffins on earth. They would melt in your mouth. My mom would make blueberry pies (Mom always made the best pies no matter what flavor). Last year when I took my twin boys berry picking I told them this story. They started smiling and one said, "Mom, you tell us each year." I told them, "It's my way of keeping Nanny with us."

Annie Wolfe
Gooseberry Patch

When I was a little girl, my grandfather planted sweet peas along the side of the garage each spring. My grandmother and I would pick bouquets together. I loved their beautiful colors, sweet smell and the way the vines wound themselves around the string supports. Now that I have my own home, I also plant sweet peas every spring. Each morning as I pick a bouquet, that sweet smell brings back wonderful memories of lazy summer days spent in my grandparents' backyard.

Michel Johnson

He loves me...
he loves me not...
he loves me!

Sunny Garden Memories

My family and its history has always been of great interest to me. Several years ago when my house became overflowing with furniture, family pictures, antique knick-knacks and such, I began looking to the flower gardens that surround my home as a place to show off my family treasures. Among the weeping cherry trees, honeysuckle, clematis, larkspur and miniature roses stands an old plow, hand hewn by a great uncle more than fifty years ago. In another garden an old bench stands vigil among the pink coneflowers and black-eyed Susans. Over the years milk cans, old watering cans, garden signs made of old wood and lanterns have found themselves as part of a flourishing garden setting. Even some of the rocks that can be found among the flowers of spring and summer have a family history. Several of them are stone blocks chiseled from an eastern Kentucky mountain by my grandfather and great-grandfather, and used in the chimney that was once part of my grandparent's home. My flower gardens are special to me not only because of the floral beauty, but because of the family memories that can be so easily evoked when I see some memento of the past.

Martha Haught

My most treasured childhood memories grow from my relationship with my grandparents and their gardens. When I was little I would follow my grandpa through his daily gardening chores. I would trail behind him pushing my wheelbarrow filled with my own child-sized tools. I would stop and watch everything he did. Then I would get down upon my knees, into the dirt, turn the soil, pull the weeds, plant the seeds and water faithfully.

Often I would follow him into his formal gardens at the front of the house. These gardens were enclosed with a high rod-iron fence and encircled with neat box hedges. Within these gardens were a sea of blue and white hydrangea bushes which towered over me. These giant snowballs could easily hide me from my sisters and cousins. None of the other children seemed particularly interested in these gardens, but I never missed an opportunity to follow my grandpa within. Often I would bring my dolls, blanket, and tea set and play upon the lawn beneath.

But the gardens where I spent the majority of my time were in the backyard. They also were enclosed with a fence and gate. You were only allowed to pass through the gate when grandpa unlocked it. I often felt as if I was passing into a magical land filled with wonderful delights. Beside the gate stood the tool shed where pots, cans and garden tools were stored. It reminded me of Mr. MacGregor's garden shed where Peter Rabbit hid within the watering can. Beyond the fence were rows and rows of cabbages, carrots, cucumbers, peppers, tomatoes, corn and lettuce. There were also box gardens with herbs and spices. Vines of eggplants, squash, watermelons, pumpkins, berries and trees full of apples, peaches and figs.

Often grandma would come out into the garden to visit with us. She would bring tall glasses of lemonade and we would break off leaves of mint and put them in our drinks. Then grandma would gather up the most succulent greens, herbs, vegetables, and fruits for our dinner. Many of the midmorning and afternoon snacks came directly from the garden. Nothing tasted better than a sun-warmed tomato or an overly ripened fig.

Nancy Rootland

Sunny Garden Memories

As I think back to my grandparents, to their love and tenderness, it is all intertwined within their gardens. And just as they nurtured their plants, they nurtured my essence and allowed me to grow and develop at my own pace. Through my journeys around their gardens I learned about tender caring; I learned about sharing; I learned about hard work; I learned about seasons and cycles; and I learned about the rewards of my labor. Those simple shared experiences have followed me throughout my life and at any moment I can reach into my treasure chest of memories and pull out the magic they shared with me.

Nancy Rootland

Experiencing the farm life of southwest Kansas, I have many gardening memories. Our garden was always plentiful because of our family of nine. One particular gardening season my brother and I had the job of planting pumpkins and watermelons. We had two areas to choose from; one was in the cool shade of the shelter belt and the other was a few yards away in the blazing sun. Being the older "big brother" his first choice was the cool shade, so he could plant, weed, and harvest without sweltering sun. I settled for the sunny spot and worked at it as if the constant heat didn't bother me. When it came to harvest time, the fruits of my labor were far more superior than my brother's. Final analysis...mine were kissed by the sun!

Jeanette Urbom

When our sons were young, we started a tradition of casting their footprints, handprints, date and their signatures in a cement stone or block every summer. Now the grandchildren have continued the tradition. The stones are laid in a marvelous "sitting" patio in the garden. When we had only a few stones, they formed part of a walk. So great to re-cord growth and change in a child through the years and a wonderful conversation piece.

Dorothy Hanford

99

The year my first child was born, I planted 100 red and yellow tulips under the large tree in our front yard. Every spring I set him in the mass of color and took his picture playing with the flowers. After many years, the tree roots crowded out the bulbs and we moved from that house. But the pictures I took of him smiling in the tulips will last forever.

When I was younger, staying at grandma and grandpa's was at the top of my list, especially in the summer. They had a garden so big I thought I might get lost in it, if I dared to enter alone. I always begged to pick all the vegetables. Grandma knew that peas were my favorite. She would chuckle when I came out of the garden with my pail, because she knew it would only be half full (the other half in my tummy). She would ask me, "How did they taste dear?" Grandpa would bring a clean bowl from the house and we would shuck the peas on the front step. After we cleaned all the vegetables outside, Grandma would carry me into the house, sit me on the counter and wash off all the mud on my feet (gardening was much more fun when barefoot!). Grandpa is gone now, and grandma doesn't garden as much as she used to, but the fond memories of staying at their house those long-ago summers live on.

Michelle Urdahl

I have a wonderful childhood memory about when my grandpa and I were the best of friends. Grandma worked second shift, leaving the afternoons for just grandpa and me. One summer afternoon, he sat in his lawn chair watching me as I played in my sandbox. When I would get so dirty he couldn't stand it, he would just throw me in my swimming pool to clean me off a bit. Back into the sandbox I would go. This went on all afternoon. After hours of fun, it was time to settle down for the evening. That night when my grandma came in from work, she saw the two of us together, sound asleep and dirty from our heads to our toes...only my eyelids were clean (because I never closed my eyes all day!). Every time my grandma tells this story she smiles and tears come to her eyes. My grandpa passed away over 7 years ago, and remembering the "good ol' days" helps us to remember what grandpa meant to all of us.

Crystal Parker
Gooseberry Patch

Sunny Garden Memories

It was a cold, snowy January, and as my seed catalogs arrived in the mail, an idea spouted...why not plant my own flowers for my wedding coming up in July? I've always gotten raves about my wildflower garden, and my wedding was going to be a country theme, so I plotted, planned and ordered seeds. The girls carried long stemmed black-eyed Susans, sweet peas, cosmos, daisies, baby's breath, and purple, pink and white statice tied with pink tulle ribbons. I carried the same theme with a few roses and carnations added, with white tulle and a few pearls and ivy (for good luck). We got up at 6:00 am, picked the flowers, had a big breakfast and time together before the big moment. For the reception and church, I had blue ball mason jars with the same flowers tied with country pink ribbons with tiny hearts. I got so many compliments on the centerpieces, I didn't have one left (58 total)! I was so happy that everyone enjoyed my theme as much as I did. Weddings are special, and growing my own flowers made mine extra special.

Tammy Moon

When I think of summer, I think of rhubarb. My father was the rhubarb lover in our family. We lived in the country and he always made sure that several plants grew along the ditch banks. We would go out in the morning and pick the large, juicy stalks for rhubarb sauce, pie, or other treats. For me, the tart taste of rhubarb had to be acquired. To temper the tangy taste, rhubarb sauce can be made using equal parts rhubarb and applesauce. Sweeten to taste with sugar or honey and a touch of cinnamon.

Glenna Tooman

My grandmother loved peonies...any color! She literally had fences of peonies growing around her yard. One day as I wandered among these beauties, amusing myself while grandmother worked inside, I grabbed the large open blossoms and put them to my nose to breathe in their most wonderful scent. However, I became very alarmed when I began to focus on the bushes with unopened buds...they were covered with ants! I knew that my grandmother would be horrified to see these ants destroying (or so I thought) her beauties. I began to "de-ant" all the infested buds by filling empty jars with insects. I was determined to conquer and save! I worked feverishly for there were so many ants. Finally after quite some time, my grandmother came out to see if I was all right. Upon catching sight of her, I quickly ran to tell her of the horrible infestation and how I had been working to save her peony buds. Instead of the heroic commendation which I expected, she quickly began to educate me about peonies and ants. Didn't I recognize that the ants were working for her, not against her? The ants, she informed me, helped the peony bud to open into all those beautifully scented and gorgeously large flowers. It was then that I realized why she always kept her beautiful bouquets of peonies on stands on her front porch and never in the house...she knew how hard it was to rid the flowers of these helpful insects before entering the house. Tens-of-years have passed since the incident and my grandmother is no longer living, but my peony buds in my garden are crawling with ants and my beautiful bouquets are placed in the same vases that she once used, but they are now on my porch instead of hers. Needless to say, the peony brings back not only memories of my loved one, but memories of a valuable lesson learned.

Judy Hand

Each time a child (or grandchild) is born into a family, plant a tree in your garden. On each birthday, take a photograph of the child in front of "his or her" tree, and remember to date each picture. You can keep a special album of this yearly growth or frame the photos and add to your collection as time goes by.

Kristen Eddy

Homegrown & Made by hand

Easy-To-Make Gifts from the Garden

Hanging Wire Baskets

Line a wire basket with plenty of moss (you can buy moss at craft and garden stores). I use Spanish moss because it grows wild in my area. In the center of your basket put a pot or basket of small-sized plants, well established. I like caladiums; they will give good height. Fill in with soil and any kind of starter plants. I use begonias, impatiens, airplane plants, jew and ivy; even small amounts of Boston fern. I like to add plants all around the baskets by pulling the wire and moss apart, pushing the plants into the soil, and then bending the wire back; even very near the bottom of baskets it will all start to grow and the basket will be high and beautiful. I have half wire baskets also that will fit on gates or any fence.

Jean Stokes

Butterfly Sachets

Stitch potpourri inside a double layer of scalloped eyelet material and tie tightly in the middle with a colorful narrow ribbon. Form a loop to hang on a door knob or in your closet. The potpourri will show through the eyelet in the material.

Mary Murray

Patchwork Pot

Supplies you will need:

1 clay flowerpot **green moss or Spanish moss**
crinkled newspaper **assortment of dried flowers**
1 styrofoam ball, **(you may also use small**
**   diameter of flowerpot** **   shells, or cones and pods)**

Fill the bottom of the flowerpot with newspaper. Glue styrofoam ball so that 1/2 shows above the rim. Glue moss lightly onto the styrofoam ball. Arrange patches of flowers onto the moss so it looks like a patchwork quilt. Glue in place.

Carol Steele

Country Garden Birdbath

Make a country garden birdbath by using an old porch post and an old granite dishpan. Cut an old (or new) porch post off to approximately 4 feet. Place post in the ground so that it is buried at least 1 foot and stands securely. Screw your dish pan into the center of the top of the post. Surround with country flowers.

Denise Green

Handmade Victorian Sachet Hanger

As a young girl I remember my mother making beautiful clothes hangers which she covered with pastel satins and embroidered her own designs of Victorian florals. She sold these to specialty gift shops. I decided to give my mother's craft a new twist when finding I had more potpourri at the end of the season than I needed for my own use. It's easy, here's how:

Place a plastic hanger on a piece of newspaper and outline a pattern (leaving a 1/2" seam allowance). Cut out a covering for the hanger from lace or a Victorian print material. Sew edges and leave a small opening to turn inside out. Place covering over plastic hanger and slip stitch shut after filling with potpourri. Now add lace edging, ribbons or dried flowers using your imagination. These make lovely gifts and the scent can be restored with a few drops of refresher oil.

Nancy Stahl

Decorate an old-fashioned garden hat with pretty posies, fragrant herbs and ribbons.

Garden Markers

Begin with wooden hearts found at a craft store. Paint desired color and allow to dry. Print desired flower or herb name. Let dry. Sand lightly to give an aged look. Glue a large craft stick on back for a stake to place in a flowerpot or flower bed.

Unique Lamps

Turn almost any unique item into a lamp. The most fun is hunting for old watering cans, crocks, old tins, teapots and such. Simple lamp-making kits can be found at hardware stores. My favorite lamp is one I made from an old watering can. I decoupaged a vintage seed packet on the front and added a lampshade covered with seed packet design fabric. Inexpensive plain white lampshades can be found at discount stores for a song and covered with whatever fabric you like. Spray adhesive makes it simple.

Fridge Magnet Idea

Use large wooden craft sticks. Paint desired color. Dry and sand. Draw on desired saying, an example would be, "Never Enough Thyme."

Fragrance Logs

Combine lavender, dill, sage and scented geraniums. Roll into small compact bundles and tie with raffia. May be tied into a fragrant wall hanging by the fireplace. Toss them in a crackling fire for a wonderful fragrance!

Chair Rails

This idea would work for a garden/sunroom or any room with a gardening theme. Use a plain board wide enough to decoupage vintage or regular seed packets to. The board should be stained or painted prior to adding seed packets. Use modge-podge to glue packets on. A large wall that needs a focal point would be best suited. The same idea would work great in a bathroom using bath seed or bubblebath packets. The bonus of collecting the packets is either a garden filled with flowers of every hue or a great time relaxing in the tub!

Jeannine English

License Plate Birdhouses

I like to pick up old license plates at the flea market and use them for the roofs of my birdhouses. They help protect them from the weather and they also are a great conversation piece. I've also found a bicycle license plate that I put on a smaller birdhouse. You have to make sure to center the license plate over the roof of the birdhouse with some overhang, and then bend and secure with a few small brads or finishing nails.

Susan Koronowski

Coleus Topiary

Pick a single stemmed coleus plant and pinch out all the side growth until the stem reaches a height of 12 to 18 inches. You will need to stake the stem to keep it straight and for extra support. When the plant reaches this height, begin to pinch back the top. When each of the two branches develop four leaves, pinch their tips. Continue pinching the tips that form from the top branches after their four leaves develop. The main stem (trunk) will get very woody and square. Fertilize your coleus topiary every two weeks with diluted fertilizer and pinch out all blooms that may form.

Mel Wolk

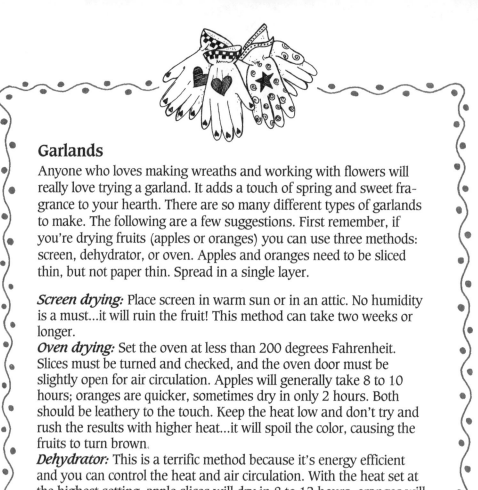

Garlands

Anyone who loves making wreaths and working with flowers will really love trying a garland. It adds a touch of spring and sweet fragrance to your hearth. There are so many different types of garlands to make. The following are a few suggestions. First remember, if you're drying fruits (apples or oranges) you can use three methods: screen, dehydrator, or oven. Apples and oranges need to be sliced thin, but not paper thin. Spread in a single layer.

Screen drying: Place screen in warm sun or in an attic. No humidity is a must...it will ruin the fruit! This method can take two weeks or longer.

Oven drying: Set the oven at less than 200 degrees Fahrenheit. Slices must be turned and checked, and the oven door must be slightly open for air circulation. Apples will generally take 8 to 10 hours; oranges are quicker, sometimes dry in only 2 hours. Both should be leathery to the touch. Keep the heat low and don't try and rush the results with higher heat...it will spoil the color, causing the fruits to turn brown.

Dehydrator: This is a terrific method because it's energy efficient and you can control the heat and air circulation. With the heat set at the highest setting, apple slices will dry in 8 to 12 hours, oranges will look their best if dried at a lower temperature and given more time. For a dehydrator or oven, the trick is to set a timer and constantly check them until they are tough and leathery to the touch. If they're too dry, they'll be brittle; and if they're too soft, they'll spoil! It sounds difficult, but it's not. Just keep checking and be patient.

Stringing: This is the fun part! You'll need thin twine or fishing line, and a large-eyed tapestry needle. Decide how long you'd like your garland and remember to cut your twine 6 to 8 inches longer to allow for a knot in the end. Tie a loop at one end of the string and secure it with a knot. Then thread the other end of the string through the needle. The idea is to puncture your material and gently push them onto the string.

You can string all kinds of goodies for your garland...fruits, bay leaves, nuts (will need a hole drilled in them first), everlastings, cinnamon sticks, pinecones, Indian corn or pomegranates (holes drilled here too). The list goes on! Roses are beautiful or try black-eyed Susans for a more country look. They will stay fresh for a day or two, or let them dry. Slip your materials over the twine, carefully pushing them close together. When you're finished, remove the needle, tie another loop, and knot securely. Hang and enjoy!

Mary Murray

Summer Fun With Hollyhock Flowers

When I was a little girl way back in the late 40's, my friends and I loved to make hollyhock dolls from the flowers of the wild hollyhocks that grew in our backyards. We would make a bride and the bridesmaids, each with a different color of dress. Pick a hollyhock flower and insert a toothpick through the center, exiting out of the stem end. On the end of this, place a small hollyhock bud (for the head of the doll). Use a petal from a matching flower for a veil or headpiece. Insert another toothpick crossways through the body of the flower for the arms. Put a smaller bud on the ends for arms. Here comes the bride!

Pat Akers

Recipe for a Happy Potpourri

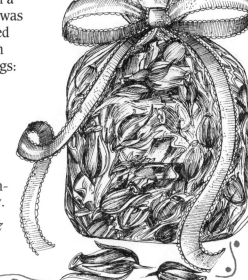

I made this as an "Anniversary Potpourri" for my parents 50th anniversary, and each guest at the party was given a bag to take home. The potpourri was put into cellophane bags, then tied with a golden bow and a tag with the ingredients and their meanings:

**rosebuds for love
chamomile for patience
lavender for devotion
marjoram for joy
rosemary for remembrance**

Blend with wisdom, age with constant attention; share generously.

Susan Mroz

Tussie Mussie

Supplies you will need:

fresh flowers
fresh herbs
florist tape, pipe cleaners or yarn
cellophane tape or floral pins
tiny satin ribbons in compatible colors
a white, lacy 4" doily
a small attractive recycled pill or
  aspirin bottle

Choose one small flower or rose for the center of your bouquet. Remember, your whole bouquet should fit in an aspirin or pill bottle. Gather herbs such as rose geranium leaves, lamb's ears, basil or any small fragrant herbs. Cut all stems to about 4" long on the diagonal and place in a glass of water for several hours. To start your bouquet, begin with your flower. Surround your flower with a small circle of one of the herbs. Add another circle of a different herb. Use floral tape or a pipe cleaner to hold stems together. Continue until you have a small bouquet, always keeping in mind the size of your container.

Take a 4" doily, fold it in half and make a small cut at the center of folded side. Unfold doily and refold in the opposite direction in half. The cut you first made will now be parallel to folded edge. Make a cut at center as before. Unfold doily, there will be a small "X" cut in center of doily. Dry off any moisture around the stems and slip stems through the doily. Press doily close up around stems and secure with cellophane tape, floral pins or floral tape. Now tie ribbons underneath doily. You may tie "love knots" in ribbon streamers. Now carefully set "tussie mussie" in its small container (labels removed of course). Be careful to only add enough water to "vase" to cover bottom of stems, but not so much that doily becomes wet. Take your tussie mussie to a sick friend or one who needs cheering up. If you have used fragrant herbs and flowers, the bouquet will smell wonderful. Depending on the plant material, it will probably dry well.

There are many definitions suggested for the origin of the word "tussie mussie." The one I've always enjoyed is "to tickle the nose."

In Victorian times, certain flowers and herbs were designated as having specific meanings, such as "rosemary for remembrance." Thus, depending on the plant material in your bouquet, the medium became the message. A tussie mussie could say, "I love you" or perhaps "I do not like you at all!"

Tamara Gruber

Sunflowery Favor

This is great as a party favor, hostess gift, stocking stuffer, or for your child's favorite teacher! You'll need:

plastic baggie & twist tie
potting soil
2 1/2" clay pot
white notepaper
sunflower seeds

tulle
1/8" width white, green, and red ribbon (or any color scheme you choose)

Fill a baggie with enough potting soil to fill the clay pot and close with twist tie. Place the baggie inside the clay pot. Make a small packet out of notepaper and seal 3-4 sunflower seeds inside. Place the seed packet on top of the baggie inside of the clay pot. Gather tulle around outside of the pot and tie with ribbon. Finish it off by using Gooseberry's sunflower rubber stamp on a square of notepaper as a gift tag. Include some simple planting instructions for starting flowers indoors and transplanting them outside. This makes a great gift for children to give because they love to watch things grow and with sunflowers they get some big results! My eight year old daughter gave one to each of her grandmothers for Christmas and is looking forward to helping them plant them this Spring and watching them grow all summer!

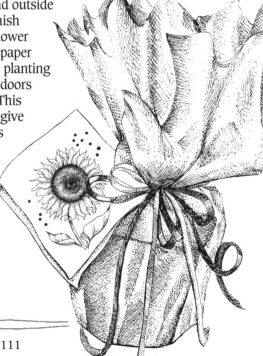

Twig Basket Love

My daughter gave me a wonderful, thoughtful, extra special gift when I graduated from college several years ago. She had carefully selected an assortment of plants, each with its own message. They were arranged in a loosely woven heart-shaped twig basket. Included were:

Sage - wisdom
Marjoram - joy
Bay - achievement and fame
Basil - love and good wishes
Scented Rose Geranium - happiness
Rosemary - remembrance and friendship
Dill - cheer and survival in the face of odds

I treasure the thoughts, support and time spent on this one-of-a kind gift from her heart.

Nancy Campbell

Decorated Clay Pots

To add country charm to your landscaping, or make your porch say "welcome," start with painted clay pots. Clay pots can be painted with acrylic paints as long as they are sealed with a clear acrylic sealer. To decorate, buy flat sponges that expand when wet. While still flat, trace cookie cutter shapes. For example, sponge a sunflower, add a stem and leaves. You could add a post with a sign "No Crows Allowed." Of course you need to put a crow on top of the sign! The rims can be painted solid.

Cindy Ziliak

Decorate a pair of inexpensive canvas gardening gloves with old buttons, fabric yo-yo's, homespun ties, stenciling, quilt remnants, scraps of lace, or ribbon rosebuds. Paperbacked fusible webbing and washable glue make this project fun and easy!

Wreath in Bloom

This wreath is great for showcasing the prettiest blossoms from your garden. It's also pretty with silk flowers when your garden isn't blooming.

1. Attach a hanging loop to a grapevine wreath.
2. Attach floral wire securely around the neck of several small bottles. (Probably five, depending on size of wreath.) Baby food or spice bottles work well.
3. Wire bottles to wreath at evenly spaced intervals, leaving a space at the top for a bow. You may wish to further secure the bottles to the wreath with hot glue.
4. Cover the wiring with ribbon bows. Add streamers as you wish.
5. Add a bow at the top of the wreath. You might want to put the bow on a floral pick to make it easier to change.
6. Add water to bottles, fill with bouquets of fresh flowers, greenery and baby's breath. (Water can be removed with a meat baster or a small sponge.)

Jackie Hoover

Living Wreath

Fashion a tubular frame out of chicken wire by cutting the wire wide enough to achieve the tube diameter you desire. Roll wire into a tubular shape, securing with florist wire. Carefully join the tube ends to form a circle. Attach a loop for hanging. Fill this compactly with spaghnum moss. Soak. Insert plants with roots into frame. Impatiens, ivies, and morning glories look beautiful! Water with a weak solution of household plant fertilizer twice a week. Mist daily. Likes morning sun only. These look great on a potting shed, garage or porch.

Toni Shawl

Kathryn's Everlasting Flora Favorites

Potpourri...fragrances that you can take right from your garden, and enjoy all year long! These garden recipes, created from bits and pieces of nature, were shared with me by a true lover of herbs and flowers. She is truly as sweet as a rose.

Herbal Garden:

1 c. dried parsley
1 c. dried sage
2 c. dried rosemary
1 c. dried thyme

1 c. dried mint of your choice
1 c. dried cranberries
10 medium-size
   pinecones

Mix together and display in a favorite basket.

A Touch of Lavender:

4 c. dried lavender blossoms
1 c. dried ivory globe
3 T. orris root
amaranth blossoms
1 c. dried salvia (blue) blossoms
1 c. dried rose petals
several drops of lavender oil

Mix ingredients and store in a sealed container for 5 to 6 weeks. Then enjoy the lovely fragrance and share some with a friend.

Rose Garden:

3 c. dried rose petals
   (pink, rose and red)
1 c. rose hips
7 to 8 drops of rose oil

10 to 12 ivory
   strawflower heads
1 c. star anise

Mix the ingredients together and store in a sealed container for 4 weeks. Makes a great gift idea for a bride-to-be.

Elaine Ross

Pressed Flower Crafts

Pressed flowers can be used to create many charming and useful things to keep or give. I like this method because it's easy. Thin flowers and greenery work best (violets, pansies, daisies, baby's breath). Wildflowers are especially good. You can use a flower press, or an old phone book will work. Weigh it with books or bricks. After flowers are dry, keep them in a tin. Collect all year long. Arrange in pleasing pictures or forms. Mount with a bit of glue to either frame as a picture, make notecards, or bookmarks. Notecards and bookmarks can be covered with wide clear strapping tape to preserve. Cover pictures with glass. Dried, pressed Queen Anne's lace can be hung from a Christmas tree. They make wonderful snowflakes. Best of all there is no cost involved.

Elizabeth Phillips

Sunflower Art

Making sunflower designs is a fun thing to do with giant sunflowers still growing in the garden. After the seeds have formed, pull out enough seeds to create a face. The dark seedbed (eyes, nose, smile) will show up nicely against the lighter seeds left in the head. You could also do a heart, star, or any other country shape.

Sue Carbaugh

Garden Signs

Recently, rustic garden signs have become very popular, so I decided to try my hand at making them. I purchased single, unfinished fence pickets and a large, alphabet stencil at my local hardware store. I painted the pickets overall and then stenciled the picket with letters to read, horizontally, "veggie garden," "herbs," and "thyme." Stake them in the garden to identify your plants.

Nancie Gensler

Garden Shirts

Here's a fun summer and fall project for kids and adults. Pick lots of flat flowers...hibiscus, impatiens, pansies; and pretty shaped leaves from trees, ferns and garden plants. Lay out the plants on the front of a T-shirt in a pleasing pattern. One at a time, paint the fronts of each plant with acrylic paints and lay back in place on the shirt. Cover with a sheet of paper and roll with a rolling pin, or press onto the shirt without wiggling the plant. When the entire design has been printed onto the shirt, press with an iron set on cotton to set the colors. Instant garden shirt!

Egg-Heads

Carefully crack the small end of an egg open and make breakfast. Rinse out the egg shell and fill with potting soil. Draw a silly face on the egg and plant a large pinch of grass seed in the soil inside of the egg shell. Set the egg-head in a sunny windowsill on an empty cellophane tape circle, or make a whole family of egg-heads to set in the bottom of an egg carton. Add a tablespoon of water and keep watering sparingly until grass sprouts. Turn the little egg-heads every day to make sure their hair grows straight. When it gets too long, just give them a haircut!

Mel Wolk

Sunflower Wreaths

What do you do with all those sunflower heads at the end of the growing season? Turn them into wreaths for the birds! Just before the heads get too dry, cut them from the stem as close to the head as possible. Then cut a hole in the very center (you'll have a donut shape!). Let them dry. When they are dry, make a small bouquet of millet, wheat and other autumnal foliage. Glue gun or wire it on the sunflower wreath. Hang the wreath using string or raffia outside where you (and the birds!) can enjoy it. Makes a great gift as well!

Edith Beck

Preserving Flowers with Hot Wax

You will need:

2 lb. paraffin   **1 1/4 c. mineral oil**
large bowl of ice water

Refrigerate flowers for 2 to 3 hours. Melt paraffin and stir in mineral oil. Cool mixture to 130 degrees! Dip flowers in the wax. Shake off excess, then place in ice water for 15 minutes.

Dottie Dobbert

Cinnamon-Applesauce Ornaments

I like to decorate the jars of my canned goods using cinnamon-scented ornaments. The ornaments can then be hung in the kitchen for a pretty decoration and a wonderful scent.

To make ornaments, you will need:

1 c. ground cinnamon   **1 t. ground nutmeg**
1 t. ground cloves   **applesauce**

Mix cinnamon, nutmeg, cloves and enough applesauce to form a dough. Using Gooseberry Patch mini cookie cutters (I love the apple one, and like to use it when I can applesauce, applebutter, apple jam or apple pie filling), cut out ornaments. Poke two holes in the center of each ornament using a small straw. Let dry. Using raffia, twine, ribbon, yarn or material, thread your cinnamon ornaments through the two punched holes, then tie around the neck of your jar, making a pretty bow.

Peggy King

Indoor Garden

Use an old wooden glass paned window to create an indoor garden. Make a simple flower box out of old weathered wood, or new wood that has been painted a desired shade and sanded to look old. Even peeling paint on an old wooden window lends instant charm. Attach the wooden flower box to the window and presto...a garden spot on any wall! Fill the box with Spanish moss, green florist's moss and dried flowers of every color and height you like. You could even use real ivy plants in a spot where sufficient light is available. This idea is perfect for a room without a window. The top can be decorated with old lace or pretty fabric to coordinate with your furnishings. Remember to reinforce for hanging as the finished product may be heavy.

Country Swag

Decorate a wall or fence with this easy country swag. You will need quite a few bay leaves, several mini terra cotta pots with small holes drilled on each side, a mini watering can and strong jute or twine. String the bay leaves and pots alternately, with the watering can in the middle. Use homespun fabric strips or ribbon to tie on whatever you choose.

Jeannine English

Gardening Pins

At the beginning of each school year, each staff member draws a folded slip of paper. Written on the paper is the name of a secret pal, their birthdate, favorite color, favorite food, and favorite hobby or pastime. Then the fun begins! Approximately once a week, each staff member receives a small gift from their secret pal. How pleasant it is to arrive at school and, sometime during the day, receive a surprise gift anonymously. My secret pal knew that I loved gardening and one day last spring I received an "I ♥ Gardening" pin, which she had made for me to wear. Simply attach a pin clasp (using glue) on the back of a wooden heart, and write "I ♥ Gardening" with a Sharpie pen on the front. Paint a decorative edge around the edge of it. Fill in the heart red and when it's dry, varnish it! You could also write sayings like I ♥ Cooking, I ♥ Reading, I ♥ Baking, etc.

Judy Schulze

Garden Glove Decorations

Paint or stencil a design (using acrylic paints) on the back of an inexpensive pair of muslin garden gloves. How about a slice of watermelon, a sunflower, or even a ladybug? Stuff with or attach a matching packet of seeds. Tie together with raffia. You could even fill with birdseed. Hang indoors for a unique decoration!

Seed Packet Magnets

Save empty seed packets, fill with Spanish moss and a tiny home-made or store-bought muslin bunny. Then glue a magnet on back! You can also use them to decorate a wreath.

Lisa Sett

Weathered Garden Signs

Any old weathered wood will work like barn siding, fence pickets...use your imagination! Letter sayings to be hung around yard or garden. A few hints:

"Never Enough Thyme"
"Thyme Began in a Garden"
"Thyme for Ewe" (this one would be cute for a spot
   in the garden just for yourself and no one else!)
"Thyme Will Tell"
"Please Touch the Herbs"
"Garden Sweet Garden"
"Garden of Weedin"

Jeannine English

Sage Wreath

10" straw wreath
sage bundles

wire loop for hanging
floral pins

In the early spring plant some extra sage for drying. Mid-summer and again in late fall clip small bunches (4" to 5") of sage branches and secure with rubber bands. Hang or lay flat in a dark, dry location for a couple of days. Wire a hanging loop on back of straw wreath. Working on a flat surface, secure one bunch of sage at a time with floral pins around the inside of the wreath. Overlap the bunches and make sure all branches are going in the same direction. Secure sage around the outside circle of the wreath. Secure remaining sage bundles on top of wreath working in the same direction and overlapping. This wreath is beautiful as is, or you may wish to add sprigs of dried purple larkspur or yarrow as a finishing touch.

Linda Lee

Bird Cakes

I like to attract birds to my garden all year round. In the winter they look forward to my bird cakes. These can be kept in the freezer until ready to put out in a mesh bag or wire suet cage. The little clinging birds like tufted titmouse, chickadee, and woodpeckers wait in line to get a bite. To make your own suet, save bacon drippings and chicken fat all year long. Keep in the freezer and melt down when ready to use. Ask friends to save some for you and in exchange give them some bird cakes for their yard. This also makes a nice gift for a bird watcher friend. Use festive muffin wrappers and gift tags.

1 part peanut butter
2 parts bird seed

5 parts cornmeal
2 parts melted suet

Melt suet and add to other ingredients in a large bowl. Mix with a wooden spoon. Line muffin cups with paper liners. Press mixture into cups and place in refrigerator until firm. Transfer to plastic bags and keep in freezer. Can also be kept in a cold garage or enclosed porch.

Donna Moran

Birdhouse Gourds

Take a gourd that is 8" or larger and drill a 2" hole in the front of it. Let the gourd dry out over the winter. When it is dry, pull out anything inside the gourd through the 2" hole. Add a few small holes on the bottom of the gourd to be used for drainage. Remember to add a hole at the top so you can hang it. String up the gourd and it's ready for tenants!

Carla Huchzermeier

Silk Flower Writing Pens

When a close friend was moving away, I had three of her closest friends over for an outdoor brunch, and wanted to make a special gift for each one to place at their plate. In keeping with her departure from us (and to encourage everyone to keep in touch) I bought a simple writing pen for each, removed the top "plug" and inserted a beautiful silk flower into the opening until the base of the flower was flush with the top of the pen, then secured it with a dab of hot glue. I wrapped the base of each pen in floral tape and attached each person's name on a small card (pinked around the edges), to a petal with a baby safety pin. The pens were beautiful, and now every time I see my pen I think of our friend, and am reminded to keep in touch. You could use each friend's favorite flower to personalize them even more!

Deena Funk

Lavender Drawer Liners

Try a few drops of lavender oil on pieces of pretty wallpaper cut to fit your dresser drawers. Roll and tie in a plastic bag and leave for a few days. The best paper to use is not coated paper. Roll a few pieces and tie with a ribbon for a great gift. Drop a few drops of lavender oil on pretty writing paper too.

Elizabeth Timmins
Gooseberry Patch Artisan

Herbal Calendar Box

A kind and thoughtful gift that can be made for as little or as much money as you choose, by putting your own special brand of creativity to work. A lovely gift for either a gardener or a cook.

pretty 4"x6" file box   **4"x6" cards**
12 plain subject index cards   **seeds**

1. Write the months of the year on the 12 index cards.
2. Buy pretty packets of herbal seeds for each month of the year. Place these seeds in the index for suitable planting times. In cold climates where some months may be inappropriate for planting outside, include seeds that can be started indoors. In that event, write instructions for how to start seeds indoors. In cold climates when even starting seed indoors would be ill advised, give a gift certificate from a local nursery or florist for an indoor flowering herb, plant, or perhaps some bulbs like paperwhite or narcissus, to be planted in pots and forced for indoor blooming.
3. Consider in which month your seeds would be ready to harvest and write recipes for using that herb. File under the proper month.
4. All kinds of gardening information can be included for the proper month, depending on the expertise of your cook or gardener.
5. File box can be decorated with paint or contact paper in garden tool, or kitchen tool design; or simply tied with a pretty bow.

Tamara Gruber

Scented Floral Water

32 oz. distilled water   1/4 oz. rose oil

Combine distilled water and rose oil in a jar. Shake well and let steep for one week. Transfer to decorative bottles after steeping. Interesting old bottles can be found at yard sales, flea markets, etc. This rose water is said to be good for strengthening of the heart and refreshing of the spirits.

Jeannine English

Peach Facial

For over-ripe peaches, making a peach facial can be beneficial. Mash peach, add 1 teaspoon honey, and 1 teaspoon oatmeal. Add just enough milk to make a paste. Coat face and neck and let dry. Wash off with warm water, followed by a cool rinse. The enzymes of the fruit removes the deadened outer layer of skin.

Sonia Bracamonte

Herbal Facial Steam

Place 4 tablespoons of herbs in a bowl. Pour 4 1/2 cups boiling water over. Cover head with towel and lean over bowl to prevent steam from escaping. Remain for 10 minutes. Wipe face with a damp cloth. Apply a freshening lotion. Very relaxing!

Susan Mroz

Chamomile Hair Rinse

Place 1 cup of fresh or dried chamomile flowers in a large jug and pour in 3 3/4 cups of boiling water. Cover with a plate and leave until cool. Wash and rinse your hair as you would usually. Strain the chamomile infusion and use as a final rinse. A chamomile rinse is a good conditioner and brings out the highlights in blonde hair.

Sue Carbaugh

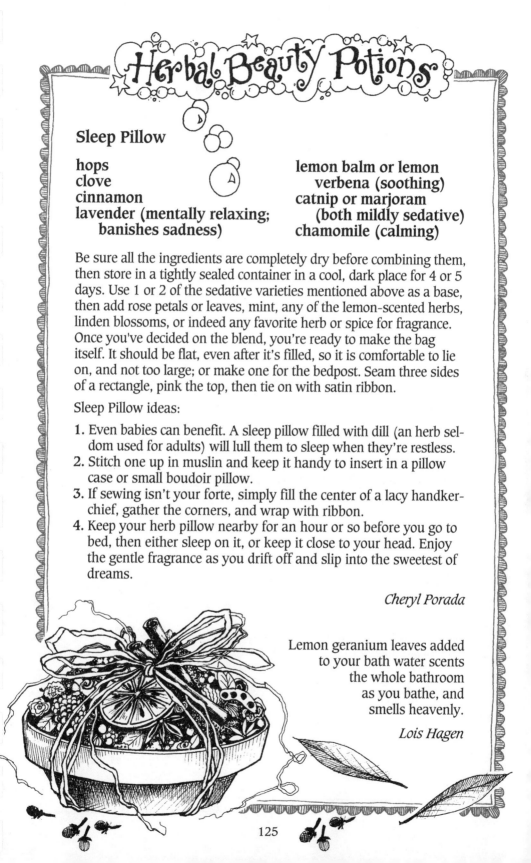

Herbal Beauty Potions

Sleep Pillow

hops
clove
cinnamon
lavender (mentally relaxing;
 banishes sadness)

lemon balm or lemon
 verbena (soothing)
catnip or marjoram
 (both mildly sedative)
chamomile (calming)

Be sure all the ingredients are completely dry before combining them, then store in a tightly sealed container in a cool, dark place for 4 or 5 days. Use 1 or 2 of the sedative varieties mentioned above as a base, then add rose petals or leaves, mint, any of the lemon-scented herbs, linden blossoms, or indeed any favorite herb or spice for fragrance. Once you've decided on the blend, you're ready to make the bag itself. It should be flat, even after it's filled, so it is comfortable to lie on, and not too large; or make one for the bedpost. Seam three sides of a rectangle, pink the top, then tie on with satin ribbon.

Sleep Pillow ideas:

1. Even babies can benefit. A sleep pillow filled with dill (an herb seldom used for adults) will lull them to sleep when they're restless.
2. Stitch one up in muslin and keep it handy to insert in a pillow case or small boudoir pillow.
3. If sewing isn't your forte, simply fill the center of a lacy handkerchief, gather the corners, and wrap with ribbon.
4. Keep your herb pillow nearby for an hour or so before you go to bed, then either sleep on it, or keep it close to your head. Enjoy the gentle fragrance as you drift off and slip into the sweetest of dreams.

Cheryl Porada

Lemon geranium leaves added
to your bath water scents
the whole bathroom
as you bathe, and
smells heavenly.

Lois Hagen

Bath Bags

Pamper yourself with an herbal bath! Herbs to use:

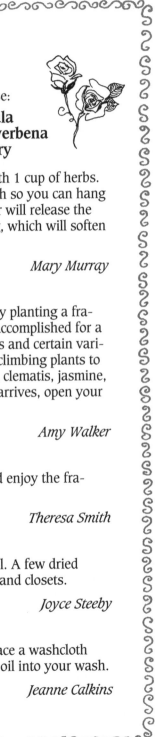

chamomile
rose geranium leaves
   or lavender

calendula
lemon verbena
rosemary

Take muslin or cheesecloth bags and fill them with 1 cup of herbs. Close tightly with ribbon or string; leaving enough so you can hang the bag from the faucet. The warm running water will release the fragrance. You might also add oatmeal to the bag, which will soften the water and soothe your skin.

Mary Murray

Create a romantic atmosphere in your bedroom by planting a fragrant garden outside your window. This can be accomplished for a first or second floor room by using window boxes and certain varieties of climbing plants. Allow the runners from climbing plants to encircle the window. Some favorites are wisteria, clematis, jasmine, gardenia, and some antique roses. When spring arrives, open your window to enjoy the soothing scents.

Amy Walker

Tie a bunch of lavender to your shower head and enjoy the fragrance as you shower.

Theresa Smith

Lavender will sweeten linens and soothe the soul. A few dried lavender spikes can be added to linens, drawers and closets.

Joyce Steeby

To give your sheets a fresh scent of lavender, place a washcloth sprinkled with a few drops of lavender essential oil into your wash.

Jeanne Calkins

Herbal Beauty Potions

Herb Soap Balls

Cut up 3 bars of white soap and 2 bars of green into small pieces. Pour 1 1/2 cups of boiling water over 2 teaspoons of an aromatic herb (sage, mint, thyme, rosemary, lavender, chamomile, bergamot, or anise). Allow to steep for a few minutes and then strain out herbs (I often leave them in the soap) and pour mixture over cut up soap pieces. Mix well with your hands (wait until cool enough to handle). Soap chips should be moist, not "swimming." Set aside for approximately 15 minutes, or until mixture is mushy. Mix softened soap again and divide into five parts. Place each part onto a piece of muslin or flannel; cheesecloth will also work. These squares of fabric should be approximately 8 inches. Using your hands, form soap into balls. Pull cloth tightly around soap ball, gather at the top and tie with string or pretty ribbon. Hang soap balls to dry in a warm place. This will take approximately 3 days. Soap is dry when it is completely hard. Unwrap and use, or give as a gift by wrapping in a pretty fabric with a ribbon! Kids and adults can all enjoy this project and reap the benefits as well...a luxurious bath! You can combine aromatic herbs and spices for all kinds of wonderful scents. It's good clean fun and can be a downright artistic endeavor if you care to experiment. I like to tie a small bundle of dried herbs into the ribbon on the soap ball...it makes a small, but lovely gift.

Judy Hand

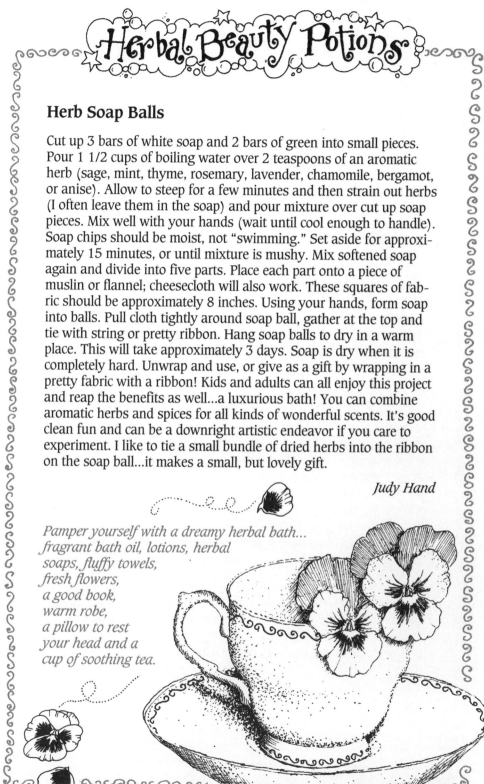

Pamper yourself with a dreamy herbal bath...
fragrant bath oil, lotions, herbal
soaps, fluffy towels,
fresh flowers,
a good book,
warm robe,
a pillow to rest
your head and a
cup of soothing tea.

Elizabeth Timmins, one of our Gooseberry Patch artisans,
"lives and loves" herbs and flowers. A special "thanks" to her
for sharing her beauty of herbs chart and so many of her
recipes for herbal beauty potions with us!

Strawberry & Cream Mask

One of my favorite things to do in the Spring is make a strawberry
& cream mask. Just mash strawberries, add a little cream and pat
on your face. Then lay down for about 20 minutes; rinse off. One
day the UPS man came and I think I scared him...after I saw myself
in the mirror, I can just imagine what he thought. My face was nice
and smooth and felt so good after!

Herb & Flower Splash

Place 6 tablespoons chopped fresh herbs and 1 pint of spring water in
a non-metal pan and bring to a gentle boil. Cover and simmer for 20
minutes. Cool completely, strain and put in a bottle. A spray bottle is
great. Keep in refrigerator in the warm months. It will keep up to two
weeks. When I have my Herb Gathering in June, I always have several bottles of this...when it looks like everyone needs a pick-me-up,
I bring out the herbal splash and everyone loves it. Rosemary, lavender and peppermint are especially refreshing. I search for unusual
bottles for my herbal delights. If I have a plain bottle I make little
flower wreaths for around the necks of the bottles or use fancy
French ribbons.

Herb and flower splashes are great to keep in the bedroom or bath.
Great when you feel tired and sluggish. They replenish some of the
moisture in your skin. Rose, lavender and thyme are refreshing
and fragrant, while chamomile and lemon balm are soothing. Herb
and flower splashes are always left to dry on your skin.

Flowers always make people better, happier, and more helpful;
They are sunshine, food, and medicine to the soul.
Luther Burbank

128

Herbal Bath Vinegar

Cider vinegar added to the bath will soften the skin. Fill a glass jar half way with chopped fresh herbs. Pour cider vinegar over the herbs to fill jar. Cover and place in a sunny window for three weeks. Strain off the vinegar and add an equal amount of spring water. Put in a clean jar and leave for one week. Another method is to heat 1 cup each spring water and vinegar to just below the boiling point in a non-metal pan. Pour in a jar that is half full of chopped fresh herbs. Cover and leave for 12 hours. Strain and bottle. To use bath vinegars, add 1 cup to bath water while running. Shake well.

Rosemary vinegar to comfort an aching head and soothe the skin...pat on forehead and face. Victorian ladies wore tiny bottles of herb and floral vinegars around their necks.

Elizabeth Timmins
Gooseberry Patch Artisan

lavender

Herbal Hair Rinse

For dark hair...1 part strong rosemary tea and 4 parts water.
For light hair...1 part strong chamomile tea and 4 parts water.
Pour over washed hair, catching water and repeating until rinse
is used up.

Easy Dusting Powder

Just find a little jar or box, add puff and tie with a pretty bow. Grandmothers love this! I remember going into my aunt's bathroom and I
always had to smell the powders. I probably had it on my nose when
I came out too!

1 part dried herbs or   **4 parts corn starch**
    flowers, finely ground

Lavender is a traditional Victorian choice; rose petals are great
alone or with lavender; lavender and mint are nice; other good
combinations are orange peel and lemon peel, or rose and mint.

Remember When Bath

To refresh the memory and bring out the child in you...place 1 cup
of rosemary and 1 cup peppermint leaves in a non-metal pan and
bring to a boil. Lower heat and simmer for 10 minutes. Strain and
pour into bath water. Put on your favorite music, light some candles, lay back, relax, close your eyes and remember those carefree
days of your childhood. Enjoy!

To relieve sore muscles from bending while gardening,
make hot compresses by placing dampened finger towels
in the microwave on high for 30-45 seconds.
Turn the towel over after 20 seconds.

Garden Bath Bag

2 T. dried rosemary   **8 fresh mint leaves**
2 T. dried thyme

Crush all ingredients and place in a bath bag. Let bag soak in tub while water is running, then massage your body with the bag!

Herbal Bath Bags

Stimulate and delight your body with the joy of herbal baths! Herbal baths can relax and calm you, revive and stimulate you, ease aching limbs, or help a tired circulation. First shower, giving your entire body a thorough soaping and rinsing. Hang your herbal bath bag under the faucet as you draw a warm bath. Now turn on your favorite music, reach for a good book, put a pillow under your head and step into your herbal bath. Relax, enjoy and have ready a large, warm, rough towel.

Lavender... added to bath water by the Greeks and Romans. The name means "to wash."

Rosemary... used by the Romans to relieve tired limbs after a long march.

Bay Leaves... a symbol of glory, honor and greatness.

Roses... for love; soothing both physically and emotionally.

Lemon Balm... causeth the mind and heart to become merry.

Bath bags may be air dried and reused. You may also steep the bath bags in water, in a non-metal pan for 10 to 20 minutes and add to bath.

Elizabeth Timmins
Gooseberry Patch Artisan

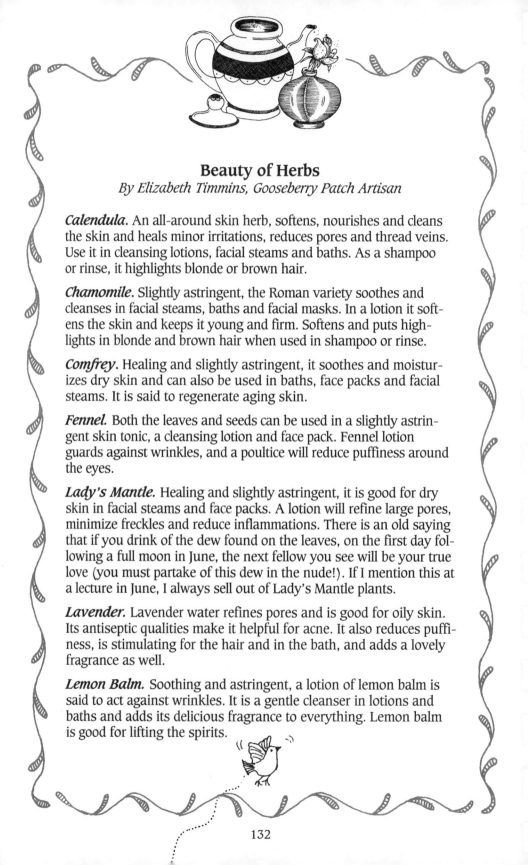

Beauty of Herbs
By Elizabeth Timmins, Gooseberry Patch Artisan

Calendula. An all-around skin herb, softens, nourishes and cleans the skin and heals minor irritations, reduces pores and thread veins. Use it in cleansing lotions, facial steams and baths. As a shampoo or rinse, it highlights blonde or brown hair.

Chamomile. Slightly astringent, the Roman variety soothes and cleanses in facial steams, baths and facial masks. In a lotion it softens the skin and keeps it young and firm. Softens and puts highlights in blonde and brown hair when used in shampoo or rinse.

Comfrey. Healing and slightly astringent, it soothes and moisturizes dry skin and can also be used in baths, face packs and facial steams. It is said to regenerate aging skin.

Fennel. Both the leaves and seeds can be used in a slightly astringent skin tonic, a cleansing lotion and face pack. Fennel lotion guards against wrinkles, and a poultice will reduce puffiness around the eyes.

Lady's Mantle. Healing and slightly astringent, it is good for dry skin in facial steams and face packs. A lotion will refine large pores, minimize freckles and reduce inflammations. There is an old saying that if you drink of the dew found on the leaves, on the first day following a full moon in June, the next fellow you see will be your true love (you must partake of this dew in the nude!). If I mention this at a lecture in June, I always sell out of Lady's Mantle plants.

Lavender. Lavender water refines pores and is good for oily skin. Its antiseptic qualities make it helpful for acne. It also reduces puffiness, is stimulating for the hair and in the bath, and adds a lovely fragrance as well.

Lemon Balm. Soothing and astringent, a lotion of lemon balm is said to act against wrinkles. It is a gentle cleanser in lotions and baths and adds its delicious fragrance to everything. Lemon balm is good for lifting the spirits.

Herbal Beauty Potions

Peppermint. Healing and astringent, it's stimulating in facial steams and face masks. It's also an invigorating and a cooling bath herb for hot summer days. Peppermint is a great splash for the face, and it's very cooling.

Nettle. Eat the young leaves like spinach to improve the complexion. Good for oily skin, it's cleansing and stimulates the circulation in face steams and baths. Use in shampoo for healthier hair; as a rinse to condition and prevent dandruff.

Parsley. Good for oily skins. Adds shine to dark hair when used as a rinse. A lotion reduces freckles, thread veins. Eat generous amounts for the Vitamins A and C.

Rosemary. Good for oily skin. Invigorating in the bath or in facial steams. Use in a shampoo or rinse for dark hair to give it body and shine, and keep it healthy.

Roses. Lightly astringent, rose water cleanses and refreshes skin and acts as a hydrating agent to help keep it young looking. Mix rose water and glycerin for a soothing lotion for chapped hands. Refreshing and fragrant in the bath.

Thyme. Deodorizing, antiseptic and tonic in the bath. Lotion good for cleansing and for helping spots and pimples. Soothing and gentle.

Yarrow. Quite astringent. Used for oily skin in face packs, and facial steams. Cleansing in the bath and for the skin in a lotion. Helps thread veins, stimulates hair growth (they say!). Healing herb for oily skin. In Old England, a little pillow stuffed with yarrow was said to produce a dream vision of future husband when placed under the pillow of a young girl.

Marjoram. Joy, happiness, kindness. Brought to America by the colonists in 1640. Used to crown young married couples in Greek and Roman days. Mildly antiseptic properties, stimulating herb.

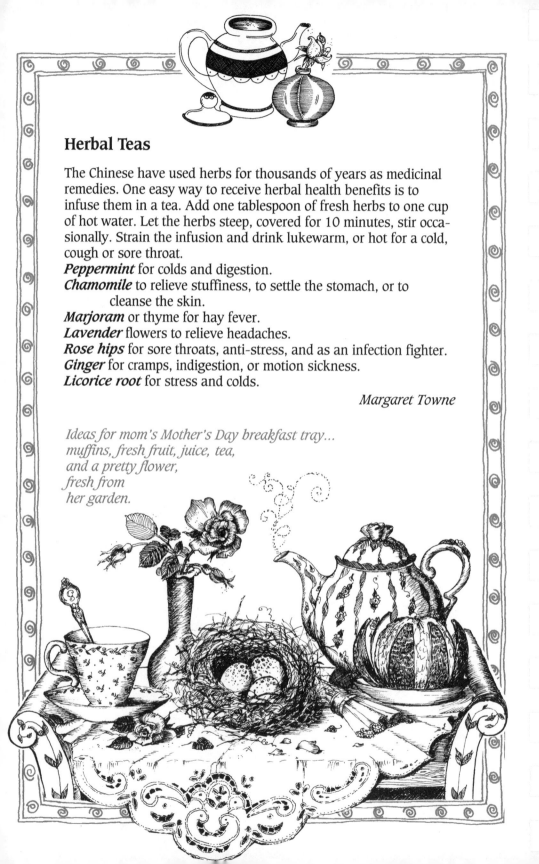

Herbal Teas

The Chinese have used herbs for thousands of years as medicinal remedies. One easy way to receive herbal health benefits is to infuse them in a tea. Add one tablespoon of fresh herbs to one cup of hot water. Let the herbs steep, covered for 10 minutes, stir occasionally. Strain the infusion and drink lukewarm, or hot for a cold, cough or sore throat.

Peppermint for colds and digestion.

Chamomile to relieve stuffiness, to settle the stomach, or to cleanse the skin.

Marjoram or thyme for hay fever.

Lavender flowers to relieve headaches.

Rose hips for sore throats, anti-stress, and as an infection fighter.

Ginger for cramps, indigestion, or motion sickness.

Licorice root for stress and colds.

Margaret Towne

Ideas for mom's Mother's Day breakfast tray...
muffins, fresh fruit, juice, tea,
and a pretty flower,
fresh from
her garden.

Outdoor Living
backyard Entertainment

Icy Decanters

To create interesting decanters put a wine bottle or vodka bottle (without labels) into a paper milk carton or a cut-off 2 liter, plastic soft drink bottle. Fill the container with ice and immerse fresh flowers and greenery into the water. Freeze solid, remove outer container and serve liquor over a plate or bowl (to catch the melting ice water). You will get lots of wonderful comments about how clever you are.

Use fresh herbs (tarragon, basil, oregano) to put under the skin of a fresh chicken or turkey. Stuff if desired. Tie the bird together using twine soaked in oil, and roast.

Jan Sofranko

This is a wonderful idea for children's parties or holiday time. Give each child a special teacup with hot water. Give each young guest a peppermint stick with a sprig of lemon balm or lemon verbena tied to it with a pretty ribbon. The children can use the peppermint stick to stir the herb into the hot water to make a delicious tea...just like the grown-ups!

Laura Steuk-Mastropaolo

For a cozy Sunday brunch, here's a menu that's easy and sooo good! Serve 2" to 3" wedges of cantaloupe melon. Top each with 4 to 5 slices (rounds) of banana and sprinkle with coconut. Tuck home-made oatmeal-apple and blueberry muffins in a homespun or pretty cotton tea towel and put in baskets. Cook up some breakfast sausages. Serve omelets containing chopped green and red (sweet) pepper, chopped onion and cooked cubed chicken. Top omelets with a dollop of dill dip. Cook enough eggs and sausages for number of guests (2 eggs per person as a rule). Serve coffee and orange spice tea. Freshly squeezed orange juice makes this brunch complete.

Kathleen Griffin

When having friends over for tea, have them bring their own teacup and saucer to use. It is fun to see the variety, and also becomes a great conversation starter, as each person shares how they acquired their teacups, often providing sentimental stories and memories to share. We even did this at a recent church ladies' tea, and it was delightful to see over 100 different teacups arrive at the tables! Surprisingly, no two were alike.

Deena Funk

My sister-in-law adds fresh orange slices to her homemade lemonade for additional sweetness. It's the best I've ever tasted!

Ildiko Mulligan

When I entertain, I love to give favors to my guests... fresh herbs and flowers. At each place on the table I arrange them in antique medicine jars, brown snuff bottles (especially pretty with zinnias), or any other kind of old bottle. Not only do they look and smell beautiful in place of a centerpiece, but my guests are so excited to take them home (but not as excited as I am to give them). I also take the favors to a restaurant when I'm treating friends to lunch.

Judy Gidley

Each season is filled with wonder, but my favorite time of the year is autumn, when the ground is carpeted with newly fallen leaves. Each October, I gather up a group of children and we go for a "nature hike" in the woods adjacent to my parents' home. They enjoy finding their own special spot and lying down as I cover them with speckled, crunchy leaves. With only their faces showing through this thick autumn blanket, they lie very still and quiet, looking up into the surrounding trees. They actually feel as if they become part of the forest, as they listen to and see nature from this point of view.

Wednesday Szollos

Pair herb pots with a folk art birdhouse as a centerpiece.

Judy Carter

Fourth of July is a big day at our house, as we host a huge annual barbecue. We decorate very inexpensively with things I've collected over the years, and set up big tables on our back deck to accommodate the 40 to 50 people who come every year. Each person brings a dish and my husband and I supply a huge platter of smoked chickens to compliment all the side dishes. Everyone arrives about 2 p.m. for volleyball, games in the pool, and badminton on the lawn. Dinner is about 6:00 p.m., and then fireworks at 9:00 p.m. It's a wonderful day filled with family, friends and fun. Some of our decorations include:

•Long tables set with red and white checked tablecloths with flag motif, pitchers filled with baby's breath, and red, white and blue carnations in the centers.
•A big, blue dining canopy covers the "eating" part of the deck, decorated on the corners with huge bunches of red, white and blue balloons.
•Flags hang on the front and side porches of the house, to welcome everyone; as well as around the perimeter of the backyard on the fence.
•Old blue and white stoneware crocks hold eating utensils, paper plates, and flag napkins on the food table that is covered with my prize...a red, white and blue log-cabin quilt.
•Baskets tied with red, white and blue grosgrain ribbon hold cookies, chips, and breads for festive dining.

To provide lots of atmosphere, and keep away bugs as well, we purchased reproduction railway lanterns. They were $5 each and can be filled with citronella oil. Placed around the perimeter of the pool or in the gardens, they provide a wonderful romantic, festive light; yet keep away those pesky mosquitoes, as we entertain outside on warm summer evenings.

Gay Hanby

It's fun to serve cold beverages from a big galvanized tub filled with lots of ice...looks festive too!

The garden is a special place for me, especially being raised in an urban setting like San Francisco where garden space can be limited. The garden is where you come face to face with some of the wonders of the world... trails of ants carrying huge objects to and fro, butterflies lighting on your hand for a snack of sugar water from a cotton ball, or the discovery of roly polys (pill bugs) under a log. It's no wonder that the garden is also a favorite place of my daughter who chose to have her third birthday celebrated there, having some backyard fun. The activities and menu were themed around bugs and plants. For example, the sandwiches were sourdough rolls of bread with their fixings arranged in the shape of a caterpillar on a platter. Olives and toothpicks were attached to the sides of each roll to form the "feet" of the caterpillar. The hit of the celebration was the unusual birthday cake which surprised everyone because it looked like a potted plant rather than the delicious pudding and cream surprise that it was. Dirt cake can be made the day before and takes less room in the refrigerator than a layered cake...great news for the busy hostess.

To control bees during a garden party, discreetly suspend a piece of bacon or meat over a tub of soapy water. When the bee is baited to the bacon and eats some of the fat, it becomes heavy and falls into the soapy water below. Discard soapy water and bait.

Robin Kato

Ice Bowls

Ice bowls are easy to make and create beautiful containers for fruit salads. Even on a hot day, they will last at least two or three hours.

You will need:

2 bowls that fit inside each other with at least 1" to spare*
tape

Put a layer of ice cubes in the bottom of the larger bowl. Center smaller bowl on top and weigh it down with a heavy can. Half fill the space between the bowls with ice, then stabilize the bowls by joining them with strips of tape. Pour water into the space to about 1 1/2" below the rim. Arrange decorative fruit in the water (flowers and leaves are also pretty). Freeze for at least 24 hours. Remove from freezer, let stand on counter until bowls can be removed. Store in freezer until ready to use. Set ice bowls on trays to catch the drips.

*Hint: the wider the gap between the bowls, the thicker the ice and the longer your bowl will last.

Rhonda Harrison

When everything is blooming, put on an old-fashioned garden party. Get out the hats and gloves, or a least pin a flower in your hair.

Maria Vaz Duarte

Watch sheet sales and pick up a bandanna or print sheet in double size to pop over the table. Colorful and easy to launder.

Charlene Robedee

Say good-bye to dry hamburgers. Add a half cup of applesauce for each pound of ground beef, plus salt and pepper. Then shape into patties for the juiciest hamburgers you can imagine.

If you are a garlic lover, you might want to throw several garlic buds on the coals as you grill your meat for a little extra garlic flavor.

Mary Dechamplain

Use Gooseberry Patch rubber stamps on colored 3"x5" cards for recipes to give or to keep. Include these with a potted herb in an attractive flowerpot for a gift. Recipe should include the herb being given.

Freeze 2 cups of hand-packed fresh herbs with 1/2 cup oil (vegetable, canola or olive) in baby food jars. You can then use it to baste chicken, sauté veggies and meats, or spread it on breads or breadsticks.

Carrie Shapiro

For a special touch, try adding to your favorite drop biscuit recipe a cup of grated cheddar cheese, and fresh herbs from your garden such as parsley, chives or basil. Delicious!

Janey Schultz

My sisters, mother and I recently gave my cousin a bridal shower with a garden theme. First of all we had everyone bring their favorite recipe on a card that we had sent to them. The bride-to-be then drew two cards out of a basket, and they were the winners of two potted plants. The bride-to-be then kept all the recipe cards to get her married life off to a good start. We played two more games and had various garden prizes, including wooden seed packet plaques and a little watering can filled with potpourri. On the table we had gardening gloves with the name of the bride and groom painted on them. We served an egg dish, fresh fruit kabobs, mini muffins (strawberry and banana nut), garden salad and punch. Our dessert was "pudding in a pot" served with a new gardening hand shovel. Everyone went home with a favor... a little mini potted plant, wrapped at the base with fabric and tied with a ribbon.

Janice Ertola

When serving friends summer beverages, I sometimes float various colors of pansies in their glasses. It's easy to refill glasses when guests remember the color of their flower (the pansies are also safe to eat).

Inexpensive bandannas make great cloth napkins for an outdoor barbecue. I tie a bandanna around the eating utensils of each guest. This makes picking up your flatware in a buffet line easier. If you purchase several colors of bandannas you can distinguish whose napkin is whose.

Carol Jones

As a table decoration for our summer picnics, I pick a large bouquet of peppermint and spearmint from my yard and place in a cut-glass vase. Alongside, I place a pair of scissors (the fancy grape scissors are neat to use!) and encourage my guests to snip off the mint and place a leaf, or better still, a stalk or two in their glasses of iced tea. My table looks summery and the mint certainly adds a wonderful and refreshing taste to the iced tea!

Carol Begley

Use Christmas lights around your deck or in your trees for a festive nighttime party look.

Shelly McHugh

Snip three thick chives evenly to 7" length. Place chives parallel on counter. Weigh down one end of chives (about 1") under a bowl. Braid the 3 strands tightly. About 1" from end, stop braiding and tie off end of braid with another shorter chive. Remove bowl and tie off end of braid with another chive. Float several in soup, or use as a garnish.

Geraldine Knatz

Mason jars make great summer drinking glasses.

Erin Clary

During the dreary months of winter, my gardening friends and I meet at one of our homes, with an herbal delight in hand. It picks up our spirits to sip warm herbal teas, taste each other's treats and discuss our spring gardening lists.

Form a "Weeding Co-Op." Once a month visit a neighbor's, relative's or friend's garden and share the burden.

Jacqueline Lash Idler

Take an old family heirloom suitcase, line with fabric and equip with picnic supplies. You're now ready for a summer's day picnic.

Enjoy a summer fest with friends, having them over for dinner on the lawn, with the herbal garden in their view. At the close of the evening, send your guests home with fresh herbal bouquets.

Place a fresh sprig of rosemary, the friendship herb, at each place-setting to welcome guests.

Make an herbal wreath and garnish the neck of a wine bottle.

Tessa Adelman

Ice Vase for Cut Flowers

Sure to be a hit at any party, shower, wedding or reception. You will need 1/2 gallon and 1 quart clean empty milk cartons, sand and paper towels. Pour 1" of water into 1/2 gallon carton; freeze. Pad upper edge of 1/2 gallon carton with paper towel cuff, so that 1 quart carton stands centered in larger carton. Remove small carton; fill with sand. Add water to larger carton. Slip 1 quart carton into 1/2 gallon carton, if necessary adjust water level; freeze. Remove sand and paper towel cuff. Peel outer carton away. To remove inner carton, run tap water between carton and ice. Gently pull out carton.

Jeannine English

To make your sugar cookie an extra special herbal treat, just add 1 teaspoon of dried lavender flowers, or 2 teaspoons dried mint leaves to your dough before you chill and roll out. Proceed as usual with your cookie recipe instructions. These are wonderful cookies for a teatime treat.

For a special wedding gift or just to introduce a friend to herbs, make up a small planter of cooking herbs such as parsley, sage, thyme, oregano and rosemary. Then include a book on herb gardening and maybe an herbal cookbook. Mark the recipes you have tried and know to be good.

For a special teatime treat, make herbal sugar. Just put a few leaves of lemon balm, rose geranium or mint of your choice in a blender with about 1/2 cup of sugar. Blend well on high until herbs are pulverized into sugar. You may add food coloring of your choice for colored sugar.

When you place your sun tea out in the morning, put a few sprigs of mint, lemon balm, scented geraniums, lemon verbena, or some rose petals in your jar. Strain out when you are ready to serve.

When serving baked potatoes with your meal, place a few sprigs of parsley, basil, chives, and oregano in a small vase of water. Have a small, sharp pair of scissors by the vase of herbs and encourage your dinner guests to snip their own fresh herbs onto their baked potatoes. Yummy!

Jeanne Calkins

Make floral ice cubes for summer drinks. Pick small edible, unsprayed flowers and herbs...lemon verbena leaves, Johnny jump-ups, borage flowers, violets, and rosebuds. Fill ice cube trays half full with distilled water (this keeps ice cubes clear, so posies can be seen). Freeze for an hour or two, until completely solid throughout. Remove from freezer and quickly place a small flower on top of each frozen cube. Add a little more distilled water (do not completely fill) and freeze trays again. When solidly frozen, fill each tray with water and freeze solid. Flowers should be suspended in ice. Use cubes for tea and lemonade. An ice ring for punch bowls can be made in the same way. Lovely!

Tamara Gruber

For a very special herbal touch at your next picnic or special dinner, rinse and wring out clean washcloths and wrap several sprigs of scented geraniums, lavender, lemon balm or lemon verbena in each cloth. Fold in half and roll up. Place closely together on a plate and heat for 1 1/2 minutes on HIGH in your microwave. After your meal, pass the heated "finger towels" around to each guest, instructing them to empty herbs out onto the tray. If towels are hot, serve them with tongs.

Tori Jones

To keep decorating simple, easy and elegant...for a centerpiece take a shallow dish (can be crystal, ceramic or porcelain), fill it with water and float candles and cut flowers (chrysanthemums, daisies, carnations or roses) in it. The candles add a soft glow to the table and the low profile centerpiece allows guests to converse freely.

Cherie Kawaguchi

Toss boiled new potatoes in butter and sprinkle in a little chopped rosemary.

Add chopped rosemary to your favorite bread recipe. To each cup of flour add 1 tablespoon freshly chopped or 1 teaspoon dried.

Dip frozen biscuits in melted butter and a mixture of parmesan cheese, garlic and a little crushed rosemary and bake.

Elizabeth Timmins
Gooseberry Patch Artisan

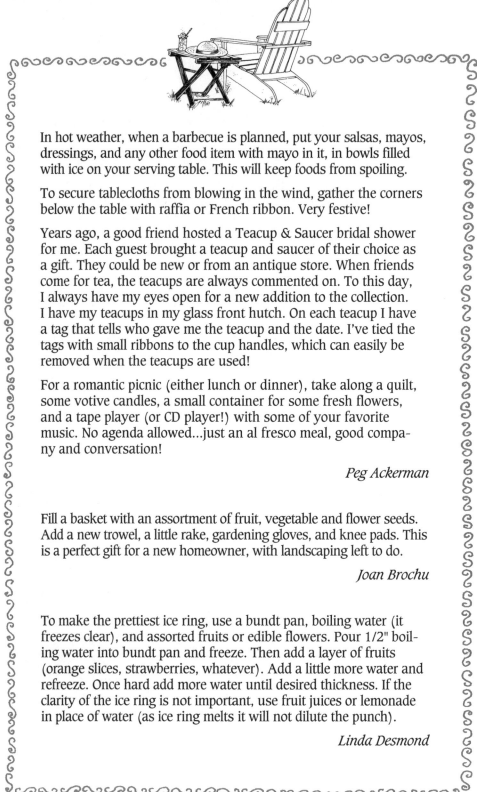

In hot weather, when a barbecue is planned, put your salsas, mayos, dressings, and any other food item with mayo in it, in bowls filled with ice on your serving table. This will keep foods from spoiling.

To secure tablecloths from blowing in the wind, gather the corners below the table with raffia or French ribbon. Very festive!

Years ago, a good friend hosted a Teacup & Saucer bridal shower for me. Each guest brought a teacup and saucer of their choice as a gift. They could be new or from an antique store. When friends come for tea, the teacups are always commented on. To this day, I always have my eyes open for a new addition to the collection. I have my teacups in my glass front hutch. On each teacup I have a tag that tells who gave me the teacup and the date. I've tied the tags with small ribbons to the cup handles, which can easily be removed when the teacups are used!

For a romantic picnic (either lunch or dinner), take along a quilt, some votive candles, a small container for some fresh flowers, and a tape player (or CD player!) with some of your favorite music. No agenda allowed...just an al fresco meal, good company and conversation!

Peg Ackerman

Fill a basket with an assortment of fruit, vegetable and flower seeds. Add a new trowel, a little rake, gardening gloves, and knee pads. This is a perfect gift for a new homeowner, with landscaping left to do.

Joan Brochu

To make the prettiest ice ring, use a bundt pan, boiling water (it freezes clear), and assorted fruits or edible flowers. Pour 1/2" boiling water into bundt pan and freeze. Then add a layer of fruits (orange slices, strawberries, whatever). Add a little more water and refreeze. Once hard add more water until desired thickness. If the clarity of the ice ring is not important, use fruit juices or lemonade in place of water (as ice ring melts it will not dilute the punch).

Linda Desmond

Plan a day to take your husband, girlfriends, the kids, or even grandma on what I call "the secret garden tour." Nobody knows the destination (except you, of course, planned in advance) until they get there. Pack a magnificent picnic in your basket, and enjoy! Their anticipation is part of the fun.

When packing a picnic, I use one whole loaf of bread (instead of individual slices or rolls). Whether using French, round, Italian, or whatever, slice horizontally. Make one huge, delicious sandwich, slicing to serve when you get there! So much easier to pack.

Create your own romantic summer hideaway, right on your very own porch. Decorate with white wicker, white tablecloths, crocks full of flowers, candles, and white trellises on the sides of the porch, crawling with anything "viney." Create as much shade as possible. Add some old flowery cushions and some iced tea or lemonade, and sit there as much as possible with those you love!

During the summer, my picnic basket goes everywhere I go. You never know where you might land! I keep it well-stocked with everything from maps and first-aid items, to little fold-up raincoats. During the winter, it sits on my kitchen floor, looking pretty in the corner, waiting for the adventurous days of summer, spring and fall to return.

Deb Damari-Tull

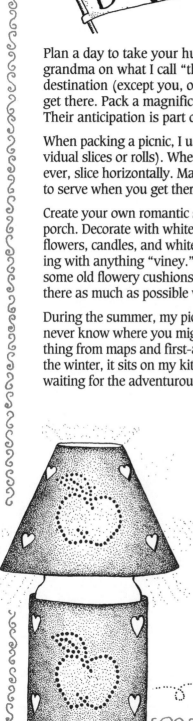

When you're cutting flowers to bring inside for an arrangement, cut a few herbs to include in the bouquet. The colors, textures and fragrance of the herbs will make your design unique.

Mel Wolk

Candles, kerosene lanterns, oil lamps and luminaries create a soft glow for evening parties.

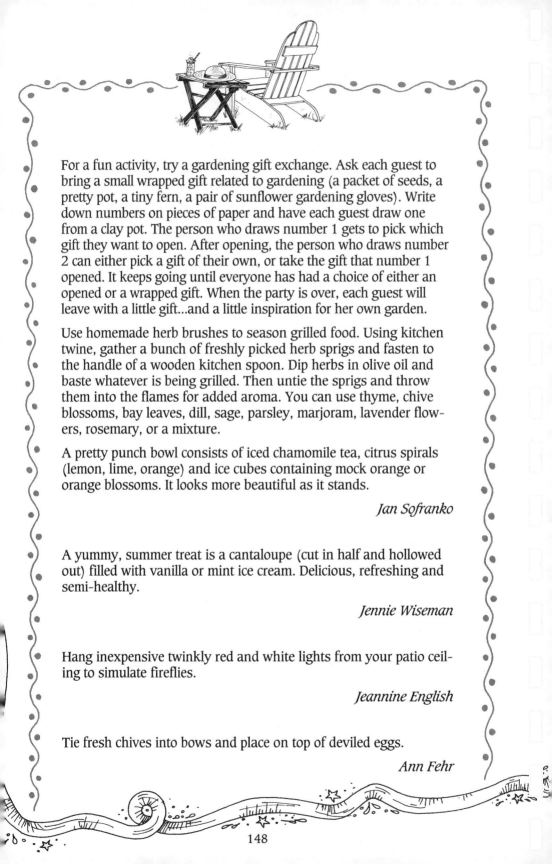

For a fun activity, try a gardening gift exchange. Ask each guest to bring a small wrapped gift related to gardening (a packet of seeds, a pretty pot, a tiny fern, a pair of sunflower gardening gloves). Write down numbers on pieces of paper and have each guest draw one from a clay pot. The person who draws number 1 gets to pick which gift they want to open. After opening, the person who draws number 2 can either pick a gift of their own, or take the gift that number 1 opened. It keeps going until everyone has had a choice of either an opened or a wrapped gift. When the party is over, each guest will leave with a little gift...and a little inspiration for her own garden.

Use homemade herb brushes to season grilled food. Using kitchen twine, gather a bunch of freshly picked herb sprigs and fasten to the handle of a wooden kitchen spoon. Dip herbs in olive oil and baste whatever is being grilled. Then untie the sprigs and throw them into the flames for added aroma. You can use thyme, chive blossoms, bay leaves, dill, sage, parsley, marjoram, lavender flowers, rosemary, or a mixture.

A pretty punch bowl consists of iced chamomile tea, citrus spirals (lemon, lime, orange) and ice cubes containing mock orange or orange blossoms. It looks more beautiful as it stands.

Jan Sofranko

A yummy, summer treat is a cantaloupe (cut in half and hollowed out) filled with vanilla or mint ice cream. Delicious, refreshing and semi-healthy.

Jennie Wiseman

Hang inexpensive twinkly red and white lights from your patio ceiling to simulate fireflies.

Jeannine English

Tie fresh chives into bows and place on top of deviled eggs.

Ann Fehr

I like to grow Johnny jump-ups. They are great because they keep seeding themselves and they pop up all over the place all on their own. For a tea or luncheon I love to decorate each tuna salad and egg salad finger sandwich served with a Johnny jump-up. All you do is pick the flowers, wash them gently, then on each little sandwich put a tiny dab of butter and the Johnny jump-up on top. It looks fabulous. I've also decorated pieces of pound cake (sliced) each with a dab of butter and a Johnny jump-up; as well as on cookies (white chocolate macadamia nut). The Johnny jump-ups add such elegance to a tea or luncheon.

Joanne Jacobellis

Stamp solid colored napkins, placemats and tablecloths with floral or botanical rubber stamps using fabric ink. This gives you a wonderful way to coordinate a garden theme. Rubber stamps can also help you create floral placecards for your tea or garden party.

Give picnic baskets as wedding gifts. Be sure to include two of everything! You can stock your basket with napkins, placemats, plates, cups, flatware and wine glasses (crystal or acrylic). Add a bottle of the couple's favorite wine and other gourmet food items, and the new bride and groom have the makings for a first meal together after they return from their honeymoon. Don't forget candles and candlesticks, or possibly a romantic tape or CD.

All you need to wrap your gift is a big bow tied onto the handle! Picnic baskets also make great Valentine's Day, anniversary or "just because" gifts. Kids would love a basket tailored just for them for special picnics with mommy and daddy, or grandparents.

Cheryl Berry

*Make homemade ice cream...
fresh strawberry, peach
and vanilla are
summertime favorites!*

149

For a special summertime beverage, layer ice, rose petals and mint in chilled glasses and fill with lemonade. Delicious!

Laurinda & Courtney Dawson

A watermelon can be used to keep fresh flowers perky and make a summer buffet or tea table charming and seasonal. Select a melon with an unblemished, well-colored rind. Its shape depends on the shape and size of the table where it will be used. Cut a wedge from the top of the melon ("top" is determined by experimenting to find on which side the melon rests without rolling, which is the "bottom") and place the slice beside the melon on a pretty tray or platter. Arrange a variety of flowers, greens, and baby's breath by inserting stems into the meat of the melon until the cavity is filled and overflowing. The juice of the melon will keep the flowers fresh and the whole arrangement can be kept refrigerated for extended use.

Rebecca Welsh

To keep certain foods cold (like potato salad), freeze a stoneware bowl ahead of time. Just before leaving on your picnic, transfer food into the frozen bowl and cover with foil. This will keep the food cold for a longer period of time.

Deirdre Barnett

Add 1 tablespoon of rose water while mixing up your filling for apple pie. This addition makes a unique and wonderful apple pie. It's not only a nice addition for entertaining, but friends and family always request this treat.

Judy Hand

Here's a "recipe" for a romantic country garden wedding reception.
Menu:

**fresh fruits & whole berries
   (strawberries, blueberries, raspberries)
finger sandwiches or deli platters (tiny buns)
mini muffins (several varieties)
fresh vegetables & dips
fresh salads
cheeses
punch, tea, coffee
wedding cake**

Cover your serving tables with white (to the floor) tablecloths, then cover with old quilts or quilt tops. Use baskets lined with floral napkins to hold silverware, napkins, and the breads; and baskets lined with waterproof plastic liners to serve the cheeses, fruits and vegetables. Old plates and platters are great to serve the meats and sandwiches, and garnish with edible flowers.
Fill old crocks with wildflowers to decorate the serving tables. Use old blue or white mason jars as candle holders. Put white votive candles in the jars, tie thin silk ribbons around the tops of each jar. Put a few flower sprigs around each jar base. Use a large pickle crock, well washed, as your punch bowl. Surround the base with a ring of flowers.

Have your bakery bake a plain (non-decorated) tiered wedding cake, and your florist make a nosegay bouquet in your wedding colors for the top of the cake. Purchase several yards of thin satin ribbon (in several colors), tuck under nosegay, letting the ribbon stream and cascade over the sides of the cake. Each guest table should have several mason jar candle holders, with ribbon and flowers around each jar. Each table should also have a basket of flowers as the centerpiece. Keep the lights low for the best effect!

Carol Bull
Gooseberry Patch

Elegant Garden Tea Party Invitations

You can create beautiful invitations and placecard settings for your special garden tea, by using fresh flowers such as pansies or rose buds. Press your fresh-picked flowers in a flower press and let dry. Use your imagination to create party invitations using elegant colored papers. Decorate with your pressed flowers and use ink colors that compliment your choice of flower colors. Additional decorations could include lace and fine ribbon trim for a Victorian look, buttons and bows for contemporary. To create placecards, simply hot glue one pressed flower in left hand side of placecard and use colored ink to write the name of your guests.

Juanita Williams

Try cutting shapes from softened butter and place on a terra cotta saucer. Use Gooseberry Patch miniature cookie cutters!

Sharon Scurto

A wheelbarrow filled with fresh straw makes a wonderful serving cart for a summertime picnic.

He who plants a garden plants happiness.
Old Chinese Proverb

Super Starters

Surround a candle with a bed of parsley, radish roses, cauliflower, carrots, cucumbers and celery sticks. This makes a colorful and edible centerpiece for a luncheon or casual meal.

Marion Pfeifer

Toasted Brie

Michele Dafgek

A delicious and simple appetizer!

wheel of brie at room temperature
1/4 c. whole blanched almonds

2 T. butter or
margarine

Sauté almonds in margarine. Place brie on cookie sheet with almonds on top. Bake at 350 degrees for 12 minutes. Serve warm with apples, pears, bread or crackers.

Hot Broccoli Dip

Sandy Bessingpas

This recipe works equally well with fresh or frozen broccoli. It is an excellent topping for new red potatoes, which are both ready about the same time in my garden. We also like it as a topping for baked potatoes in the winter and also an excellent hot dip for tortilla chips any time of the year. Your kids just might LOVE broccoli if you try this recipe.

l lb. fresh broccoli or 16 oz. pkg. frozen
16 oz. pasteurized processed cheese spread
2- 4 oz. cans sliced mushrooms, drained
1 can cream of mushroom soup
1 can cream of onion soup

Cook broccoli, drain and chop into bite-size pieces. Melt cheese in microwave. Stir all ingredients together into a crock pot. Cook until hot and well blended.

Dilly Shrimp Dip
Mary Murray

Great for a summer dinner party!

8 oz. pkg. cream cheese, softened	1 T. mustard
8 oz. shrimp, cleaned and chopped	1 T. ketchup
1 c. celery	1 T. onion, chopped
2 T. sour cream	1/2 t. dill
1 T. mayonnaise	1 t. parsley

Put all ingredients in your blender or food processor and blend until smooth. Chill and serve with crackers or bagel chips.

Sausage-Cheese Balls
Mary Murray

This recipe makes about 100 pieces, terrific for a crowd!

1 lb. uncooked sausage	1/2 lb. cheddar cheese, grated
4 c. biscuit mix	2 t. crumbled sage*

Combine all ingredients and roll into balls. Bake on ungreased cookie sheet until cooked thoroughly. Approximately 20 minutes at 350 degrees. These could be frozen and reheated before the party!

*Don't forget when you're using fresh sage, rub the leaves between the palms of your hands. This will crumble the sage nicely, as well as separate out the stems which should be discarded.

Shrimp Mousse
Barbara Truax

8 oz. pkg. cream cheese	1/2 c. celery, diced
1 envelope plain gelatin	1/2 c. onion
1 c. mayonnaise	2 c. small salad
1 can cream of mushroom soup	shrimp, frozen or fresh

Melt cream cheese over low heat (double boiler best). Dissolve gelatin in 1/4 cup warm water. Add to softened cream cheese and stir until smooth. Add other ingredients and pour into an oiled fish-shaped mold. Refrigerate until solid. Unmold and surround with parsley.

Zucchini Appetizers

Susan Harvey

3 c. unpeeled zucchini, thinly sliced
1/2 t. oregano
1/2 c. onion, finely chopped
1/2 c. parmesan cheese, grated
1 clove garlic, finely chopped or 1 t. garlic powder

1/2 t. seasoned salt
1 c. biscuit baking mix
1/2 t. salt
1/2 c. vegetable oil
4 eggs, slightly beaten
2 T. snipped parsley
dash of pepper

Heat oven to 350 degrees. Mix all ingredients together and spread in a greased 13"x9" pan. Bake until golden brown (about 25 minutes). Cut into small pieces for appetizers or large pieces for a side dish.

Summer Vegetable Pizza

Mel Wolk

This is a lovely summer appetizer or lunch and can be made ahead. Fresh fruit, iced mint tea and summer vegetable pizza served under a shady tree, is a perfect way to curl up with a Gooseberry Patch book and dream!

1 tube refrigerated crescent rolls
2- 8 oz. pkgs. cream cheese

1 1/2 T. mayonnaise or yogurt
1 t. dillweed

Press crescent rolls onto a 13" pizza pan or baking stone, pinching seams together to seal. Bake at 350 degrees until lightly browned. Let crust cool completely. Soften cream cheese and mix together with mayonnaise and dillweed. Spread evenly over top of the cooled crust.

Topping:

(All finely chopped) zucchini, mushrooms, green peppers, green onions, tomatoes, cucumbers (well drained), grated carrots. Thinly slice some to use as a garnish. Sprinkle a layer of each vegetable over cheese layer. Chill before serving. Cut in wedges or squares. Makes 1 pizza.

Parsley-Bacon Sandwich (Canapé)   *Carol Carr*

2 bunches fresh parsley or watercress, chopped
1 lb. bacon, drained and cooked until crumbles
1/4 c. mayonnaise (scant amount, should be stiff)
1 t. worcestershire sauce
1/4 t. garlic powder
1/2 c. butter, softened
1 loaf very fresh sandwich bread, crust trimmed

Combine chopped parsley, bacon, mayonnaise and worcestershire to spreading consistency. Mix garlic powder with softened butter. Roll the bread with a rolling pin. Spread bread with garlic butter mixture. Spread parsley mixture over the butter. Roll the slices up and wrap in waxed paper and twist ends. Freeze. To serve, unwrap and slice 5 per roll. Thaw. Makes 10 dozen.

Rose Petal Sandwiches   *Judy Hand*

8 oz. pkg. cream cheese, softened
3 T. rose water
12 thin slices white bread, crusts
    removed
6 UNSPRAYED roses, red or pink

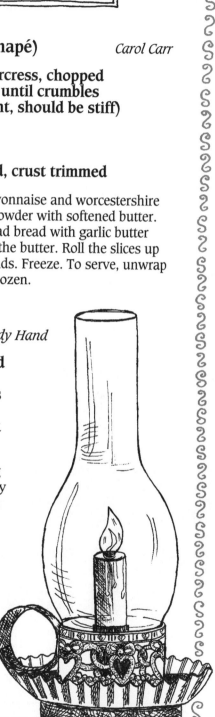

Mix cream cheese and rose water into a smooth spread; divide evenly among slices of bread, spreading very carefully on all pieces to edge. Cover each bread slice with rose petals, pressing them well into cheese spread. Cover and firm in refrigerator. After firming, cut in half, then fourths. Place on plate garnished with several roses. Other edible flowers may be used in sandwiches or for garnishes on plates, cakes, or floated in beverages...try nasturtiums, Johnny jump-ups, marigolds, or violets.

Faux Carrots

Judy Hand

Peter Rabbit would have loved these...your guests will too!

3 oz. pkg. cream cheese, softened　　**1 c. carrots, grated**
4 to 5 drops worcestershire sauce　　**1/4 t. salt**
dash of cayenne pepper　　**1 T. onion, grated**
fresh parsley to imitate carrot tops

Mix all ingredients, except parsley, together. Form mixture into a roll and chill. Once roll is chilled, take small pieces from it and roll into small carrot shapes. Place sprig of parsley at the top of each carrot shape.

Baked Dip

Jeanne Calkins

These two recipes are two of my all-time family-tested and family-requested recipes. At each special family event my twin sisters request the combo as top choice for pre-meal munchies. They are absolutely made to go with each other.

1 c. sharp cheddar cheese, grated　　**1/2 t. thyme, dried**
1 c. mayonnaise　　**1/2 t. marjoram, dried**
1 small onion, grated

Mix well and bake at 350 degrees in oven until hot. Serve with crackers or cheese straws. Yields 2 cups.

Cheese Straws

Jeanne Calkins

2 c. cheddar cheese, grated　　**yolk of 1 egg**
1/2 c. butter　　**1 1/2 c. flour**
dash of hot pepper sauce or　　**1/4 t. salt**
**　　sprinkle of cayenne pepper**

Mix like pie crust. Roll out, cut in narrow strips and bake at 350 degrees for 10 to 15 minutes. Serve with baked dip.

Spinach Dip

Marlene Wetzel-Dellagatta

1.2 oz. envelope vegetable
  soup mix
1 can water chestnuts,
  chopped
1 pkg. frozen chopped spinach
  (defrosted and drained well)

1/2 t. lemon juice
1 pt. sour cream
3 green onions,
  chopped
1/2 c. mayonnaise

Drain all liquid from spinach. Mix all ingredients. Refrigerate 2 hours. Hollow out round loaf of black bread and spoon spinach dip into bread. Serve. (Bread removed from inside of loaf may be broken into bite-size pieces and served with the dip.)

Stuffed Tulips

Cora Baker

These stuffed tulips make a beautiful addition to a special Easter or spring buffet table.

6 tulip blossoms
6 eggs
1/4 t. salt
4 T. sour cream
2 T. chives, chopped
1 T. dill, chopped
1 T. tarragon, chopped

Remove the inside stem and gently wash and pat dry the tulips. Boil the eggs for 12 minutes then cool them quickly in cold water. Shell them and chop fine, add salt, sour cream, chives, dill and tarragon. Mix well. When using dried herbs use half the amounts. Fill the tulip blossoms with the egg salad. The tulips may be eaten.

10-Layer Mexicale Dip

Wendy Lee Paffenroth

This is excellent with fresh garden tomatoes, green peppers, etc. Only make a few hours before or it can get runny. I cut up veggies ahead and place in baggies, then when I want to make it, I just start layering. You will find that on a day when it is too hot to cook or no one feels like eating much, this is great. Just put it out on the porch along with a basket of tortilla chips, serve some cool drinks and watch it disappear! They will clean it up and look for more. Serves 6 to 8.

16 oz. can refried beans
1 pt. sour cream, divided
large green pepper
12 oz. jar salsa
8 to 12 oz. sharp cheddar
 cheese, shredded

large tomato, diced
medium onion (red or
 yellow), diced
8 to 12 oz. mozzarella
 cheese, shredded

Using a fork, spread refried beans on the bottom of a 9"x9" pan (or double recipe and go for a 13"x9" pan). Stir 1/2 pint of sour cream until pourable, spread over beans. Cut green pepper into thin slivers, and place half of them over sour cream. Put salsa (mild, medium or hot, your choice) in a strainer for a few minutes to drain a bit. When drained, pour over pepper slices. Spread cheddar cheese evenly over salsa. Stir the other 1/2 pint of sour cream until pourable, spread over cheese. Add diced tomato (if it is really juicy, put in a strainer for a few minutes). Next add the rest of the green pepper slivers. Placed the diced onions on top of the pepper slices. Top with mozzarella cheese (or a pre-packaged taco cheese).

Guacamole

Debbie Parker
Gooseberry Patch

2 c. (2 large) avocados, mashed
2 T. lemon juice or 1 T. lemon
 juice and 1 T. lime juice
1 tomato, diced (optional)
2 green chilies, finely chopped

1/4 t. salt
1/4 t. chili powder
1 T. onion, grated or
 finely chopped
1/8 t. garlic powder

Combine all ingredients. Chill and serve.

Mango Salsa

Suzan Turner

1 c. mango, cubed and peeled
1 c. tomato, cubed and seeded
1/2 c. onion, finely chopped
1/4 c. green onion, finely
    chopped

2 T. chopped cilantro
2 T. olive oil
2 T. fresh lime juice
1 jalapeno pepper,
    seeded and minced

Combine all ingredients in a small bowl. Season to taste with salt and pepper. Can be prepared 2 hours ahead; cover. Serve with grilled chicken, fish or shrimp. Very low-fat!

Fresh Garden Salsa

Deborah McClellan

4 to 5 ripe tomatoes
1 to 1 1/2 fresh green chilies
1/4 onion
salt to taste
fresh cilantro to taste

lemon juice, lime juice
    or vinegar to taste

Whirl tomatoes, chilies (can be of several varieties, depending on taste, from very mild to very hot) and onion in food processor to a "dipping" consistency. Add lemon juice, lime juice or vinegar; then salt and cilantro. Fresh cilantro adds a very fresh taste to the salsa, but dried cilantro can also be used.

South of the Border Basket

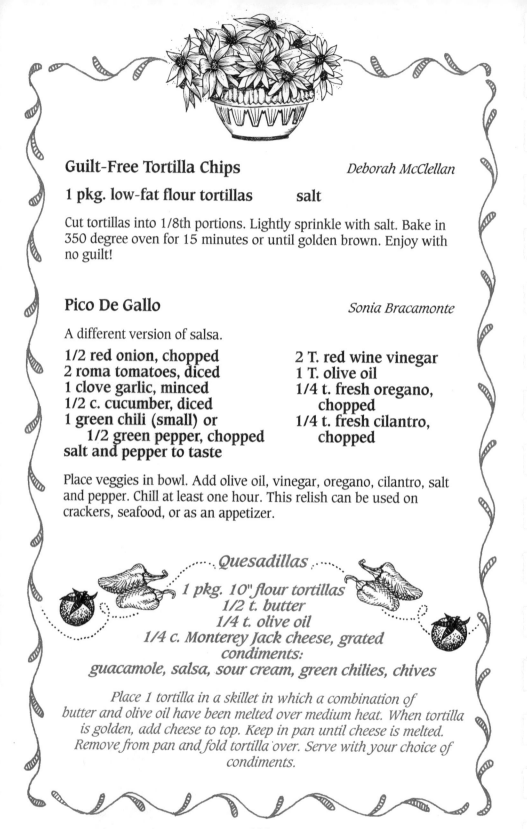

Guilt-Free Tortilla Chips

Deborah McClellan

1 pkg. low-fat flour tortillas   salt

Cut tortillas into 1/8th portions. Lightly sprinkle with salt. Bake in 350 degree oven for 15 minutes or until golden brown. Enjoy with no guilt!

Pico De Gallo

Sonia Bracamonte

A different version of salsa.

1/2 red onion, chopped
2 roma tomatoes, diced
1 clove garlic, minced
1/2 c. cucumber, diced
1 green chili (small) or
    1/2 green pepper, chopped
salt and pepper to taste

2 T. red wine vinegar
1 T. olive oil
1/4 t. fresh oregano,
    chopped
1/4 t. fresh cilantro,
    chopped

Place veggies in bowl. Add olive oil, vinegar, oregano, cilantro, salt and pepper. Chill at least one hour. This relish can be used on crackers, seafood, or as an appetizer.

Quesadillas

1 pkg. 10" flour tortillas
1/2 t. butter
1/4 t. olive oil
1/4 c. Monterey Jack cheese, grated
condiments:
guacamole, salsa, sour cream, green chilies, chives

Place 1 tortilla in a skillet in which a combination of butter and olive oil have been melted over medium heat. When tortilla is golden, add cheese to top. Keep in pan until cheese is melted. Remove from pan and fold tortilla over. Serve with your choice of condiments.

Sun-Dried Tomato and Roasted Garlic Pesto

Jeannine English

Delicious tossed over pasta of your choice or as an appetizer spread on toasted sourdough bread.

1 whole head of garlic
3 T. extra-virgin olive oil
1 c. sun-dried tomatoes, packed in olive oil
1/3 c. packed fresh flat-leaf parsley sprigs
2 T. garlic chives or green onions, chopped
2 T. parmesan cheese, freshly grated

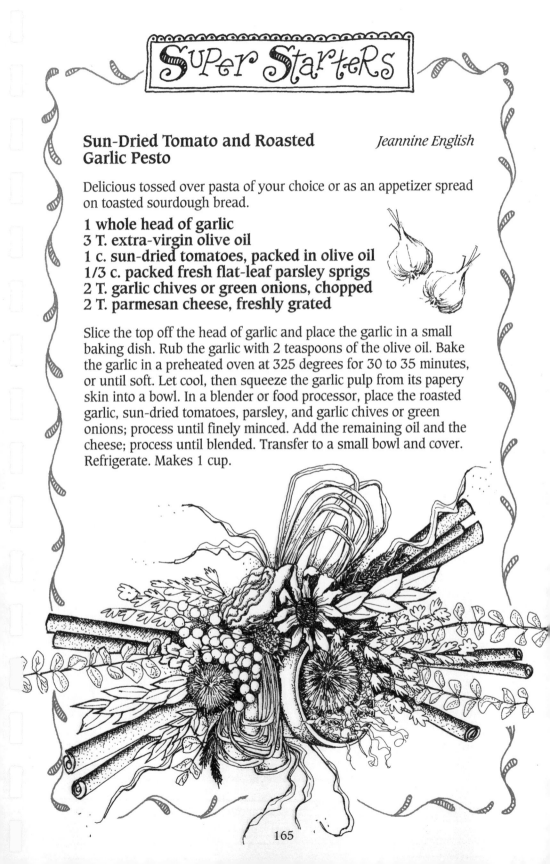

Slice the top off the head of garlic and place the garlic in a small baking dish. Rub the garlic with 2 teaspoons of the olive oil. Bake the garlic in a preheated oven at 325 degrees for 30 to 35 minutes, or until soft. Let cool, then squeeze the garlic pulp from its papery skin into a bowl. In a blender or food processor, place the roasted garlic, sun-dried tomatoes, parsley, and garlic chives or green onions; process until finely minced. Add the remaining oil and the cheese; process until blended. Transfer to a small bowl and cover. Refrigerate. Makes 1 cup.

Herb Cream Cheese

Nancie Gensler

Delicious served with a basket of mixed crackers or vegetables!

**8 oz. pkg. cream cheese, softened
1/4 to 1/2 c. fresh herbs, chopped*
fresh ground pepper and salt**

Combine all ingredients and press into small crock or other attractive dish. Refrigerate until needed. For something really special, line small heart molds with cheesecloth, press herb cream cheese into mold and refrigerate until firm. Carefully remove cheese from mold and place on individual serving dish (I like to use small, antique china plates) and garnish with sprig of fresh herbs or flowers from the garden (chive blossoms, nasturtiums, or Johnny jump-ups). Remember, any herbs or edible flowers from the garden should be grown organically and washed thoroughly before use in recipes.

*Use combination of parsley, cilantro, rosemary, lemon thyme, chives, watercress, dill, whatever is available.

Pumpkin Dip

Joan Limberg

This is a good way to use the apples you've harvested. Cut into wedges or you can use on breads (apple, date or nut). For a festive Halloween, cut the top off a pumpkin from your garden and scoop out the insides. Fill with dip and use ginger snaps for dipping.

**2- 8 oz. pkgs. cream
    cheese
1 lb. powdered sugar
1/2 t. cinnamon
1/4 t. nutmeg
1 large can pumpkin
1/4 t. pumpkin spice**

Mix all ingredients well.
Serve with fresh fruits.

Radish Chive Spread

Susan Koronowski

8 oz. pkg. cream cheese
1 T. butter or margarine, softened
1 c. homegrown red radishes, chopped
1/2 c. chopped chives, or freeze-dried chives to taste
1/2 t. salt, or to taste
1 pkg. pumpernickel cocktail bread

Make sure radishes are DRY. Soften cream cheese, add butter and mix well. Add chopped radishes, chives and salt mixing well. Chill. Serve in bowl letting guests make their own open-faced sandwiches.

Pumpkin Porcupine

Carol Bull
Gooseberry Patch

1 small to medium pumpkin   dip of your choice

Wash pumpkin well, cut off top, and clean out just like you would a jack-o'-lantern. Fill the empty pumpkin shell with dip. Cut up a vegetable assortment (broccoli, cauliflower, green pepper, carrots, celery, cherry tomatoes) into bite-sized pieces. Thread the veggies onto toothpicks and stick the toothpicks all over the outside of the pumpkin. Now your pumpkin porcupine can be the centerpiece of a holiday buffet!

Flowerpot Pesto

Elizabeth Timmins
Gooseberry Patch Artisan

Garnish with basil sprig and serve with bread, crackers or vegetables.

1 lb. cream cheese   **1 lb. butter, softened**

Beat together until smooth; set aside.
Prepare pesto.

2 c. basil leaves, lightly packed
2 large cloves garlic
1/2 c. pine nuts
3/4 c. parmesan cheese,
  grated
2/3 c. olive oil

Combine basil leaves and garlic
in a food processor. Blend to a fine
paste, scraping down sides of bowl
as necessary. Add pine nuts and
parmesan cheese, process until
smooth. With machine running, pour
olive oil through feed tube in a slow,
steady stream. Mix until smooth
and creamy. Line two small flowerpots or one medium flowerpot with
damp cheesecloth, making sure the
cheesecloth is large enough to fold
over the top. Alternately layer
cheese mixture and pesto, starting and finishing with cheese
mixture. Fold cheesecloth over
the top and press down lightly
with your hand to compact.
Refrigerate at least 2 hours.
If made ahead, cover with
plastic wrap and refrig-
erate for up to 5 days.
When ready to serve,
invert onto a serving dish
and gently pull off cheesecloth.

Relaxful Refreshments

When having an outdoor party for children, borrow your child's red wagon, fill it with ice and put cold drinks and juice boxes in it. You can also use a new garden hand spade to scoop ice into paper cups. Be sure you clean the wagon first!

Jill Buser

Purple Cow

Deb Damari-Tull

Good summertime drink. So cool and purple!

vanilla ice cream   **grape juice**
carbonated water

Put 1 scoop of vanilla ice cream in a tall glass. Fill halfway with grape juice and top with carbonated water.

Summer Slush

Debbie Felt

I remember having this slush on hot summer afternoons on my grandmother's back porch.

46 oz. can of pineapple juice   **3 c. sugar**
12 oz. can frozen orange juice   **46 oz. water**
lemon-lime carbonated drink

Combine all of the above ingredients in a saucepan and boil until sugar dissolves. Pour into a 13"x9" pan and a loaf pan. Cover with foil and freeze until firm. To serve, cut out chunks with a knife, place in a glass and pour your favorite lemon-lime carbonated beverage over it. Head for the shade or the back porch!

Tomato Juice

Mary Dungan

I'll be 76 in September. My mother prepared this juice when I was a child. I have been doing the same for 50 years.

8 qt. very ripe, red tomatoes   **2 t. onion salt**
2 t. celery salt   **3/4 c. sugar**

Wash tomatoes and remove core. Put in a 10-quart pot and cook for 5 minutes over medium heat; put through ricer. Measure 6 quarts, add onion salt, celery salt and sugar. Put all in a large pot and bring to a boil. Fill quart jars, sealing according to approved way. Let set overnight before removing rings. Store and use to drink, for soups or in stews. Delicious!

Relaxful Refreshments

Old-Fashioned Lemonade

Karen Wald

Nothing beats a glass of cold lemonade on a hot summer day!

4 lemons　　　　　　　　　**3/4 c. sugar**
4 c. cold water

Cut lemons into thin slices, remove seeds. Place slices in a large non-metal bowl; sprinkle with sugar and let stand for 10 minutes. Press lemons with the back of a spoon to extract juice. Add water, stirring and pressing lemons. Remove lemon slices and serve over ice. Garnish with additional lemon slices. Makes 4 servings.

Mint Lemonade

Marion Pfeifer

Best reason I know to grow mint!

2 c. sugar　　　　　　　　　**juice of 6 lemons**
2 1/2 c. water　　　　　　　**1 c. mint leaves**
juice of 3 oranges

Cook sugar and water 5 minutes. Cool. Add juices. Pour over mint leaves, cover and let sit one hour. Strain into jar, keep in refrigerator. Fill 8-ounce glass with 1/3 cup syrup, then add ice and water. Makes 10 to 12 servings.

Take time out from gardening and cool off with an old-fashioned root beer float!

Punch Slush
Paula Griffen

The kids just love this and it's good to have in the summer months when it's so hot!

1 pkg. strawberry drink mix
1 pkg. cherry drink mix
12 oz. orange juice concentrate
enough water to fill the pail

1 1/2 c. sugar
lemon-lime carbonated drink

Mix all of the above (except lemon-lime carbonated drink) in a 1-gallon ice cream pail and freeze. Put in glasses and add lemon lime carbonated drink.

Friendship Punch
Elizabeth Timmins
Gooseberry Patch Artisan

3 T. dried rosemary or
   1 1/2 T. fresh
1 c. water
6 oz. can frozen limeade

1 t. vanilla
12 oz. can apricot nectar
2 qt. ginger ale

Simmer rosemary in water for 2 minutes. Cool completely and strain. Combine remaining ingredients (well chilled) and serve in a punch bowl decorated with an ice ring. Johnny jump-ups, violets, or rosemary flowers may be floated on punch for a special touch.

Rosemary Lemon-Pineapple Punch
Helene Hamilton

46 oz. can unsweetened
   pineapple juice
3/4 c. sugar (may add 1/4 c.
   more if you prefer sweeter)
1 1/2 c. fresh lemon juice

2 c. water
1 liter ginger ale, cold
4 or 5 fresh rosemary
   sprigs, crushed gently

In a large saucepan, bring pineapple juice, sugar, lemon juice, water and rosemary sprigs to a boil. Remove from heat, cover and steep for 15 minutes. Remove rosemary. Chill. Add ginger ale, stir and serve. Garnish with fresh rosemary sprig. Very refreshing! Serves 12.

Relaxful Refreshments

Sparkling Grape Punch
Barbara Truax

2/3 c. sugar
2 c. water
1 pt. grape juice
2 c. orange juice

1 c. lemon juice
6- 7 oz. bottles of lemon-
   lime carbonated drink
additional lemon-lime
   carbonated drink

Simmer sugar and water for 5 minutes, chill along with fruit juices. Pour additional lemon-lime drink into two ice cube trays and freeze. Mix juices and slowly pour in lemon-lime carbonated drink. Add ice cubes. Float fresh fruit and mint leaves on top.

Peppermint Grape Punch
Elizabeth Timmins
Gooseberry Patch Artisan

1/2 c. sugar
1 1/2 c. water
1 c. peppermint leaves

1/4 c. lemon juice
2 c. grape juice
12 oz. ginger ale

Cook sugar and water and pour over peppermint leaves and lemon juice. Steep for one hour. Strain and add grape juice. Chill. Before serving add ginger ale. Makes 2 quarts.

Summer Strawberry Cooler
Carol Jones

4 c. fresh strawberries
1 1/2 c. sugar

4 2/3 c. orange juice
2/3 c. ginger ale
4 c. ice cubes

In a blender combine strawberries, sugar and 1 cup of orange juice. Process until smooth. Pour mixture into pitcher. Slowly blend remaining orange juice with ice until mixture is slushy. Mix orange "slush" with berry mixture and ginger ale in large container. Serve. Makes approximately 4 quarts.

Citrus Mint Tea Cooler

Sheri Berger

3 regular-size tea bags
4 to 6 sprigs fresh mint
2 c. boiling water
2 c. cold water
2/3 c. sugar

2/3 c. grapefruit juice
1/2 c. lemon juice, freshly
   squeezed
lemon slices for garnish

Place tea bags and mint in 2-quart pitcher. Add the 2 cups boiling water; cover and steep for five minutes. Discard tea bags and mint. Add cold water, sugar, grapefruit and lemon juice; stir to dissolve sugar. Chill. Serve over ice. Garnish with lemon slices. Makes 1 1/2 quarts.

Strawberry Iced Tea Fizz

Sheri Berger

1 pt. fresh strawberries,
   stemmed and sliced
1/2 c. sugar
5 c. boiling water
1 tea bag

1 qt. club soda
12 oz. can frozen lemonade
   concentrate, thawed
ice cubes

Combine strawberries and sugar. Pour water over tea bag. Steep 5 minutes. Cool to room temperature and discard tea bag. Stir in strawberries and lemonade concentrate. Chill. To serve, stir in club soda and ladle over ice cubes. Serve with spoons. Serves 12.

Joy's Special Iced Tea

Joy Camille Kokenge

Delicious anytime! We serve it year round.

family-size decaf tea bag
3 strips orange rind

1 cinnamon stick
1/2 c. sugar (or more)

Place orange rind and cinnamon stick in cheesecloth bag. In a 1 quart saucepan of water bring tea bag, sugar, orange rind and cinnamon stick to a boil. Let steep for one hour. Remove cheesecloth bag, pour into pitcher and add cold water to your likeness. Pour over ice. Serves 4 to 6 8-ounce glasses, depending on how much water is added.

Relaxful Refreshments

Tennessee Fruit Tea

MaryAnne Osesek

Especially refreshing after gardening!

4 to 5 T. unsweetened
    instant tea
4 c. water
1 1/2 c. sugar

12 oz. can frozen
    lemonade
12 oz. can frozen
    pineapple orange juice

Stir together tea, water and sugar; bring to a boil, then let cool. In a gallon container mix lemonade and pineapple orange juice. Add these to the tea mixture along with enough water to make 1 gallon. Refrigerate. Serve over ice.

Sun Tea

Mary Ann Nemecek

Take a one gallon glass jar and fill with cold water; add 8 regular tea bags, tied together. Let the papers hang on the outside placing the lid over them to hold the bags. Place in a sunny spot in your flower garden. Depending on the temperature and the sun exposure, it will take from 2 to 6 hours. Do not leave over night or in the rain as the flavor is not as good.

As your herb garden begins to produce, you may want to add to your tea such herbs as lemon balm, spearmint, peppermint, or licorice mint. Each adds a nice touch to summer tea. Take approximately 1/2 cup of fresh leaves and add to your tea prior to setting outside. I suggest tearing the leaves in small pieces before placing them into a cheesecloth bag or tea diffuser. By brushing the leaves they will release more flavor.

Rose Petal Tea

Marie Alana Gardner

2 c. firmly packed fragrant rose petals*   1 c. tea leaves

Preheat oven to 200 degrees. Place rose petals on an ungreased baking sheet. Leaving oven door slightly open, dry petals in oven for 3 to 4 hours or until completely dry, stirring occasionally. In a food processor, fitted with a steel blade, process rose petals and tea leaves until finely chopped. Store in an airtight container.

To brew tea: Place 1 teaspoon tea for each 8 ounces of water in a warm teapot. Bring water to a rolling boil and pour over tea. Steep tea 5 minutes. Stir and strain. Serve hot or chilled. Serves 3.

*About 15 large roses, wash and pat dry.

Rose Petal Ice Cubes

Jolie Halm

These look so pretty floating in a bowl of punch or a pitcher of iced tea or lemonade. A perfect touch for an outdoor wedding, bridal shower or garden tea party!

Collect pesticide-free rose petals. Rinse under warm water and blot dry. Fill ice cube tray half full with water and freeze. Place a rose petal on each cube, cover with a teaspoon of water; freeze again. Fill cubes completely with water and freeze, remove from trays. Makes 16 cubes per tray.

Main Medley

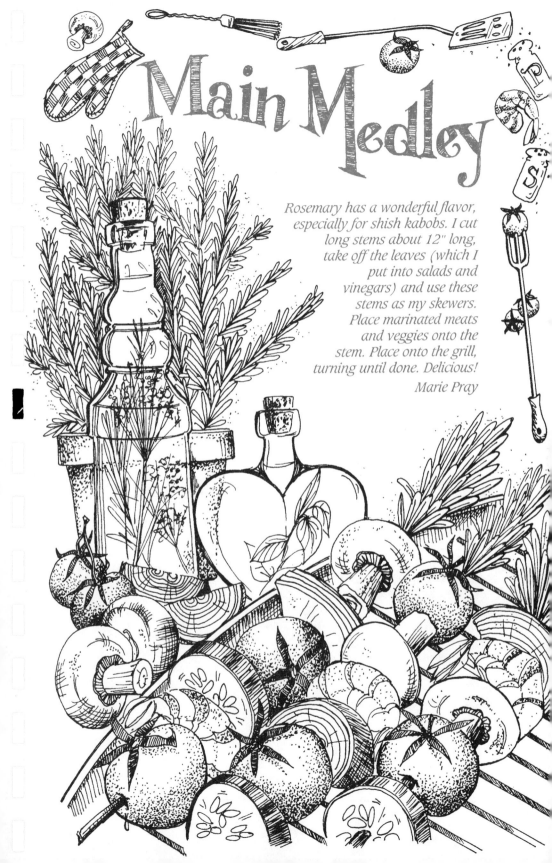

Rosemary has a wonderful flavor, especially for shish kabobs. I cut long stems about 12" long, take off the leaves (which I put into salads and vinegars) and use these stems as my skewers. Place marinated meats and veggies onto the stem. Place onto the grill, turning until done. Delicious!

Marie Pray

Flowerpot Pies

Frances Guch

You will need 6 new clay flowerpots, each measuring 4"x4", aluminum foil, vegetable oil, egg yolk glaze, butter pastry and chicken pot pie filling.

Butter Pastry:

2 c. all-purpose flour
1 t. salt
1 1/2 sticks butter, chilled

3 T. shortening
1/3 c. ice water

Place flour in a large mixing bowl along with the salt. Cut the butter into thin slices. Using a pastry blender or two knives, blend the butter and shortening into the flour mixture until it resembles coarse meal. Work quickly so the butter does not soften. Sprinkle the ice water evenly over the top. Mix rapidly with a fork. Gather the dough into a ball and flatten it; wrap in aluminum foil and refrigerate for 3 hours or overnight.

Chicken pot pie filling:

3 T. butter
1/2 c. celery, finely diced
1/2 c. onion, finely diced
1 small bay leaf
3 T. flour
1 1/2 c. chicken stock
1 1/2 c. milk or cream
salt and pepper to taste
2 c. chicken, cooked and diced
2 c. potatoes, cooked and diced
2 c. carrots, cooked and diced
2 c. peas or green beans, cooked
  (beans cut in 1" pieces)
1/2 c. fresh dill, chopped

Melt the butter over low heat in a large saucepan. Add the celery, onion and bay leaf; cover and cook about 10 minutes or until the vegetables are

soft. Remove the bay leaf. Sprinkle the flour over the vegetables, stir well to incorporate, then cook for about 5 minutes. Stir in the chicken stock and milk or cream. Cook the sauce over low heat for 15 minutes, stirring occasionally. Stir in the chicken, potatoes, carrots, peas or beans and dill. Cool to room temperature. Cut six 12" squares of foil. Shape the foil around the outside of each flowerpot. Remove the foil shape and carefully reposition so it conforms to the inside of the flowerpot, making sure it doesn't tear. Remove the foil and trim away the excess all around with scissors. The top of the foil should reach near the top of the pot without being included in the pastry. Do the same for all 6 flowerpots.

Preheat oven at 425 degrees. Brush the outside of each flowerpot with vegetable oil and blot with a paper towel to remove excess oil. Spoon chicken pot pie filling into each lined flowerpot. The filling should come to within 1/2" of the top of the flowerpot. On a lightly floured surface, roll out the pastry to 1/8" thickness. Cut six 6" circles of pastry. Top each of the filled flowerpots with a circle of pastry and turn the edge under all around. Use your fingers to make a decorative edge all around. Cut 3 small steam escape holes in the center of the pastry.

Egg yolk glaze:

Place 1 egg yolk in a small bowl with 1 tablespoon cold water; mix thoroughly with a fork or wire whisk. Using a pastry brush, paint the tops of each pie with the glaze. Carefully place the flowerpot pies in the center of the oven, directly on the oven rack. Line the bottom of your oven with foil when baking pies because one may drip while baking. Bake the pies for 30 to 35 minutes or until pastry is crisp and golden brown and filling is hot. Serves 6. For decoration, place seed packets glued to sticks on the flowerpot pies. Serve with a crisp green salad.

At the first sign of frost, pick your tomatoes, wrap each individually in newspaper and store in a loosely covered box in a cool, dark spot. They'll ripen slowly and keep for weeks.

Lobster Mousse

Jeannine English

Delicious served with table water crackers and a romaine salad.

2 c. lobster meat,
  coarsely chopped
1 T. lemon juice
3/4 c. heavy cream, whipped
1/2 t. lemon zest
1/2 t. paprika
1/4 c. plus 1/2 c. dry vermouth
lemon slices and fresh dill sprigs

1/2 c. mayonnaise
1 T. shallots, finely
  chopped
1 t. salt
1 envelope unflavored
  gelatin
1 T. fresh dill or
  chervil, chopped

Lightly coat a 3-cup ring mold with a vegetable oil spray. In a small bowl, sprinkle gelatin over 1/4 cup vermouth. Let stand until gelatin is softened. In a small saucepan, bring shallots and 1/2 cup vermouth to boiling. Boil gently until reduced by half. Mix in softened gelatin until dissolved. Cool until warm about 15 to 20 minutes. In another bowl combine the gelatin mix, mayonnaise, salt, dill, paprika, lemon juice and zest. Whisk well. Add lobster. Gently fold in whipped cream just until blended. Pour into mold. Cover and refrigerate 3 or 4 hours, until set. When unmolded, garnish with lemon slices and dill sprigs.

Grilled Salmon

Serve with raspberry-mustard sauce or cucumber dill sauce...delicious!

**salmon steaks
vegetable or olive oil
lemon
salt and pepper, to taste
rosemary, dill or tarragon (optional)**

Brush salmon with oil and lemon juice; sprinkle with salt, pepper and rosemary, dill or tarragon (optional). Place salmon over charcoal for about 5 minutes. Turn carefully. Brush with oil and lemon. Sprinkle with salt and pepper. Broil only until fish flakes easily with fork (about 4 or 5 more minutes).

Main Medley

Shrimp and Fresh Fruit Platter

Debbie Parker
Gooseberry Patch

assorted fresh fruits (melon, kiwi, pineapple,
   strawberries, mandarin oranges)
chilled shrimp, peeled and deveined

Arrange on a salad plate. Drizzle with raspberry dressing (can be purchased) and garnish with mint leaves.

Crabmeat Quiche

Marlene Wetzel-Dellagatta

6 oz. pkg. crabmeat
4 eggs
9" pie shell
1 c. half & half
dash pepper
1 t. salt

4 oz. can sliced
   mushrooms, drained
1 t. chives, chopped
dash nutmeg
1/2 c. Swiss cheese, grated

Thaw and drain crabmeat. Beat eggs, add half & half along with the seasonings. Place mushrooms and crabmeat at bottom of pie shell, sprinkle cheese, add egg mixture. Bake at 375 degrees for 35 to 40 minutes or until center is firm.

Raspberry-Mustard Sauce

A nice accompaniment to grilled salmon!

1/2 c. raspberry mustard   1/2 c. heavy cream
1 T. raspberry vinegar

*Mix raspberry mustard, raspberry vinegar
and heavy cream together. Heat to a simmer
but be sure not to boil. Keep at a simmer
for a few minutes. Makes 4 servings.*

Italian Zucchini Crescent Pie
Susan Harvey

4 c. zucchini, thinly sliced
1 c. onion, chopped
1/4 to 1/2 c. margarine
1/3 c. parsley, chopped
1/2 t. salt
1/2 t. pepper
1/4 t. oregano leaves

2 eggs, beaten
2 c. (8 oz.) mozzarella
  cheese, shredded
8 oz. tube refrigerated
  crescent rolls
2 t. mustard

Cook and stir zucchini and onion in margarine for 10 minutes. Stir in parsley, salt, pepper, and oregano leaves. Combine beaten eggs and shredded cheese; add to zucchini mixture. Separate crescent dinner rolls into 8 triangles. Place in ungreased 10" pie pan, press over bottom and up sides to form crust. Spread crust with mustard. Pour vegetable mixture into crust. Bake in preheated oven at 375 degrees for 18 to 20 minutes or until center is set. Cover crust with foil during last 10 minutes of baking. Let stand 15 minutes before serving.

Stuffed Zucchini
Julie Carwile

Great way to get kids to like zucchini!

2 medium zucchini
3 T. onion, chopped
1 slice bacon, chopped
1/2 c. fresh mushrooms, sliced
  or 4 oz. canned (optional)
1/2 c. tomato, chopped

1/4 c. chicken broth
1/2 t. basil
1/2 t. thyme
1 c. seasoned bread
  crumbs (for stuffing)
dash pepper

Steam zucchini 15 minutes. Slice lengthwise, remove pulp and reserve. Fry bacon and onion until onion is translucent. Add mushrooms, tomatoes, and reserved pulp. Cook 5 minutes stirring occasionally. Add broth and seasonings, bring to a boil.
Add bread crumbs and remove from heat.
Fill zucchini shells with mixture.
Bake at 350 degrees for
25 minutes.

Zucchini Pizza

Joan Limberg

This is absolutely delicious! Serve with salad and French or Italian bread. A great way to use some of the abundance of zucchinis from your garden.

3 1/2 c. (about 1 1/4 lb.) zucchini, coarsely grated
2 large eggs, beaten lightly
2 c. (8 oz.) shredded mozzarella cheese, divided
1/2 c. parmesan cheese, grated

1/3 c. flour
1 T. olive oil
1 c. spaghetti sauce
1 t. dried oregano
1/8 t. dried crushed red pepper

Press zucchini between paper towels to remove excess moisture. Combine zucchini, eggs, 1 cup mozzarella cheese, parmesan cheese and flour in a medium bowl. Stir well. Spread in a greased 13"x9"x2" pan. Bake uncovered at 350 degrees for 20 to 25 minutes. Remove from oven, brush surface with oil. Broil 5 1/2" from heat for 5 minutes. Remove from oven, spread spaghetti sauce on top of zucchini mixture. Sprinkle with remaining 1 cup mozzarella cheese, oregano and red pepper. Bake uncovered at 350 degrees an additional 20 minutes. Yields 6 servings.

Stuffed Bell Peppers

Debbie Meyer

2 large bell peppers
1 c. cheddar cheese, grated
1/4 c. jack cheese, grated
1/8 c. parmesan cheese, grated
1 c. cooked rice
1/4 c. cooked corn
1/2 c. tomatoes, diced
dash of basil

1/2 t. chili powder
1/2 t. garlic powder
1/2 t. onion powder
1/2 c. tomato sauce
dash of hot pepper sauce
1/2 onion, diced
salt to taste

Sauce:

2 c. tomato sauce
1/2 t. Italian seasoning
3 T. sherry wine

1/8 t. garlic powder
1/8 t. onion powder

Cut peppers in half lengthwise and wash, removing all seeds (par boil if desired). Combine cheeses, reserving 1/2 cup cheddar. Mix in saucepan with rice, corn, onion, tomatoes, spices, 1/2 cup tomato sauce and hot pepper sauce. Cook about 5 minutes stirring constantly or until cheese is melted. Taste for seasoning, adjust as necessary.

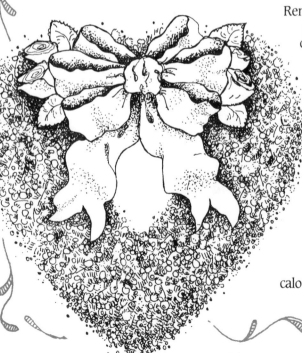

Remove from heat and let cool. Mix sauce ingredients in pan and simmer for 15 minutes. Stuff peppers with rice and corn mix. Place in covered dish. Bake at 275 degrees for 15 minutes. Add sauce and cook 15 minutes more. Top with remaining cheese and bake until cheese melts. Serve immediately. Each serving has 295 calories. Yields 4 servings.

Broccoli and Cheese Ham Rolls
Cheryl Ewer

This recipe worked well for me served as a brunch for several people. I made the rolls a day ahead and poured the mixture on just before baking. I served fresh fruit and sweet rolls alongside.

2- 10 oz. pkgs. frozen broccoli (or fresh)
8 slices of Swiss cheese
8 slices of ham

1 can mushroom soup
1/2 c. sour cream
1 t. prepared mustard

Cook broccoli, let cool. Place a slice of cheese on a slice of ham. Divide broccoli between the 8 ham-cheese slices. Roll. Place in buttered baking dish seam sides down. Pour mixture of soup, sour cream, and mustard over ham rolls. Bake uncovered at 350 degrees for 20 minutes.

Chicken with Tarragon Cream

Tastes like you worked all day...simply add a cool, crisp salad, sourdough rolls, and chilled white wine!

2 T. butter
4 boneless, skinless chicken breast halves
1 c. chicken broth
1/4 c. shallots, chopped
2 t. fresh tarragon, minced
1/2 c. whipping cream

1/4 c. sherry (optional)
1 t. fresh lemon juice
1/2 t. lemon peel, grated
salt and pepper, to taste
lemon slices
fresh parsley, chopped

Melt butter in heavy large skillet over medium heat. Add chicken and cook until lightly browned, about 1 minute per side. Stir in broth, shallots and tarragon. Cover and simmer until chicken is opaque, about 10 minutes. Transfer chicken to serving platter and keep warm.

Boil pan juices until reduced to 1/2 cup, about 7 minutes. Add cream (and sherry, if desired) and cook until reduced to sauce consistency, stirring constantly, about 5 minutes. Mix in lemon juice and peel. Season with salt and pepper. Pour sauce over chicken. Garnish with lemon slices and parsley.

Garden Lasagna

Amy Schueddig

1 c. onion, chopped
2/3 c. green peppers, chopped
2 cloves garlic, minced
2 c. zucchini, coarsely chopped
1 1/2 c. tomato, peeled
    and chopped
1 1/2 c. fresh mushrooms, sliced
1/2 c. carrots, shredded
1/2 c. celery, chopped
1 1/4 c. tomato sauce
1 T. plus 1 1/2 t. red
    wine vinegar
6 oz. can tomato paste

1 t. oregano
1 t. basil
1/2 t. Italian seasoning
1/2 t. salt
1/2 t. pepper
1/4 t. fennel seeds
1 bay leaf
6 lasagna noodles,
    uncooked
1 1/2 c. ricotta cheese
1 1/2 c. mozzarella
    cheese, divided
1 T. parmesan cheese

Spray a large pan with non-stick spray and heat to medium temperature. Add onion, green pepper and garlic, cook until tender. Add

zucchini, tomato paste, tomato sauce, vinegar, chopped tomatoes, mushrooms, carrots, celery and spices. Cover and bring to boil, remove bay leaf. Reduce heat and simmer 20 to 30 minutes, stirring occasionally. Cook noodles separately. Combine in a medium bowl ricotta cheese and 1 cup of mozarella cheese. Coat 11"x7" pan with non-stick spray. Spoon 2 cups of veggie mixture into pan, top with a layer of two noodles and add half of the cheese mixture; repeat. Top with the final layer of noodles. Cook covered, in a preheated 350 degree oven for 25 minutes. Remove from the oven and sprinkle with 1/2 cup of mozarella cheese and the parmesan cheese. Bake an additional 10 minutes, uncovered. Serves 8.

Garden Bounty Pasta
Xenia Schneider

This tastes wonderful hot, cold or reheated.

2 large tomatoes, chopped into bite-size pieces
1/2 can (#1 size) Italian plum tomatoes
1/3 c. parmesan cheese, grated
1 t. salt
pepper to taste
3 T. olive oil
1 lb. bow tie pasta, cooked

2 medium zucchini, quartered and sliced 1/4" thick
2 medium yellow squash, quartered and sliced 1/4" thick
2 cloves garlic, pressed
1/4 c. onions, chopped
1/3 c. white wine
3 T. dill weed, freshly snipped

Cook pasta and set aside. Chop 2 fresh tomatoes and add cheese, 1 tablespoon olive oil, salt and pepper. Mix and set aside. Heat 2 tablespoons oil in a large frying pan and add onion to brown lightly. Stir in squash and zucchini, brown 5 to 6 minutes. Add 1/2 can plum tomatoes, garlic and wine; heat through. Combine squash, zucchini, uncooked fresh tomatoes and pasta. Sprinkle dill over all and toss slightly. Serve with a loaf of fresh bread. Makes 6 healthy servings.

Pot Roast On The Grill
Renee Hobler & Orville Lowe

Whenever we go to Florida to visit my parents, my dad always makes this for us. He is a very creative cook and loves to try new things.

2 lb. chuck roast
6 new potatoes, quartered
1 medium onion, quartered

3 carrots, sliced
1/2 lb. fresh mushrooms
1 to 2 stalks celery, sliced

On very hot grill, brown roast on both sides, only long enough to sear. Place roast on a large piece of heavy duty foil and place veggies on top of meat. Wrap up and seal edges tightly. Bake in covered grill 30 minutes each side.

Lemon Balm Stuffed Chicken

Jeanne Calkins

This chicken will be the most flavorful chicken you have ever tasted. I use this recipe during the summer and fall seasons when the lemon balm is fresh and abundant.

**1 large whole chicken
1 small lemon, sliced
large bunch of fresh lemon balm
3 to 6 cloves garlic, peeled and sliced
a few sprigs of fresh parsley
cracked pepper and salt**

Rinse chicken out with cold water; pat dry. Stuff chicken with lemon slices, lemon balm, garlic and parsley. Sprinkle outside with pepper and salt. The chicken is now ready to be placed on your grill or may be roasted in the oven at 400 degrees for 1 1/2 hours. Serves 4 to 5 people. To complete your dinner, serve with fresh greens salad sprinkled with violet flowers, rose petals and pansy flowers; baby new potatoes and garlic bread. Dress with a light raspberry vinaigrette.

Garden Chicken Casserole

Dawn Lee

This casserole is wonderful for garden teas, picnics, gatherings of family and friends or Sunday brunches. Make sure to have extra copies of this recipe for requests. It's a sure hit!

2 c. chicken broth
2/3 c. cooking sherry, divided
6 oz. pkg. long grain and wild rice mix
1 small onion, chopped
2 small carrots, grated
1 small green pepper, chopped
1/4 c. butter or margarine
3 c. cooked chicken, diced

4 oz. can mushrooms, sliced
8 oz. pkg. cream cheese
2 c. (8 oz.) American cheese, shredded
1 c. evaporated milk
1/3 c. parmesan cheese, grated
1/2 c. almonds, sliced
carrot rounds and green onions for garnish

In a medium saucepan bring broth and 1/3 cup sherry to a boil. Add contents of rice package, cover and simmer over low heat 25 to 30 minutes or until all liquid is absorbed. In a dutch oven, sauté onion, carrots and green pepper in butter until soft, about 5 minutes. Add rice, chicken and mushrooms, mixing well. Place cream cheese, American cheese and milk in a saucepan and melt over medium heat stirring until smooth. Add to dutch oven with remaining sherry, mixing thoroughly. Pour into a buttered 13"x9"x2" casserole dish. Top with parmesan cheese and almonds. Cover and bake in a preheated 350 degree oven for 35 minutes, uncover and bake 15 minutes longer or until bubbly. If desired, garnish with carrot rounds and green onions to make a floral design on top of the casserole. Casserole may be refrigerated overnight before baking. If refrigerated, increase baking time to 45 minutes covered and 15 minutes uncovered.

Wish with all your might that summer will never end!

Stromboli

Gay Hanby

It's fun; it's low-fat; it's delicious! Use as an appetizer or serve with a fruit salad for a great, light summer supper. My family of four eats 1 1/2 of these for supper. They're also great leftovers.

10 oz. pkg. refrigerated bread dough
mustard
slices of meat

chopped fresh vegetables
shredded cheese of your choice

Roll bread dough into a 6"x10" rectangle and place on a well greased cookie sheet. Bake at 375 degrees for 10 minutes. Line bread with mustard (dijon, yellow, creole...your choice), meat (either packaged meats, leftovers, deli meats; again, your choice), chopped vegetables (I've used carrots, green onions, broccoli, zucchini), and cheese, in that order. Roll up along the long side and place seam side down on same cookie sheet. Bake an additional 20 to 25 minutes. Cool for 5 to 10 minutes, slice and serve.

Italian Beef

Glenda Nations

Great served on hoagie rolls! Especially good with potato salad, slaw and baked beans.

3 lb. rump roast
1 T. pepper
1 T. salt
1 T. garlic powder
1 T. dry mustard
1 T. worcestershire sauce

Make paste and rub on roast. Put in dutch oven and add 2" of water to pan. Bake at 350 degrees for 1 hour per pound. Shred meat and save liquid in pan or add water to make a liquid. Put in crock pot on low for an hour or so. You can make this up a day or so before and then reheat it in the crock pot.

Zucchini & Tomato Quiche
Mary Wighall

Great for a light dinner accompanied by a lettuce salad, wheat rolls and a glass of wine.

9" baked pie shell
2 c. zucchini, sliced
1/2 c. onion, chopped
1 T. butter
1/2 c. Swiss cheese,
  shredded
1 T. flour

1 large tomato, peeled
  and chopped (drain excess)
6 eggs (can use egg substitute)
1 c. half & half
1/2 t. crushed basil
1/2 t. salt
1/8 t. pepper

In large skillet, over medium heat, sauté zucchini and onion in butter until lightly browned, approximately 5 minutes. Sprinkle zucchini mixture with flour. Add cheese and tomato, pour into pie shell. Beat together eggs, half & half, basil, salt and pepper until well blended. Pour over vegetables mix. Bake at 375 degrees for 30 to 35 minutes. Let stand 5 minutes before serving.

California Quiche
Linda Desmond

Great for brunches and even weddings and baby showers! Serve with a fresh green salad and muffins.

1 deep dish pie shell
3/4 lb. hot Italian sausage
3 eggs, slightly beaten
1 3/4 c. milk

2 c. (8 oz.) Monterey
  jack cheese, shredded
4 oz. can green chillies,
  chopped

Prebake unpricked pie crust on a preheated cookie sheet in 450 degree oven for 6 minutes. Reduce temperature to 325 degrees. Remove casing on sausage, brown in skillet, breaking up meat with a fork. Drain well. In a bowl combine eggs, milk, sausage, cheese and chilies. Turn into partially baked pastry shell. Bake in 325 degree oven on a preheated cookie sheet for 45 minutes or until knife inserted comes out clean. Let stand about 10 minutes before serving.
Makes 6 servings.

Lemon Thyme Stuffed Chicken

Elizabeth Timmins
Gooseberry Patch Artisan

6 chicken breasts,
   skinned and boned
1/2 c. cream cheese
1/4 c. chives, chopped
2 T. fresh lemon thyme leaves
1/2 c. dry bread crumbs
1/2 c. parmesan cheese
1/3 c. flour

1 t. paprika
1/2 t. salt
1/2 t. pepper
2 eggs
2 t. water
fresh thyme leaves to
   garnish

Preheat oven to 350 degrees. With a mallet, pound chicken breasts between sheets of plastic wrap until 1/8" thick. Roll with a rolling pin to even thickness. Spread cream cheese lengthwise down center of each piece using a generous tablespoon for each. Sprinkle with 2 teaspoons chopped chives and 1 teaspoon thyme leaves. Roll up jelly-roll style starting at narrow end. Tuck the sides under to seal. Combine flour, paprika, salt and pepper on a dish. In a small bowl beat eggs and water. On another plate combine bread crumbs and parmesan cheese. Dip chicken rolls in flour mixture, then in beaten egg and then in bread crumb mixture. Arrange with seam side down in a single layer in a greased baking pan. Bake for 20 to 25 minutes until juices run clear. Garnish with the thyme leaves.

Pasta with Fresh Tomato Basil Sauce

Jeanne Calkins

2 1/2 lb. ripe tomatoes
   (room temp.)
1/2 c. olive oil (may
   substitute vegetable oil)
1 lb. linguine

3 garlic cloves
2 T. fresh parsley
1 1/2 c. fresh basil,
   loosely packed
salt and pepper to taste

Process all ingredients except pasta in a food processor. Set this sauce aside. Cook pasta, al dente (or about 7 minutes) in boiling water. Drain. Place in a large bowl and pour sauce over it. Toss and serve immediately. No cheese needed!

Brunch Baked Eggs

Leona Keeley

Accompanying the eggs could be a variety of quick and yeast breads, fresh fruit cups/bowl and champagne splashed with tangerine liqueur. If you decide to forego the ham, substitute Canadian bacon or smoked turkey alongside the eggs.

6 c. (24 oz.) Monterey jack
    cheese, shredded (divided)
12 oz. fresh mushrooms, sliced
1/2 medium onion, chopped
1/4 c. sweet red pepper, thinly sliced
1/4 c. margarine or butter, melted
8 oz. cooked ham,
    cut into julienne strips
8 eggs, beaten
1 3/4 c. milk
1/2 c. all-purpose flour
2 T. fresh chives, basil, tarragon,
    thyme or oregano, snipped
1 T. parsley, snipped

Sprinkle 3 cups cheese in the bottom of a 13"x9"x2" baking dish. In a saucepan, cook the mushrooms, onion and red pepper in the margarine until vegetables are tender but not brown. Drain well. Place vegetables over the cheese. Arrange ham strips over vegetables. Sprinkle remaining 3 cups cheese over ham. Cover and chill in refrigerator overnight. To serve, combine eggs, milk, flour, chives and parsley. Pour over cheese layer. Bake at 350 degrees about 45 minutes. Let stand 10 minutes. Serves 12.

Grilled Veggie and Cheese Sandwich

Debbie Parker
Gooseberry Patch

Serve with fresh fruit or herb potato salad.

Variation 1:

Texas toast or French bread, sliced
cucumbers, thinly sliced
sharp cheddar cheese slices
red Bermuda onions, thinly sliced
fresh ripe tomatoes, thinly sliced
guacamole (optional)*

*spread on after grilling

Variation 2:

rye bread, sliced
Swiss cheese, sliced
tomatoes, sliced
dijon mustard*

*spread on bread before grilling

Heat griddle or skillet. Place vegetables and cheese on bread. Butter each side. Grill until golden brown.

Herb Burgers

Candy Hannigan

These are moist, tender and delicious! We serve these on the 4th of July with all the trimmings.

1 lb. lean ground beef
1 tomato, seeded and finely chopped
1/2 c. ripe olives, chopped
1 t. pressed garlic
1/3 c. green chillies, chopped
2 t. creamy mustard blend
1 t. fresh oregano, chopped
2 t. chili powder
1 t. fresh lemon thyme, chopped

1 T. fresh dill leaves, chopped or 1 t. dried
1 T. fresh parsley, chopped
2 T. fresh cilantro leaves, chopped
1/4 c. onion, minced (I use vidalias)
2 t. fresh basil, chopped or 1/2 t. dried
2 t. fresh lemon zest, grated

Mix together all ingredients except the beef. Add beef and mix lightly (over mixing makes it more like meatloaf). Shape into 4 or 5 patties. Grill for 4 to 5 minutes on each side. Turn only once.

Main Medley

Herbed Grilled Chicken
Sandra Curtis

Low calorie and delicious!

1 T. oil
2 T. dry white wine
2 T. fresh herbs from your garden (I like lemon thyme or rosemary)

4 T. fresh lemon juice
salt and lemon pepper to taste

Marinate boneless, skinless chicken breasts in this mixture. Grill until done.

Buttery Herb Baked Fish
Judy Hand

We like to use haddock for this yummy dish.

1/2 c. butter or margarine
1/4 c. parmesan cheese, grated
1/4 t. garlic powder
1 lb. frozen fish fillets (thawed, separated and drained)

2/3 c. saltine crackers, crushed
1/2 t. basil
1/2 t. oregano

Preheat oven to 350 degrees. In a 13"x9" pan, melt butter in oven. In a 9" pie pan combine cracker crumbs, parmesan cheese, basil, oregano and garlic powder; mix well. Dip fish fillets into melted butter and then into crumb mixture, coating each piece of fish. Arrange fish in baking dish and bake near center of 350 degree oven for 25 to 30 minutes or until flaky. Serves 2 to 3.

Pizza Sauce

Mel Wolk

1/2 c. onion, chopped
1 to 2 cloves garlic
2 T. olive oil
3 c. fresh tomatoes, chopped
2/4 c. tomato paste
1/4 t. salt (optional)

pinch of ground pepper
1 t. oregano
1 t. basil, crumbled
1 t. whole bay leaf
1/4 c. fresh parsley,
   chopped (optional)

Brown onion and garlic in oil until soft and golden. Add remaining ingredients and heat to boiling over medium heat. Reduce heat and simmer, stirring occasionally, for about 2 hours or until sauce has thickened. Discard bay leaf. Makes enough sauce for 2 to 3 pizzas. You can double or triple recipe and freeze for later. Try this with Up-side Down Pizza.

Up-side Down Pizza

Mel Wolk

pizza sauce for one pizza
1 1/2 c. mozzarella cheese, grated
toppings: sausage, mushrooms, pepperoni,
   peppers, ham, ground beef, etc.

Crust:

2 c. flour
2 c. milk
2 eggs

1 t. salt
2 t. oregano, crumbled or ground
parmesan cheese

Oil the bottom of a large-rimmed pizza pan or cookie sheet. Spread the sauce evenly over the pan. Add the toppings your family loves. Sprinkle with mozzarella cheese; set aside. Combine ingredients for crust in mixer or blender and beat/blend until the batter is smooth and without lumps. Pour over cheese, toppings, and sauce, tilting pan slightly to distribute batter evenly. Bake at 350 degrees for about 30 minutes or until the crust is golden brown. To serve, cut into sections and use a spatula to scoop the piece out and turn up-side down on a plate. Sprinkle with parmesan cheese. This makes a giant pizza and will serve 4 to 6 people. Use a fork to eat this pizza.

Sprouting Salads

I use pansies or nasturtiums in a fresh salad or cold pasta salad at summer picnics and potlucks. The flowers are edible too. Your guests will think you're a gourmet cook!

Janet Mitrovich

Shrimp Dill Salad

Debbie Parker
Gooseberry Patch

2 T. green onions, chopped
1 T. garlic, chopped
1 T. dijon mustard
1 T. honey
1 T. red wine vinegar
1 T. raspberry vinegar
  (optional)

1/2 c. fresh dill, chopped
1 T. parsley, chopped
2/3 c. oil
shrimp, cooked and peeled
mixed greens
tomatoes, thinly sliced

Mix green onions, garlic, mustard, honey, red wine vinegar, raspberry vinegar, dill, parsley and oil together for dressing; beat until well blended. Pour over the shrimp and allow to marinate for several hours. Placed mixed greens and tomatoes on a salad plate. Top with marinated shrimp. Garnish with a sprig of dill.

Spinach Salad

Barb McFaden

Delicious and your friends will all want the recipe for the dressing!

fresh spinach leaves
4 oz. feta cheese, crumbled
1/2 c. walnuts, chopped
1 avocado, cut
3 to 4 T. real bacon bits

1/2 red onion, cut in
  thin rings
1/2 c. red pepper
1 tomato, chopped

Using a large bowl, fill with spinach leaves. Add all other ingredients to bowl. Toss salad with sweet and sour dressing. Great for spinach salads and pasta salads.

Dressing:

1 1/2 c. salad oil
1/2 c. red wine vinegar
3 T. sugar

1 t. chili powder
2 t. onion, grated (optional)
1 t. seasoned salt
garlic to taste
2 to 3 T. worcestershire sauce

Shake well. Pour enough dressing
to cover spinach leaves. Toss.

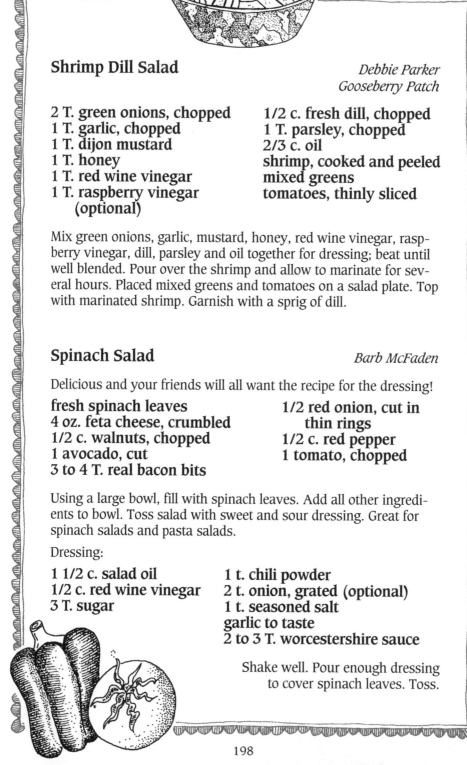

Spinach Salad With Strawberries
Janet Myers

A different, attractive salad. Great in the spring when you can pick fresh strawberries. Always brings raves!

10 oz. fresh spinach   1 pt. strawberries, sliced thin

Dressing:

1/2 c. sugar	**1/4 t. worcestershire sauce**
2 T. sesame seeds	**1/4 t. paprika**
1 T. poppy seeds	**1/2 c. oil**
1 1/2 t. onion, minced	**1/4 c. vinegar**

Make dressing in a blender. Yields 6 to 8 servings.

Grilled Chicken Salad

This is a delicious summertime salad served with crusty sourdough rolls and iced tea!

grilled chicken breast, cut into strips
salad greens (a variety is best!)
walnuts, chopped
blue cheese, crumbled
bacon, fried crisp and crumbled
red onion rings
tomato wedges

Arrange lettuce on plates; add walnuts, blue cheese, bacon and red onion rings. Top with strips of grilled chicken breast. Tomato wedges can be added for garnish. Serve herbal dressing or a raspberry vinaigrette alongside.

Warm Pesto Dinner Salad
Kristi Hartland

4 c. mixed greens*
1 c. fresh broccoli florets
1 c. zucchini, cut into
   match sticks
1/2 c. carrots, sliced
1/2 c. beets, sliced

3/4 c. chick peas
2 c. hot cooked pasta (rotini)
4 T. prepared pesto
1 large red ripe tomato, cut
   into wedges
salt and pepper to taste

Steam the broccoli florets, carrots and zucchini sticks for about 2 minutes (you want the veggies to remain crisp, but a little tender and warm). Toss together the greens, beets and chick peas in a large bowl. Add the slightly steamed veggies to the greens mixture and toss. Divide the greens mixture on two dinner plates (two dinner plates for two large salads, or four smaller plates for four small salads). Mix together the hot, cooked pasta and the prepared pesto. On top of the greens mixture, pour 1 cup of the pasta mixture (on each plate). Garnish with fresh tomato wedges. Salt and pepper.

*Boston bibb, redleaf, fresh garden lettuce, etc.

Prepared Pesto:

2 1/2 c. pesto leaves, tightly packed
2 cloves garlic
1/3 c. parmesan cheese
   (or asiago cheese is great!)
1/2 c. olive oil

1/4 c. chicken broth
1/4 c. pine nuts
1/8 t. salt
1/8 t. lemon juice

Mix all ingredients together in a blender. You may want to add chicken broth slowly while the blender is on, so the leaves can mix well. Pour into an airtight container and store in the fridge. No need to heat up the pesto when mixing with pasta. Just toss together and the pasta will warm it nicely.

*Visit a roadside stand or farmers' market
and buy the freshest produce,
flowers, jams, jellies and
home-baked goods.*

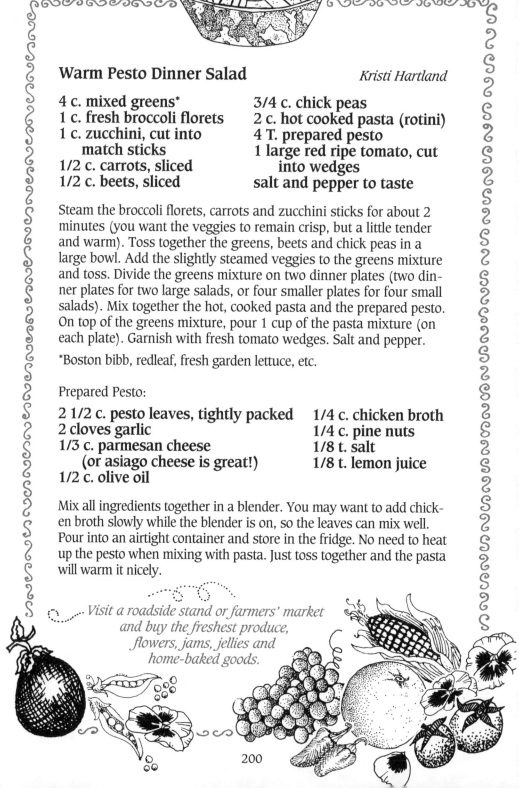

Sprouting Salads

Chicken Salad
Jeannine English

Excellent served on buttery croissants, with fruit salad and mint tea! Great recipe for weekend get-togethers or showers.

4 chicken breasts
8 oz. cream cheese, softened
4 stalks celery, finely
  chopped
1 T. pimiento, finely chopped

1 small green bell pepper,
  finely chopped
1 T. dijon mustard
salt and pepper, to taste
dried parsley (optional)

Boil chicken until tender then chop into small pieces. Combine chicken and cream cheese, mix until smooth. Add other ingredients and chill.

Layered Club Salad
Marion Pfeifer

Nice to have when tomatoes are fresh from the garden.

3 to 4 c. lettuce, shredded
2 c. ranch dressing
1 large tomato, diced
2 c. cherry tomatoes, halved
6 oz. Swiss or Monterey
  Jack cheese, cubed

small red onion, thinly sliced
6 oz. ham, cubed
6 oz. turkey, cubed
3 slices bacon, cooked and
  crumbled
1 c. seasoned croutons

In a 3-quart glass bowl layer lettuce, 1 cup dressing, then diced tomato, cherry tomatoes, seasoned croutons, red onion, cubed ham, cubed turkey, cheese. End with 1 cup of dressing and bacon garnish.

Black Bean & Salsa Salad
Margaret Riley

12 oz. can corn, drained
15 oz. can black beans, rinsed
  and drained*
1 1/2 c. celery, chopped
1/2 c. green onion, chopped

1/4 c. cilantro, chopped
14 oz. can salsa
1/4 c. red wine vinegar
  dressing

In a large bowl combine corn, beans, celery, onion and cilantro; mix well. Blend the salsa with the red wine vinegar dressing, pour over salad and toss well. Cover and chill. Serves 8.

*You can also use navy, pinto or kidney beans.

New Potato Salad

Rebecca Suiter

2 lb. new potatoes
1/2 c. celery, diced
3 hard cooked eggs, sliced
8 oz. carton sour cream
1 T. fresh dill weed, chopped
   or 1 t. dried whole
   dill weed

2 T. vinegar
1 t. sugar
2 t. prepared horseradish
1/2 t. salt
1/2 t. dry mustard
1/8 t. pepper, freshly
   ground

Cook potatoes in boiling water and cover for 20 minutes or until tender. Drain well, and let cool. Peel potatoes, and slice into 1/2" slices. Combine potatoes, celery and eggs in a large bowl and toss gently. Combine sour cream, dill weed, vinegar, sugar, horseradish, salt, dry mustard and pepper in a small bowl. Pour over potato mixture and stir gently to coat. Chill thoroughly. Yields 6 to 8 servings.

Peanutty Broccoli Slaw

Sheri Berger

16 oz. broccoli slaw
2 red apples, cored,
   cut in chunks

1/2 c. raisins
1/2 c. dry roasted
   peanuts, chopped

Dressing:

2/3 c. mayonnaise
4 t. sugar
2 T. vinegar
1 t. salt
1 t. celery seed

Combine slaw, apples and raisins. Toss with dressing. If desired, cover and refrigerate several hours. Top with nuts just before serving. Serves 8.

Sprouting Salads

Freezer Slaw
Kay Oglageo

**1 medium head cabbage
   (garden cabbage is best)
1 green pepper**

**1 red pepper
1 carrot**

A fast way to shred cabbage, peppers and carrot is to use a blender on grate (DO NOT grate them at the same time). Put 5 cups cabbage with 2 cups water in blender, turn blender off and on for only a few seconds. When shredded, drain. Grate pepper and 1 cup of water, one pepper at a time. Grate carrot and 1 cup of water. Drain well all ingredients, then mix well. Let stand for 1 hour.

Dressing:

**1/2 c. vinegar
1/2 c. water
2 c. sugar**

**2 t. salt
1 t. celery seed**

Mix all ingredients together, boil for 1 minute. Cool completely, pour over slaw. (If the dressing is warm, it will wilt the cabbage.) Mix well, place in an airtight container. Freeze.

Cabbage Salad
Eleanor Miller

Our family loves this salad. It always disappears quickly at family gatherings. Many of the ingredients come right out of our garden. And...it's very low in fat!

**1 medium head cabbage,
   shredded
1 green pepper, chopped**

**1 c. celery, chopped
1/2 c. onion, chopped**

Dressing:

**2 c. sugar
1/2 c. vinegar
2 t. salt**

**1 t. celery seed
1/2 t. dry mustard**

Mix dressing ingredients. Pour dressing over cabbage and leave overnight. The salad forms its own juice. When salad is refrigerated, it keeps 7 to 10 days (but there is never any left over). Serves 8 to 10.

Pasta Salad
Arlene Roberts

Good served with deviled eggs or French bread.

8 oz. pasta shells
1/2 c. green onions, sliced
1/2 c. fresh parsley, chopped
1 c. celery, sliced
1 c. frozen peas
1 c. fresh tomato, diced
1 c. ripe olives, sliced
1/2 c. mayonnaise
2 T. soy sauce (optional)
3 c. cooked chicken, sliced
  (or 2 c. cooked shrimp)

2 T. lemon juice
2 T. red wine vinegar
1 t. dijon mustard
1 t. sugar
1/2 t. garlic powder
1/2 t. paprika
1/2 t. ground ginger
1/8 t. red hot pepper
  sauce
1/8 t. ground black pepper

Cook pasta according to directions on package until just tender (don't overcook). Rinse with cold water and drain. Place in a large bowl; add onion, parsley, celery, peas, tomato and olives. Combine mayonnaise with soy sauce, lemon juice, vinegar, mustard, sugar, garlic powder, paprika, ginger, pepper sauce and black pepper. Add to pasta mixture along with chicken or shrimp; mix well. (Adjust seasonings to your taste.) Chill overnight. To serve, pile into serving bowl or onto platter and garnish with tomato wedges, parsley or lettuce. Makes 6 generous servings.

Low-Fat Herbal Pasta Salad
Laura Steuk-Mastropaolo

This salad is so colorful and healthful for summertime or anytime picnics.

2 lb. rotini pasta, cooked
  and drained
6 oz. feta cheese, crumbled
10 to 15 black olives
2 to 3 T. olive oil
1/2 c. fresh basil, chopped
  or herb of choice

1/2 t. dried red pepper flakes
1 red pepper, sliced into strips
1 yellow pepper, sliced into
  strips
1 green pepper, sliced into
  strips

Combine all ingredients, toss to coat. Best if left in refrigerator overnight. This recipe makes a lot. You can cut in half if you wish.

Sprouting Salads

Garden Pasta Salad
Debbie Hefty

4 medium tomatoes, peeled
   and seeded
1 medium cucumber, seeded
1 small green pepper, seeded
1 onion, sliced

1/4 c. snipped parsley
fresh herb dressing
8 oz. spaghetti or
   fettucini
1 c. feta cheese, crumbled

Dice tomato, cucumber, green pepper and onion. Put into a mixing bowl with parsley. Pour fresh herb dressing over vegetables. Toss to combine. Cover and chill. Cook pasta until tender. Drain and rinse in cold water. Put pasta in a large bowl. Spoon vegetables over the top. Sprinkle with cheese. Toss to coat.

Dressing:

1/4 c. cooking oil
1 T. sugar
3 T. dry white wine
1/4 t. fresh ground pepper
2 T. lemon juice

1 T. snipped fresh basil (or
   1 t. dried basil, crushed)
1 t. salt
several dashes bottled hot
   pepper sauce

Combine ingredients in a screw-top jar. Cover and shake well.

Cucumber Salad
Loretta Nichols (Vickie's mom)
Gooseberry Patch

For extra crunch, soak cucumbers in salt water in the refrigerator for about 20 minutes before making this salad!

1/2 c. sugar
2 1/2 T. white vinegar
1/3 c. mayonnaise-type
   salad dressing

3/4 c. half & half
2 cucumbers, peeled and sliced
small onion, chopped
1 T. fresh dill, minced

In a small bowl, combine sugar and vinegar, then add salad dressing and half & half. Stir until well blended. Pour dressing over cucumbers and onions. Add fresh dill. Chill for about an hour to allow flavors to blend. Serves 4.

Garden Spirals Summer Salad
Nancy Campbell

Wonderful, colorful summer salad for a crowd. My friend serves it often on her deck, to family and friends.

12 oz. bag garden spirals
   pasta
1 c. broccoli florets
1/2 c. red bell peppers
1 c. zucchini, sliced
1/2 c. yellow crooked neck
   squash, sliced
1 t. dill weed
1/2 t. oregano

1/4 t. sweet basil
1/4 t. tarragon
1 small tomato, diced
1 c. green onions, chopped
1 1/2 c. skinless, bone-
   less chicken breasts,
   cooked and cubed
1/2 c. parmesan cheese

Dressing:

2 t. salt
3/4 c. olive oil
1/2 c. mayonnaise

1 t. ground black pepper
1/3 c. red wine vinegar

Cook pasta as directed. Drain well. Blanch broccoli, red bell pepper, zucchini and crooked neck squash for 3 to 5 minutes. Drain and chill. Add spices to pasta and toss well. Combine all dressing ingredients in a mixing bowl and hand whip until smooth. Add dressing to pasta, mixing thoroughly. Add blanched vegetables, tomato, onion and chicken. Sprinkle with parmesan cheese. Serves 12.

Tuna Salad
Debbie Parker
Gooseberry Patch

6 1/8 oz. can tuna
1 T. lemon juice
1/4 c. celery or cucumbers
1/4 to 1/2 c. mayonnaise

2 T. red onion, minced
   or finely chopped
1 to 2 T. fresh herbs,
   chopped (your choice)*

Combine ingredients and place in tomato cups, cucumber boat or pepper halves for edible bowls.

*Such as dill or lemon balm.

Tomato Pepper Salad
with Basil Mint Dressing

Cora Baker

2 large red peppers	1 T. basil or chive vinegar
1 medium red onion, sliced	1 T. lemon juice
6 large ripe tomatoes	1 T. fresh basil, chopped
1/4 c. good quality olive oil	1 T. fresh mint, chopped

Cut the red peppers in half vertically and remove seeds. Place them on a baking sheet along with the onion slices and broil for about 5 minutes until the pepper skins start to pucker. Cut up the tomatoes. Peel the peppers and slice them into strips. Place tomatoes, peppers and onions in a bowl. Combine the oil, vinegar and lemon juice in a small bowl and whisk to blend. Stir in basil and mint and toss the dressing with the vegetables. Cover and refrigerate for at least 2 hours.

Fresh Tomato
and Mozzarella Salad

Margaret Zellhofer

1/4 c. olive oil	2 to 3 large ripe tomatoes, sliced
2 T. red wine vinegar	
1 1/2 t. fresh basil, chopped	8 oz. mozzarella cheese
1/4 t. black pepper	(deli), thinly sliced
1/4 t. salt	red onions, sliced

Mix together oil, vinegar, basil, pepper and salt. Arrange tomatoes and cheese, alternately, on a large serving plate. Pour oil and vinegar dressing over tomatoes and cheese. Garnish with onions. Serve extra dressing with salad. Makes 4 servings.

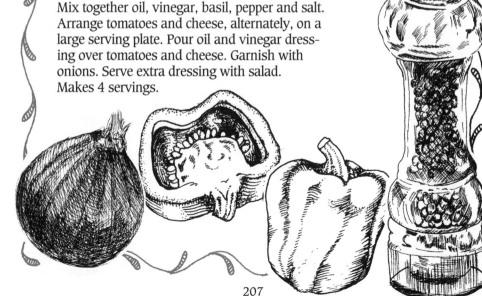

Marinated Tomatoes

Sandra Bowman

6 large ripe tomatoes, peeled
1/4 c. fresh parsley, minced
1 garlic clove, minced
2 T. fresh thyme leaves or 1/2 t. dried
1/4 c. scallions or spring onions (including some of the
    green), thinly sliced
1 t. salt
1/4 t. black pepper, freshly ground if possible
2/3 c. vegetable oil
1/4 c. red or white wine vinegar

Cut the tomatoes into thick slices and place on shallow plate or
dish. In a small bowl, combine the scallions, parsley, garlic, thyme,
salt and pepper. Sprinkle the mixture over the tomatoes. In a jar,
mix together the oil and vinegar and pour over the tomatoes. Cover
and refrigerate for several hours or overnight. Spoon the dressing
over the tomatoes from time to time. You may wish to drain off the
dressing before serving. Serves 6.

Greek Style Tomato Salad

Marie Alana Gardner

6 medium tomatoes, sliced
1/4 lb. feta cheese, crumbled
1 small onion, thinly sliced
1/3 c. red wine vinegar
2 T. parsley, minced
3 1/2 oz. can pitted ripe olives,
    drained and sliced

4 t. sugar
1/2 t. basil
1/4 t. salt
1/4 t. pepper
1/2 c. olive oil
lettuce leaves

Make about 2 1/2 hours before serving or early in the day. Place in
order: tomatoes, olives, feta cheese and onion in a 13"x9" baking
dish. Set aside. In a small bowl, with fork, mix olive oil, vinegar,
parsley, sugar, basil, salt and pepper. Pour dressing over tomato
mixture. With rubber spatula, gently lift tomato slices to coat with
dressing. Cover baking dish and refrigerate at least 2 hours to
blend flavors. To serve...line chilled platter with lettuce leaves.
Arrange tomato mixture on lettuce. Serves 8.

24-Hour Salad

Mary Brehm

1 lb. fresh spinach, washed and broken in pieces
1 onion, chopped
1/2 lb. bacon, cooked and crumbled
1 pkg. frozen peas, thawed and drained
6 hard-boiled eggs, sliced
1 head lettuce, broken in pieces
1/2 head broccoli or cauliflower, washed and broken in bits

Dressing:

1 c. sour cream
1/2 c. Swiss cheese, grated

2 c. mayonnaise

Mix sour cream and mayonnaise. Spread over top of salad to edges to seal in flavor. Refrigerate for 24 hours. Just before serving, sprinkle with cheese.

Cucumber Onion Salad

Mary Dungan

4 or 5- 6" cucumbers
1/4 c. sweet onions, sliced
2 T. granulated sugar

1/4 c. cider vinegar
dash of black pepper

Thinly slice peeled cucumbers, sprinkle with salt; stir and set aside. Thinly slice sweet onions; set aside. Just before serving, pour off and rinse with water the sliced cucumbers. Add onion. Sprinkle sugar, black pepper and cider vinegar over the cucumbers and onions. Stir together, serve. An extra taste treat is to add 2 to 3 tablespoons of chopped dill fern ("leafy" top part of stem, do not include any seeds). Serves 6.

Macaroni Salad

Doris Stegner
Gooseberry Patch

7 oz. elbow, shell or ring
    macaroni, uncooked
10 oz. pkg. green peas, frozen
1 c. cheddar cheese, cubed

1 c. sweet pickles, diced
3/4 c. mayonnaise
1/2 c. onion, chopped
salt and pepper

Bring 3 quarts of water and 1 tablespoon salt to a rapid boil. Drop macaroni in and boil uncovered, stirring occasionally, just until tender (7 to 10 minutes). Drain quickly in colander and rinse with cold water. Cook peas as directed on package; drain. Mix macaroni, peas, cheese, sweet pickles, mayonnaise and onion. Sprinkle with salt and pepper. Cover and refrigerate for at least 2 hours. Serves 6 to 8.

Broccoli Salad

Nancy Campbell

This delicious recipe is a favorite of patrons of the fundraiser "Soup and Salad Dinners" at my granddaughter's school.

4 to 5 c. broccoli florets
12 strips bacon (approx. 1 lb.), fried and crumbled
1 small red onion, chopped
1/2 c. raisins
1/2 c. sunflower seeds

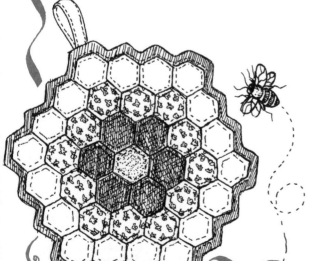

Dressing:

1/3 c. sugar
1 c. mayonnaise
2 T. vinegar
    (cider vinegar)

Combine ingredients. Mix dressing and pour over vegetables. Let stand 5 hours in the refrigerator before serving. Serves 8 generously.

Fruit Salad
Linda Ferguson

4 c. cabbage, shredded
1/2 c. mandarin oranges
1/2 c. pineapple pieces
1/2 c. apple cubes

1/2 c. salad dressing (mayo)
2 T. pineapple juice
1/4 t. nutmeg
1 t. sugar

Shred cabbage, combine with fruit. Mix nutmeg, juice, and sugar with salad dressing; add to cabbage mixture. Toss to coat well. Chill and serve. Makes 4 to 6 servings.

Stuffed Apple Salad
Charlotte Crockett

6 firm apples
1/2 c. tiny red cinnamon candies
enough water to cover apples
    in saucepan

lettuce leaves
cottage cheese
nuts and raisins
low-fat salad dressing

Wash, peel and core any firm type of apple of your own choosing. Simmer them gently in water with tiny red cinnamon candies that have been added. The candies help with the flavor, sweetening and color. Simmer until desired softness. Take out of water and cool apples on platter. Discard water. Place on lettuce leaves and fill the centers with cottage cheese, raisins and/or nuts. Add a low-fat salad dressing and serve. The salad dressing is an option. Makes 6 servings.

Black-Eyed Pea Salad
Linda Ferguson

16 oz. can black-eyed peas,
    drained
1/2 c. green pepper, chopped
1/4 c. green onion, chopped

1 tomato, chopped
1 c. cole slaw dressing
1 c. celery, chopped
2 c. lettuce, cut into strips

Dressing:

1/4 c. wine vinegar
1/4 c. mayonnaise

3 to 4 T. sugar

Do not make ahead of time. Make and serve.

Summer Garden Bean Salad

Toni Tobin

Adds zip to any summertime meal!

3/4 c. sugar
1/3 c. vinegar
1/2 c. salad oil
salt and pepper, to taste
1 lb. yellow beans, cooked and drained
1 medium onion, sliced
1 lb. green beans, cooked and drained
1 lb. can red kidney beans, drained
1 green pepper, cut up

Mix sugar, vinegar, oil, salt and pepper until sugar is dissolved. Pour over beans, green pepper, and onion. Let refrigerate overnight.

Antipasto Salad

Vicki Hockenberry

Let your garden be your guide when making this antipasto salad. As summer moves on, switch the vegetables to use those that are most plentiful. Enjoy!

1/2 lb. pepperoni
1 sweet red pepper, cut into squares
1 c. cauliflower or broccoli
1/2 green pepper, cut into squares
1/2 c. black olives, sliced
1/2 c. yellow squash or zucchini
1/2 lb. Swiss cheese, cubed in small squares
1/4 c. Italian salad dressing

In a large bowl, combine all vegetables; add black olives, pepperoni and cubed Swiss cheese. Pour dressing on top, toss to coat. Cover and chill for at least 2 hours. Stir before serving. Serves 4.

Red Leaf Lettuce Salad

Sheri Berger

Everyone loves this and nobody can figure out what makes the dressing taste so good (honey!).

red leaf lettuce, torn into pieces,
1 pt. strawberries, quartered
1 large can mandarin oranges, drained
1 can artichoke heart, quartered
1 pkg. Italian dressing mix
2 T. honey

Depending on size of lettuce, use 1 or 2 heads. Mix lettuce pieces, strawberries, oranges and artichoke hearts. In a separate container, mix up Italian dressing as directed on package. Add honey and mix well. Refrigerate salad and dressing separately and combine just before serving.

Marinated Mushrooms

Amy Schueddig

This lightly seasoned salad gives color to your plate without competing with other dominant flavors.

1/2 lb. fresh mushrooms, halved
1 T. fresh parsley, minced
12 cherry tomatoes

1/2 c. oil-free sweet
and sour dressing

In medium bowl, combine all ingredients. Cover and refrigerate several hours or overnight. Makes 4 servings.

You never realize how creative you are until it comes time to figure out what to do with all the zucchinis in your garden!

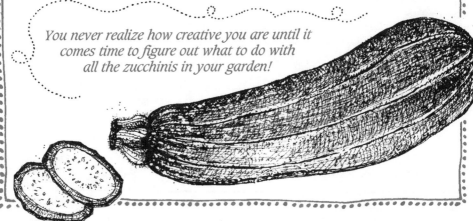

Sweet and Sour Potato Salad
Eleanor Miller

I have been asked to make this perennial favorite for a wide variety of occasions over the past 25 years and have passed on the recipe so often I have it memorized! I have modified the recipe to lower the fat content...but not the taste. Friends have appreciated this feature!

5 lb. potatoes	2 stalks celery, finely chopped
1 T. salt	2 hard boiled eggs,
1 to 2 t. celery seed	sliced (optional)
(more if desired)	1/2 onion, finely chopped

Boil potatoes (with skins on) in a covered pan, adding salt and enough water to cover the potatoes, for approximately 45 to 60 minutes (depending on the potato size). Test doneness with a fork. Drain. Peel potatoes while hot and cube into small pieces. Add celery seed, celery, onion and eggs. Mix dressing ingredients well and pour over potatoes.

Dressing:

1 c. whipped non-fat dressing	8 T. vinegar
(or non-fat mayo, if preferred)	8 T. sugar

Mix ingredients together, adding the vinegar in 1/4 amounts so dressing does not get lumpy. Refrigerate. When salad is chilled, stir again. Add additional salad dressing or mayo and salt if needed. This is best done 6 to 8 hours before serving so dressing flavors can permeate the potatoes. Put into a pretty bowl on a bed of lettuce, sprinkle with paprika and garnish as desired with tomato wedges, olives or additional sliced eggs.

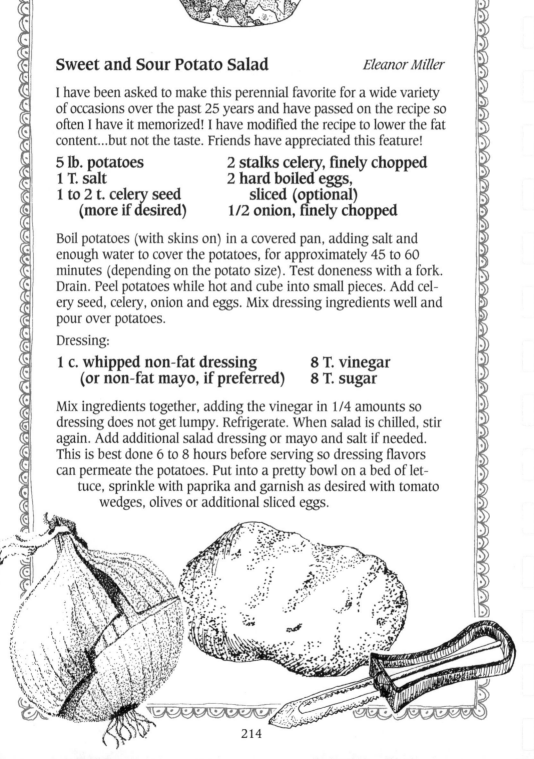

savory sides

Most of us agree, we can't improve on Mother Nature, so
let's use fruits and vegetables as serving containers, instead
of man-made ones. The garden outdoors suddenly
grows indoors. Here are some suggestions:

lemons and limes filled with ice-cream or sorbet
cantaloupes filled with chicken or tuna salad
red, yellow and green peppers filled with dip
tomatoes stuffed with shrimp salad
oranges filled with marmalade or jam
watermelon filled with fruit balls
pumpkins and squash as soup tureens

Sandra Bowman

Summer Tomatoes

Ruth Kangas

There is nothing better in the summer than big red tomatoes...home grown with loving care in your own garden.

4 large tomatoes	**1 green pepper, sliced**
1 big red onion, sliced in rings	**in rings**

Alternate layers of above in big wide bowl.

Marinade Sauce:

1/4 c. lemon juice	**1 t. salt**
2 T. fresh parsley, chopped	**1/2 c. salad oil**
1/2 t. white sugar	**1/8 t. savory**
1 1/4 oz. blue or roquefort cheese	

Mix lemon juice, parsley, sugar, salt, oil and savory. Pour over layered veggies. Sprinkle crumbled cheese over top. Marinade overnight in refrigerator to blend. Serve as side dish.

Asparagus Casserole

Sandi Stewart

This casserole is great served as a side dish for a large crowd. I usually double it and bake in a 13"x9" pan because it serves so many. You can make it with fresh asparagus, but it is equally good made with fresh broccoli or cauliflower/broccoli mix. Canned or frozen vegetables may be used.

1 to 1 1/2 lb. fresh asparagus or 2- 14 1/2 oz. cans
10 3/4 oz. can creamy chicken mushroom soup
1/2 c. cheddar cheese, shredded
1/2 c. mayonnaise
1 T. grated onion
8 to 10 crushed buttery crackers for topping

Clean, trim and blanch asparagus for 1 to 2 minutes. Drain and pat dry. Place in lightly buttered casserole dish. In mixing bowl combine soup, cheese, mayonnaise, and onion. Mix well. Pour ingredients over asparagus and bake covered about 30 to 40 minutes at 375 degrees (or until hot and bubbly). The last 10 minutes of baking, remove cover and sprinkle top with crushed cracker crumbs. Serves 6.

Grilled Mushrooms

Amy Schueddig

Combine several types of mushrooms to create a truly unique flavor.

2 T. butter, melted
1 clove garlic, minced
3/4 t. chili powder

1/4 t. salt
3 c. (8 oz.) white
   mushrooms, sliced

In medium glass bowl combine butter, garlic, chili powder and salt. Add mushrooms, tossing to coat. Divide mushrooms between two 12" squares of heavy-duty aluminum foil and wrap securely. Place packets on grill over hot coals. Grill 8 to 10 minutes. Serve hot. Mushroom packets may be baked in 400 degree oven for 10 minutes. Makes 4 servings.

Bootlegger Beans

Betty Asberry

I tried this as the title intrigued me. Now I make three batches at a time...love it!

3 strips bacon
15 oz. can pork and beans
2 T. vinegar

1 small onion, chopped
1 T. brown sugar
2 T. catsup

Dice strips of bacon and fry. When partially fried, add onion. When onion is slightly browned, pour off most of grease and add pork and beans, sugar, vinegar and catsup. Stir well and cover. Serves 4.

Spinach Casserole

Susan Catina

This is great with steaks and baked potatoes! The first time I had this was at a local restaurant and somehow I got my hands on the recipe. Anyone who likes spinach will love this.

1 lb. fresh spinach	1 small can mushrooms,
3 eggs	chopped fine
3/4 c. mayonnaise	1/4 c. bread crumbs
8 oz. sharp cheese, grated	paprika

Tear spinach into small pieces and place in mixing bowl. Add eggs and stir lightly. Add sharp cheese and blend lightly. Mix in well the mushrooms, mayonnaise and bread crumbs. Layer in buttered casserole dish spinach mixture, salt and pepper to taste. Sprinkle bread crumbs and paprika on top. Bake 350 degrees for 15 to 20 minutes. Serves 12.

Summer Squash Casserole

Sally Grushon

This was always a favorite summertime casserole. Squash is not always a favorite with children but they love this casserole.

2 lb. (6 c.) yellow summer squash, sliced
1 can cream of chicken or cream of celery soup
1/4 c. onion, chopped
1 c. sour cream
1 c. carrots, shredded
8 oz. pkg. herb stuffing mix
1/2 c. margarine, melted

Cook squash and onion in boiling salted water for 5 minutes. Drain. Mix soup and sour cream. Stir in shredded carrots. Add squash and onion. Combine stuffing and margarine. Spread half of stuffing mixture in a 9" square pan. Spoon on vegetable mixture. Sprinkle with remaining stuffing. Bake at 350 degrees for 30 minutes. Be sure it is heated through.

savory sides

Grilled Potato Casserole

Marty Darling

These are delicious!

fresh sliced potatoes
onions, chopped
1/2 c. cheddar cheese, shredded

1/4 stick margarine
salt and pepper

Layer on double layer of foil sliced potatoes (these can be peeled or unpeeled), onions, cheese, margarine, salt and pepper. Repeat these layers and tightly seal the foil. Grill 1 hour, turning every 10 to 15 minutes.

Great Grandma Elizabeth's German Potato Salad

Wendy Lee Paffenroth

I found this recipe in an old cookbook about 35 years after my great-grandmother died. We tried it and found it good with ham or even a barbecue. Makes the kitchen smell good on those rainy summer days.

1/2 lb. bacon, diced and fried
1 c. celery, diced
1 c. onion, diced
3 to 4 heaping T. flour
1/2 to 3/4 c. water
1/2 to 1 c. cider vinegar

2/3 c. white sugar
salt and pepper to taste
parsley to taste
8 to 10 c. cooked potatoes,
    peeled and cut up

Place the cut up potatoes in a large bowl and set aside. In a large skillet, fry the bacon and when almost browned, add the celery and the onion. Continue frying until tender, do not drain. Stir in the flour until very thick, then add the water. When it boils, add the vinegar and the sugar. Stir in a bit of salt, pepper and parsley to taste. Pour the hot mixture over top of the potatoes and stir until well coated. Place into an oven-proof bowl and bake at 350 degrees for 1/2 hour and remove. Serve warm from the oven. Can be reheated the next day if you like. Also good cold.

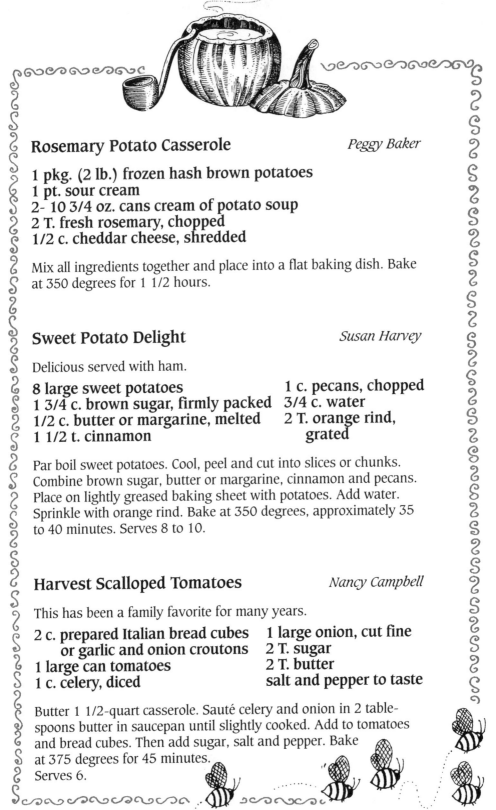

Rosemary Potato Casserole

Peggy Baker

1 pkg. (2 lb.) frozen hash brown potatoes
1 pt. sour cream
2- 10 3/4 oz. cans cream of potato soup
2 T. fresh rosemary, chopped
1/2 c. cheddar cheese, shredded

Mix all ingredients together and place into a flat baking dish. Bake at 350 degrees for 1 1/2 hours.

Sweet Potato Delight

Susan Harvey

Delicious served with ham.

8 large sweet potatoes
1 3/4 c. brown sugar, firmly packed
1/2 c. butter or margarine, melted
1 1/2 t. cinnamon

1 c. pecans, chopped
3/4 c. water
2 T. orange rind, grated

Par boil sweet potatoes. Cool, peel and cut into slices or chunks. Combine brown sugar, butter or margarine, cinnamon and pecans. Place on lightly greased baking sheet with potatoes. Add water. Sprinkle with orange rind. Bake at 350 degrees, approximately 35 to 40 minutes. Serves 8 to 10.

Harvest Scalloped Tomatoes

Nancy Campbell

This has been a family favorite for many years.

2 c. prepared Italian bread cubes or garlic and onion croutons
1 large can tomatoes
1 c. celery, diced

1 large onion, cut fine
2 T. sugar
2 T. butter
salt and pepper to taste

Butter 1 1/2-quart casserole. Sauté celery and onion in 2 tablespoons butter in saucepan until slightly cooked. Add to tomatoes and bread cubes. Then add sugar, salt and pepper. Bake at 375 degrees for 45 minutes.
Serves 6.

Potatoes "White and Green Summer Sauce"

Irmy Parrish

Serve with bratwurst. It's so delicious, we never have leftovers!

2- 16 oz. containers sour cream
salt and pepper to taste
2 c. fresh chives

8 oz. cream cheese
8 eggs, hard-boiled
3 lb. potatoes

In blender or mixing bowl mix sour cream and cream cheese until well blended and resembles a sauce (if too thick, add one tablespoon of lowfat milk). Pour into ceramic bowl, add salt and pepper to taste. Add hard-boiled eggs (chopped fine) and chives to sauce. Cover and refrigerate. Peel and quarter potatoes, boil until soft. Drain. Pour cold chive sauce over hot potatoes. The potatoes can be peeled and quartered the day before the party (as long as they're covered with cold water and are refrigerated).

Zucchini Skillet Medley

Peggy Baker

This colorful dish has been a family favorite for years. It has all of the colors of summer and is easy to prepare. We love it served with grilled meats and it is even good as a cold salad.

3/4 c. celery, sliced
1/2 c. onion, sliced
1 clove garlic
1 lb. zucchini, sliced
2 tomatoes, cubed
1/2 c. green pepper
1/2 c. carrot, shredded

1 can tomato sauce
2 t. prepared mustard
1/4 t. basil (fresh or dried)
1/4 t. salt
1/8 t. pepper

Sauté celery, onion and garlic; add zucchini, tomatoes, green pepper and carrot. Sauté 10 minutes; add tomato sauce, mustard, basil, salt, and pepper. Simmer 5 minutes. Serve warm or chilled on a leaf of lettuce.

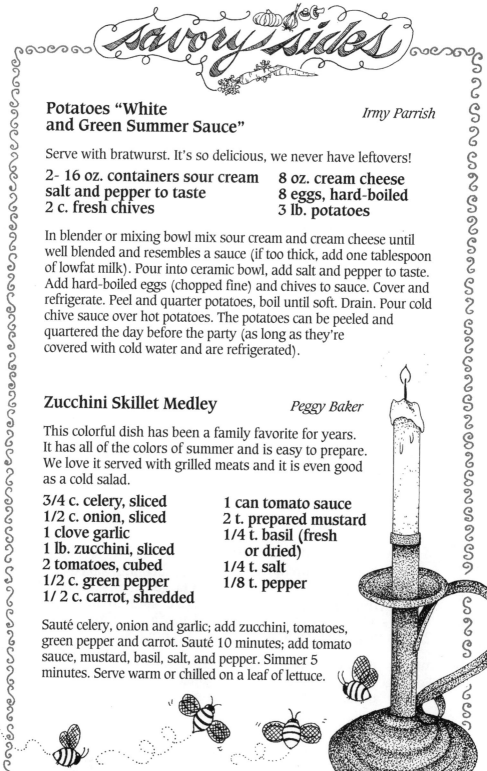

Chile Relleno Puff

Nancie Gensler

This recipe is excellent as a brunch dish. Serve with warmed flour tortillas or tortilla chips and salsa, crisp salad or vegetable.

7 oz. can whole green chiles, drained and split
4 oz. jack cheese, shredded
4 oz. cheddar cheese, shredded
2 T. cilantro, chopped (optional)
4 green onions, chopped (optional)

6 eggs, slightly beaten
3/4 c. milk
1 T. flour
1 t. baking powder
1/ 2 t. salt

Chile Sauce:

8 oz. can tomato sauce
1 t. oregano

1/4 c. salsa

In a lightly oiled 11"x7" baking dish layer split chiles and jack cheese. Combine eggs, milk, flour, baking powder and salt. Pour over chiles, top with cheddar cheese. Bake at 350 degrees for 30 minutes until puffed and browned. Heat combined tomato sauce, salsa and oregano 5 minutes. Spoon hot chile sauce over serving of chile relleno puff. Sprinkle with chopped green onions and cilantro.

Aunt Ruth's Favorite Zucchini Casserole

Elaine Ross

A delicious way to prepare your plentiful harvest of zucchini.

10 3/4 oz. can cream of chicken soup
4 c. stuffing mix (save half of stuffing for top)
2/3 c. margarine, melted

3 c. zucchini, sliced
3 large carrots, grated
1/2 c. sour cream
1 medium onion, chopped

Mix zucchini, carrots, onion, soup and sour cream together. Fold together stuffing and melted margarine, add to zucchini mixture. Place in a greased casserole, top with remaining stuffing mixture. Bake at 325 degrees for 30 to 35 minutes. Serves 10.

Yummy Zucchini Casserole

Cheryl McCullough

2 c. zucchini, grated
3/4 c. cheddar cheese, grated
2/3 c. biscuit baking mix
1 egg
1/8 t. pepper

1/4 c. vegetable oil
1/4 c. onions, chopped
1/4 t. salt
1/2 t. oregano or basil

Mix all ingredients thoroughly in a large bowl. Pour into a 9"x9" greased baking dish. Bake at 350 degrees for 45 minutes or until crusty brown on top.

Squash Casserole

Joan Limberg

8 oz. bulk pork sausage
3 small zucchinis, sliced
1 medium onion, finely chopped
2- 8 3/4 oz. cans cream style corn
2 c. (8 oz.) Monterey jack cheese, shredded
4 oz. can green chilies, chopped and drained

Brown sausage in a skillet, stirring until it crumbles; drain well and set aside. In skillet, over medium heat, sauté zucchini and onion in butter until tender. Combine zucchini mixture, reserved sausage, corn, cheese and chilies; stir well. Spoon into a lightly greased 2-quart casserole. Bake, uncovered, at 350 degrees for 30 to 40 minutes until golden. Serves 8.

Who loves a garden still his Eden keeps,
Perennial pleasures plants,
and wholesome harvest reaps.

Amos Bronson Alcott

Tomato Tart

Judy Kelly

Pastry:

2 c. all-purpose flour	1/2 t. salt
1 1/2 T. baking powder	6 T. margarine
1 1/2 t. sugar	1/2 c. plus 2 T. buttermilk

Combine flour, baking powder, sugar and salt in a large bowl. Cut in margarine with pastry blender. Gradually mix in buttermilk until dough just comes together. Gather dough and knead on floured pastry cloth a few seconds. Add more flour to cloth if dough is sticky. Slightly roll out and place in an 11"x8" baking dish. Press dough up the sides of the dish. Bake in a 400 degree oven for 15 minutes until puffed and golden. Remove from oven and gently press dough down with rubber spatula. Set aside. Reduce oven to 375 degrees.

Filling:

4 medium fresh tomatoes, diced
1/2 c. fresh basil, chopped or 2 T.
    prepared pesto sauce
1 c. cheddar cheese, grated
1 c. Swiss cheese, grated
1/2 c. mayonnaise
1/4 t. salt

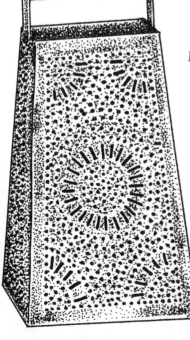

Mix tomatoes with basil or pesto sauce and salt. Spoon into crust, spreading evenly. Blend cheeses with mayonnaise and pat evenly over tomatoes. Bake for 20 to 25 minutes. Cut into small squares and serve warm. This may be prepared ahead and frozen. When ready to serve, place in a 350 degree oven for about 15 to 20 minutes or until warmed.

Onion Shortcake

Judy Kelly

2 large onions, sliced thin
1 stick margarine
8 oz. sour cream
3/4 t. dill weed
1/4 t. salt
5 or 6 drops hot pepper sauce

1 c. cheddar cheese, grated
15 oz. can cream-style corn
1/3 c. milk
1 egg, slightly beaten
7 oz. pkg. corn bread mix

Sauté onions in margarine; stir in sour cream, dill weed, salt and half the grated cheese. In separate bowl combine corn, milk, egg, hot pepper sauce and corn bread mix. Put corn mixture in buttered 13"x9" pan. Spread onion mixture over top. Top with remaining cheese. Bake in preheated oven at 425 degrees for 30 to 40 minutes. Serves 8.

Spinach Topped Tomatoes

Kathy Zenor-Horine

Delicious on a hot summer day with a cool glass of tea!

10 oz. pkg. frozen chopped spinach
2 t. instant chicken bouillon
salt to taste
3 large tomatoes, halved
1/3 c. parmesan cheese, grated
1/3 c. onion, chopped
1 c. herb-seasoned corn bread stuffing
1/2 c. margarine, melted

1/4 t. pepper
1 garlic clove
1 egg, beaten
parmesan cheese,
 shredded
 (optional)

Cook spinach according to directions with bouillon; drain well. Cool and press out excess liquid. Lightly salt tomato halves and place with cut side down on 2 paper towels for about 15 minutes to absorb excess moisture. In a small bowl, combine spinach with corn bread stuffing, parmesan cheese, onion, margarine, egg, garlic and pepper. Mix well. Place tomato halves, cut side up, in a shallow baking dish. Divide spinach mixture over tomatoes. Sprinkle with shredded parmesan cheese, if desired. Bake at 350 degrees for 15 minutes. Serves 6.

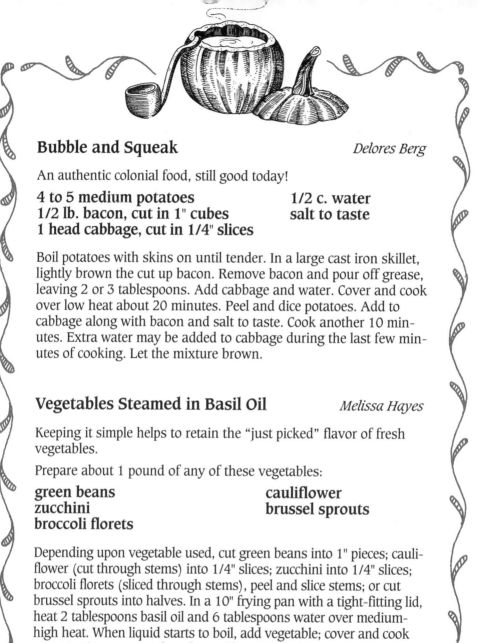

Bubble and Squeak

Delores Berg

An authentic colonial food, still good today!

4 to 5 medium potatoes
1/2 lb. bacon, cut in 1" cubes
1 head cabbage, cut in 1/4" slices

1/2 c. water
salt to taste

Boil potatoes with skins on until tender. In a large cast iron skillet, lightly brown the cut up bacon. Remove bacon and pour off grease, leaving 2 or 3 tablespoons. Add cabbage and water. Cover and cook over low heat about 20 minutes. Peel and dice potatoes. Add to cabbage along with bacon and salt to taste. Cook another 10 minutes. Extra water may be added to cabbage during the last few minutes of cooking. Let the mixture brown.

Vegetables Steamed in Basil Oil

Melissa Hayes

Keeping it simple helps to retain the "just picked" flavor of fresh vegetables.

Prepare about 1 pound of any of these vegetables:

green beans
zucchini
broccoli florets

cauliflower
brussel sprouts

Depending upon vegetable used, cut green beans into 1" pieces; cauliflower (cut through stems) into 1/4" slices; zucchini into 1/4" slices; broccoli florets (sliced through stems), peel and slice stems; or cut brussel sprouts into halves. In a 10" frying pan with a tight-fitting lid, heat 2 tablespoons basil oil and 6 tablespoons water over medium-high heat. When liquid starts to boil, add vegetable; cover and cook 6 to 10 minutes or until tender and liquid is cooked away. Stir often and add water, 1 tablespoon at a time, if liquid evaporates before vegetable is tender. Season with salt, pepper or garlic. Serves 4.

Basil Oil:

Pack fresh basil leaves (rinsed and patted dry) into a jar, then fill with salad or olive oil. Cover and store in a cool, dark place for 5 or 6 days. Strain and discard basil. Store in refrigerator.

Zia Rosa's Grilled Marinated Eggplant

Joanne Jacobellis

Two summers ago my parents, my two brothers, my husband and I went to Italy for two weeks. This was my mother's dream that we all travel to Italy together. Our relatives in Sicily were incredible, they couldn't do enough for us and the food was sensational. Best of all I loved the grilled marinated eggplant dish. I make it every summer now when I get eggplants from our garden and I go to the "Picking Patch" to get even more eggplants. Every time I make this dish I think of our wonderful trip to Sicily and our loving relatives. We all cried when it was time to leave and said that we would return in a few years, this time with our children.

2 to 3 medium-size eggplants
3/4 to 1 c. olive oil
2 to 3 cloves garlic, minced
salt and black pepper to taste
crushed red pepper flakes
**   (sprinkling to cover, more**
**   if you like it hot!)**

Cut up the eggplant lengthwise in thin slices. Brush each side of the eggplant pieces with olive oil to coat. Grill (on a barbecue grill) until golden brown. Place the grilled eggplant pieces in a bowl with the olive oil and the rest of the ingredients. Let marinate for 1 to 2 hours at room temperature. Makes 4 to 6 servings.

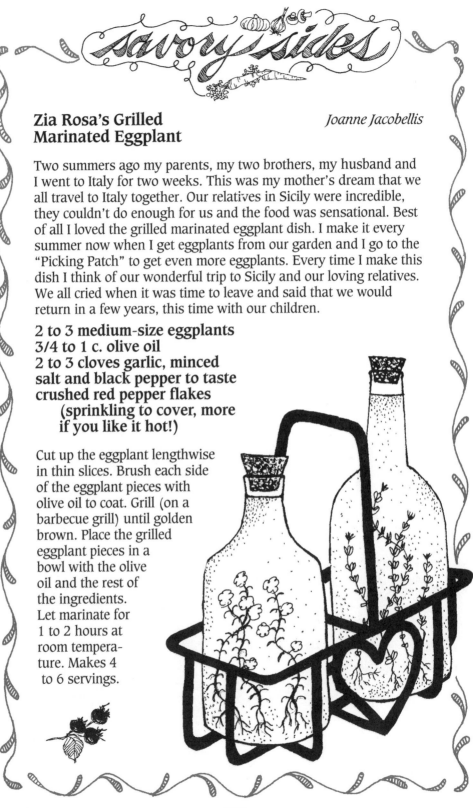

Roasted Pepper Salad

Joanne Jacobellis

6 red peppers
3 stalks celery, in bite-size pieces
8 oz. jar small black olives, pitted
2 to 3 cloves garlic, minced
1/4 c. olive oil and white wine vinegar

Cut red peppers in half, clean out the seeds. Place pepper halves on a cookie sheet. Broil until the skins turn black and the peppers are scorched. Let cool in a paper bag for 15 to 20 minutes. After being cooled, peel the black part off the pepper and easily remove the skin. Cut the halves in long thin strips, place them in a bowl. Add celery, olives, garlic, olive oil and vinegar. Toss all ingredients together. Let marinate in the refrigerator. Makes 4 to 6 servings.

Italian Fried "Pumpkin Flowers"

Bernadine Sabia

This recipe is a treat that can be enjoyed for only a few weeks out of the year. That's what makes it so special! Serve as an hors d'oeuvre at a backyard barbecue or serve with a green salad for a light summer lunch. At our house, these fritters disappear as soon as they are fried.

Pick pumpkin, zucchini or other squash flowers in the early morning, when they are fully open. Pluck carefully, leaving centers on vine so that fruit will continue to grow. A small garden may take a few days to yield enough flowers for a "batch." Immerse flowers in water to clean. Pat dry on paper towels and layer on waxed paper or foil. Store in refrigerator crisper until you have collected enough flowers for a "batch." Dip flowers in batter (below) and fry in oil until golden crisp. Drain on paper towels and lightly salt. Makes approximately 24 flowers.

Batter:

3 eggs
3 T. olive oil
1 c. warm water

pinch of salt
1 c. flour
pinch of baking powder

Beat eggs, olive oil, water and salt together. Sprinkle in flour gradually, beating after each addition. Add baking powder, stir and let stand for 1/2 hour.

Cream-Style Corn

Sara Walker

If your family likes cream-style corn, try this quick and easy freezer method.

8 to 10 c. corn, cut from the cob
1 lb. margarine
1 pt. cream

Combine ingredients in roaster. Cook for 1 hour at 350 degrees, stirring every 15 minutes. Let cool. Ladle into containers and freeze. Delicious!

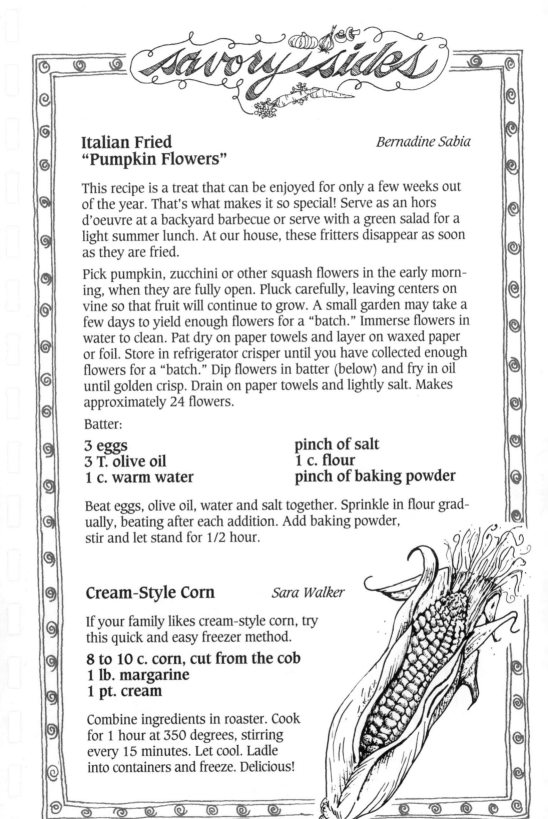

Herbed Eggs

Susan Mroz

6 hard cooked eggs
2 T. plain yogurt
2 T. mayonnaise
1/2 T. mustard
2 T. chives, chopped

1 t. dill, chopped
1 T. tarragon, chopped
1 T. chervil, chopped
salt and pepper to taste
fresh dill sprigs

Shell the boiled eggs and cut them in half lengthwise, removing yolks carefully. Mash the yolks, moistening them with the yogurt, mayonnaise and mustard. Season them with the herbs. Add salt and pepper to taste. Pile the mixture back into the egg whites, arrange the eggs on a platter and garnish with sprigs of dill. Serves 12.

Baked Apples

Juanita Williams

This is a great old-fashioned recipe you can try for a special treat or side dish with pork or ham!

1/3 c. golden raisins
1/3 c. dark raisins
1/4 c. water
2 T. bourbon
6 tart apples

4 T. butter (1/2 stick)
2 T. flour
1/2 c. brown sugar
1/2 t. vanilla extract

Heat oven to 425 degrees. In small saucepan, combine raisins, water and bourbon. Cook over low heat, stirring occasionally, until raisins are plumped. Remove from heat. Core apples and peel about half way down. Spoon raisins into center of each apple. In small saucepan, melt butter; stir in flour until smooth. Stir in sugar and vanilla; spread over apples. Bake 15 minutes or until crust is set. Reduce temperature to 350 degrees and bake apples until tender, about 30 minutes. Serve warm.

Summer-Thyme Soups

*Mince fresh herbs and put in ice cube trays,
with water, to freeze and use at will for stews,
sauces and soups. Reminds you in winter
of the flavors of a fruitful summer.*

Carrie Shapiro

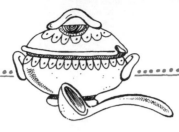

Fresh Garden Vegetable Soup

Carol Sheets
Gooseberry Patch

2 c. beef, cubed (leftover roast
   can be used)
2 T. butter or margarine
2 cans beef broth
1 to 2 c. water
2 c. fresh corn, cut off
2 medium onions, chopped
2 c. fresh carrots, thinly sliced

2 c. fresh peas
2 to 3 sprigs parsley
2 c. fresh green beans
2 c. turnips, diced
4 c. potatoes
1 c. celery, thinly sliced
4 fresh tomatoes
salt and pepper

Brown beef in butter or margarine; drain. Cook vegetables (except tomatoes) in water to cover, until tender. Combine vegetables with drained beef and broth. Add the fresh tomatoes and seasonings. Bring to a boil and simmer for 2 to 3 hours.

Strawberry Soup

Myrtle Christ

2 c. fresh strawberries
   (or 2- 10 oz. pkgs. frozen)
1 1/2 c. water

3/4 c. sugar
1 c. cranberry juice
8 oz. strawberry yogurt

Save 9 whole strawberries for garnish. Blend 1/2 cup water and the berries until smooth. Put in a large pan and add sugar, remaining water and cranberry juice; bring to a boil. Cool and whisk in yogurt. Refrigerate until cold. Garnish with the whole strawberries and mint leaves. Makes nine 1/2-cup servings.

Zucchini Soup

Barbara Burnham

Great served with French garlic bread!

12 to 16 oz. seasoned ground
   pork sausage
2 c. celery, cut into 1/2" pieces
1 c. onion, chopped
2 lb. zucchini, cut into 1/2" slices
14 1/2 oz. can tomato sauce
2 green peppers, cut into 1/2" pieces
1 t. Italian seasoning
2- 14 1/2 oz. cans stewed tomatoes

1/2 t. basil
2 t. salt
1 T. sugar
1/2 to 1 c. water
1/4 t. garlic powder
1 t. oregano
pepper to taste

Brown sausage, drain off fat. Add celery and cook for 10 minutes, stirring occasionally. Add rest of ingredients, bring to a boil, cover pan, reduce heat and simmer for 20 to 30 minutes. Ladle into bowls and top with parmesan cheese. Serves 6 to 8.

Classic French Vichyssoise

You'll enjoy this refreshing summertime soup!

*4 leeks (white part,
   include small
   amount of green),
   thinly sliced
1 medium onion, thinly sliced
1/4 c. butter
5 medium potatoes, thinly sliced*

*4 c. chicken broth
1 T. salt
2 c. milk
2 c. light cream
1 c. whipping
   cream*

Cook leeks and onion in butter until tender but not brown. Add potatoes, broth and salt. Cook 35 to 40 minutes. Rub mixture through fine sieve or place in blender and process smooth; return to heat only to thicken. Add milk and light cream. Season to taste with salt and pepper. Bring to boiling; cool. Chill. When cold, add whipping cream. Chill. Garnish with snipped chives or parsley. Serves 8.

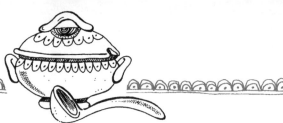

Pumpkin Soup

Barbara Burnham

This soup is sometimes greeted with turned up noses by those who have never tried it because of the unusual ingredient (pumpkin), but these same people come back for seconds whenever I serve it. It is a traditional first entree at our family Thanksgiving Dinner, but my family also loves it served up in steaming mugs topped with dollops of sour cream after a cold night of local high school football games where my granddaughter is a cheerleader!

1 large onion, chopped
1 tart apple, peeled and chopped
3 T. butter or margarine
1 can (16 oz.) pumpkin
2- 14 1/2 oz. cans chicken broth
1/8 t. nutmeg (optional)

1 bay leaf
1 t. curry powder
2 c. half & half or 13 oz.
can evaporated milk
plus 1/3 c. water

Sauté onion and apple in butter until soft. Mash fine. Add chicken broth, pumpkin (you can use canned or your own cooked and pureed pumpkin), bay leaf, curry powder and nutmeg, if desired. Simmer for 15 minutes. You can puree in food processor if smoother consistency is desired. Add half & half or evaporated milk and water. Add salt and pepper to taste. Simmer for an additional 10 to 15 minutes. Serve in bowls or mugs with desired toppings.
Toppings: sunflower seeds, croutons, parsley sprigs, sour cream.

Cold Cucumber Soup

Take the heat out of summer with a bowl of this refreshing soup!

3 cucumbers, peeled, seeded
and cut into chunks
1/4 t. salt
1 c. plus 1 c. chicken broth

1 c. sour cream
3 T. fresh chives, minced
2 T. fresh dill, minced

Combine cucumbers, salt and 1 cup of the chicken broth in a blender or food processor. Cover; blend about 1 minute or until smooth. Transfer to a bowl and stir in the remaining chicken broth. Whisk in sour cream, and herbs. Cover; chill. Garnish with fresh dill. Serves 6.

Creamed Zucchini Soup

Mary Redline

3 c. zucchini, sliced
1/2 c. water
1 T. onion, minced
1/2 t. parsley flakes
2 t. chicken stock or bouillon

2 T. butter
2 T. flour
1/8 t. white pepper
1 c. milk
1/2 c. light cream

Combine zucchini, water, onion, parsley, and 1 teaspoon stock. Cook until zucchini is tender and only small amount of water remains. Puree in blender. In saucepan, mix together 1 teaspoon stock, butter, flour, white pepper, milk and cream. Cook until blended well. Combine with zucchini mix. This makes 2 generous servings. Garnish with sour cream and paprika.

Tomato Soup

Judy Vaccaro

A quick and easy, tasty soup!

10 c. water or vegetable stock
5 c. tomatoes, peeled and chopped
1/2 c. fresh parsley, minced
3 T. honey
2 t. dill weed
1 c. milk

1/2 c. flour
1/4 c. butter
1 to 2 t. salt
vegetable seasoning
   to taste

Blend together water or vegetable stock, tomatoes, parsley, honey and dill weed; heat until hot. Blend together milk and flour until smooth, add to broth mixture; cook and stir until thickened. Season soup with butter, salt and vegetable seasoning to taste.

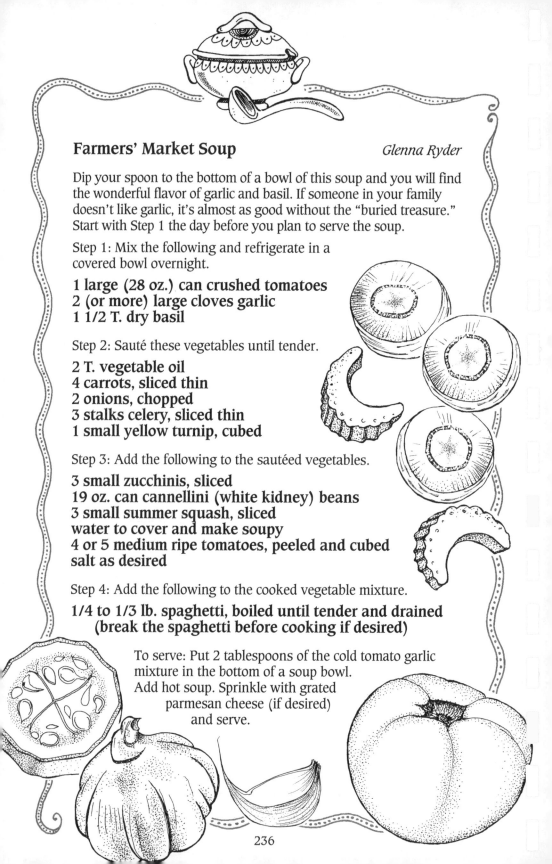

Farmers' Market Soup

Glenna Ryder

Dip your spoon to the bottom of a bowl of this soup and you will find the wonderful flavor of garlic and basil. If someone in your family doesn't like garlic, it's almost as good without the "buried treasure." Start with Step 1 the day before you plan to serve the soup.

Step 1: Mix the following and refrigerate in a covered bowl overnight.

1 large (28 oz.) can crushed tomatoes
2 (or more) large cloves garlic
1 1/2 T. dry basil

Step 2: Sauté these vegetables until tender.

2 T. vegetable oil
4 carrots, sliced thin
2 onions, chopped
3 stalks celery, sliced thin
1 small yellow turnip, cubed

Step 3: Add the following to the sautéed vegetables.

3 small zucchinis, sliced
19 oz. can cannellini (white kidney) beans
3 small summer squash, sliced
water to cover and make soupy
4 or 5 medium ripe tomatoes, peeled and cubed
salt as desired

Step 4: Add the following to the cooked vegetable mixture.

1/4 to 1/3 lb. spaghetti, boiled until tender and drained
(break the spaghetti before cooking if desired)

To serve: Put 2 tablespoons of the cold tomato garlic mixture in the bottom of a soup bowl. Add hot soup. Sprinkle with grated parmesan cheese (if desired) and serve.

Garden-Fresh Gazpacho with Shrimp

C.L. Ragland

I like to make this dish on a summer weekend morning, and let it chill while my wife and I pursue outdoor activities (usually working in the yard!). Preparation of the gazpacho and shrimp doesn't take much time out of our morning, and it's relaxing to come inside at the end of the day to a cool, refreshing meal that's simple to serve. I generally steam the shrimp myself, without seasoning. Already-prepared shrimp are also available in markets, and the preparation time is decreased if you don't have to steam and peel them yourself.

1 medium red onion
1 ripe avocado, remove peel and seed
1 medium bell pepper, remove seeds
2 cloves of garlic, chopped
3 stalks celery
24 oz. can tomato-based vegetable juice
1 large carrot
24 oz. can tomato juice
1 medium cucumber, peel and remove seeds
2 c. fresh tomatoes, peeled*
6 to 8 medium shrimp per serving chilled,
    shelled, steamed

Chop each vegetable (including canned tomatoes) very finely, using a food processor. Be careful not to process the vegetables into a puree. Combine and thoroughly mix all ingredients (except shrimp) in a glass bowl. Cover and chill in refrigerator for at least two hours before serving. Ladle the gazpacho into shallow soup bowls, placing 6 to 8 chilled, shelled, steamed shrimp on the surface just before serving. Serve with hot, crusty French bread. Provide wedges of fresh lime and some finely chopped hot peppers (or pepper sauce) and cilantro for those who may prefer the added flavors. Gazpacho may also be served without the shrimp, and "plain" leftovers are convenient to use the next day with midday sandwiches or dinner.

*If unavailable, you can substitute a 16 oz. can of tomatoes (retain juice).

Creamy Herb Potato Soup

Elizabeth Timmins
Gooseberry Patch Artisan

4 large russet potatoes
3 leeks
3 c. water
1 t. salt

2 T. dill weed
1 c. light cream
2 T. sour cream
1 T. butter

Chop potatoes and leeks and put in a heavy saucepan. Cover with water, add salt and cook till tender, about 1/2 hour. Puree in blender, a little at a time, and return to pan. Add light cream and dill weed and heat. Stir in sour cream and butter. Fresh dill makes a nice garnish.

Seafood Gazpacho

Suzan Turner

1/2 lb. cooked medium shrimp
fresh cilantro
1/4 c. olive oil
1 c. celery, chopped
2 T. red wine vinegar
1 small onion, chopped
3 garlic cloves, chopped
1 cucumber, quartered and sliced
1 green pepper, quartered and sliced
2 tomatoes, peeled and chopped
6 1/2 oz. can clams, minced
46 oz. can cocktail vegetable juice
1 1/2 t. worcestershire sauce
5 "squirts" hot pepper sauce
    (more for a really spicy taste)

Slice shrimp lengthwise. Prepare vegetables (I use a food processor to save time and effort!). Combine all ingredients in a large plastic or glass container. Salt and pepper to taste. Adjust hot pepper sauce to suit personal preference. Cover and chill well. Serve cold with croutons (homemade are easy and add a special touch). Garnish with chopped, fresh cilantro. The seafood can be omitted for real land-lubbers. This is a wonderfully refreshing summertime taste! Serves 8 to 12.

Blooming Breads

Small loaves of French bread make unusual holders for arrangements. Remove the middle of the loaf and line the cavity with aluminum foil. Then insert a piece of porous florist's foam, which has been soaked well and drained. Then you are ready for your design. You can make eggplant, squash, or other large vegetable the base as well.

Ernestine Hayes

Herbed Pizza Bread

Edwina Gadsby

This delicious fresh-from-the-garden, herb-flavored pizza bread goes great with salads. It's so quick and easy...the herb spread can be made up ahead of time and kept in the refrigerator for days.

1/4 c. olive oil
3 T. bread crumbs
1 T. fresh parsley, chopped
1 T. fresh chives, chopped
1 T. fresh basil or tarragon, chopped
1 or 2 cloves garlic, finely minced

salt and pepper to taste
3/4 c. unsalted butter, softened
16 oz. pkg. ready-made pizza crust
parmesan cheese, optional

Mix together olive oil, bread crumbs, parsley, chives, basil, garlic, salt and pepper until well blended. Mix in the butter. Preheat oven to 375 degrees. Spread herb butter mixture over pizza crust. Bake for 8 to 10 minutes or until golden brown. Sprinkle with fresh parmesan cheese, if desired. Makes 4 servings.

Zucchini Bread

Sharon Hall
Gooseberry Patch

Delicious served with a cup of tea or hot chocolate!

3 eggs
2 c. sugar
1 c. brown sugar
3/4 c. oil
1 T. vanilla
2 c. zucchini, grated

3 t. cinnamon
1 t. salt
1 t. baking soda
3 c. flour
1/2 c. raisins or
    1/4 c. walnuts, if desired

Beat eggs until frothy. Add sugars, beat until creamy. Add oil and vanilla. Blend in dry ingredients with the zucchini. Beat for 1 minute. Fold in raisins or nuts. Pour into 2 or 3 greased loaf pans. Bake for 1 hour in a 350 degree oven. For country muffins, fill paper muffin cups three-fourths full and bake at 350 degrees for 20 to 25 minutes. Freeze a few for quick morning breakfasts...just pop in the microwave!

Blooming Breads

Dilly Onion Bread

Peggy Gerch

12 to 14 c. flour*	1 T. salt
2 medium onions	4 T. honey
3 T. dry yeast	2 T. dill weed
1/2 c. powdered milk	2 T. dill seed
1/2 c. oil	2 eggs

Chop onions, quarter and put in the blender half full of water. Onions and water blended together should measure 6 cups. Place this in a mixer bowl and add half of the flour. Mix all other ingredients (except remaining flour) in bowl with the kneading arm. Add remaining flour one cup at a time. Knead for 10 minutes. Dough should clear bowl, if not, add more flour cautiously. Let dough rise in bowl for 15 minutes. Remove dough from bowl and divide into loaves on board. Shape and place in greased pans. Let rise until double and bake at 400 degrees for 10 minutes, and then 350 degrees for 30 minutes. Before bread starts to rise, cut slits in top with scissors, brush with water and sprinkle with sesame or poppy seeds. Makes 4 loaves.

*May use combination of whole wheat and white.

Lemon Poppy Seed Bread

Ann Fehr

Great any time of day. Makes really nice little "thinking of you" gifts.

18.25 oz. pkg. lemon cake mix	1 T. poppy seeds
3.4 oz. pkg. instant lemon pudding	2 T. sugar
1 c. water	1/2 c. lemon juice
1/2 c. vegetable oil	(preferably fresh
4 large eggs	squeezed)

Combine cake mix, pudding, water, oil and eggs in a large bowl; beat at medium speed. Stir in poppy seeds. Pour into three 8 3/4"x4 1/2"x2 1/2" greased loaf pans. Bake at 325 degrees for 40 minutes. Combine sugar and lemon juice, and brush over loaves.

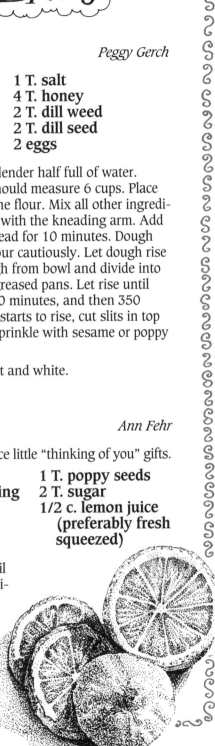

Plum Bread

Mary Dechamplain

This bread tastes best when mellowed a day or two, if you can keep your family away from it that long!

2 c. all-purpose flour, sifted
1 1/2 c. sugar (I use 1 c.)
1 t. baking soda
1 t. salt
1 t. cinnamon
1/2 t. nutmeg

1 c. salad oil
3 eggs, beaten
7 3/4 oz. jar junior baby
    food strained plums
1 c. walnuts, chopped

Combine flour, sugar, soda, salt, cinnamon and nutmeg. Stir in salad oil. Beat in eggs and blend well. Stir in strained plums and beat at medium speed for about 2 minutes, or until well blended. Stir in chopped nuts and pour into two greased 8 3/4"x4 1/2"x2 1/2" loaf pans. Bake in preheated 350 degree oven for 1 hour. Remove from pans, place on rack and while still warm brush with hot topping. Decorate as desired with decorative candies, colored sugar, candied fruit or walnuts. Makes 2 loaves.

Topping:

1/3 c. margarine
1/4 c. milk
1/2 c. sugar

1/8 t. baking soda

Mix all ingredients together in a small saucepan. Bring to boiling, stirring constantly. Boil about 5 minutes (not any longer) until clear and smooth. Let stand for about 5 minutes, until it starts to thicken, then brush tops of loaves.

Blooming Breads

Apricot-Pecan Nut Bread

Jane Gossett

2 1/2 c. flour
1 1/4 c. sugar
3 1/2 t. baking powder
2 T. orange peel, grated
1 t. lemon peel, grated
1 t. salt

3 T. salad oil
1/2 c. milk
1 egg
3/4 c. orange juice
1 1/2 c. pecans, chopped
2 c. dried apricots, chopped

Measure all ingredients into large mixing bowl. Mix for about 2 minutes by hand or 1 minute with electric mixer. Pour into a greased and floured loaf pan. Bake for 1 hour at 350 degrees. Test with pick in center to make sure it's done. Let cool. Slice and serve.

Pineapple Zucchini Bread

Laurie Dyer

I started making this recipe years ago before we learned to only plant one zucchini seed in our garden. Our six children love zucchini when it is made into Pineapple Zucchini Bread.

3 eggs
1 c. salad oil
2 c. sugar
2 t. vanilla
2 c. zucchini, coarsely shredded
8 1/4 oz. can crushed pineapple
1 c. nuts and 1 c. raisins
3 c. flour
2 t. baking soda

1 t. salt
1/2 t. baking powder
1 1/2 t. cinnamon
3/4 t. nutmeg

Beat eggs, salad oil, sugar and vanilla until thick and foamy. Add zucchini and pineapple. Combine flour, baking soda, salt, baking powder, cinnamon, nutmeg, nuts and raisins. Stir into zucchini mixture until well blended. Pour into 2 bread pans and bake at 350 degrees for 1 hour.

Potted Herb Bread

Judy Schulze

Makes a terrific and unusual bread and floral presentation for entertaining.

2 pkg. yeast	**1 t. salt**
1 c. warm water	**3 eggs**
1 c. warm milk	**1/2 c. butter**
1/3 c. sugar	**3 to 4 c. flour**
3 T. favorite herbs	

Sprinkle yeast over water in a small bowl. Stir to dissolve. Heat together milk, sugar and salt until slightly warm. Beat eggs; add yeast, milk mixture and butter. Add herbs (rosemary, garlic powder, oregano, thyme, whatever you like. If you wish to use sage, use only half the amount). Add enough flour to make soft dough. Knead lightly and place in lightly greased bowl in a warm, draft-free spot, cover and let rise until dough doubles in bulk (approximately 1 hour). In the meantime, grease well six small (5") flowerpots and flour generously. Punch down dough and shape the dough into long roll. More herbs may be added to jelly-roll style roll, if desired. Cut into six 3" rolled pieces. Shape into flowerpots (filling pots three-fourths full) and place pots onto cookie sheet. Let rise again (approximately 1 more hour). Bake at 350 degrees for 12 to 18 minutes or until golden brown. For the last 5 minutes brush with beaten egg. Sprinkle top with a mixture of dried herbs, fresh cracked pepper and salt. Note: This may be difficult to remove from flowerpots if not greased and floured enough.

Ah yet, ere I descent to the grave
May I a small house
and large garden have;
And a few friends,
and many books, both true,
Both wise, and both delightful too!
Abraham Cowley

Lemon Balm Bread
Denise Green

This bread is the perfect companion to hot or iced herbal tea.

1 stick unsalted butter
1 c. sugar
2 large eggs
pinch of salt
1/4 c. dried lemon balm leaves,
  finely chopped

1 1/2 c. flour, sifted
1 t. baking powder
grated rind of 1 lemon
1/4 c. chopped nuts
  (optional)

Preheat oven to 350 degrees. Cream butter with lemon balm leaves. Add sugar and beat well. Add remaining ingredients, mixing well. Pour batter into greased loaf pan. Bake for 30 to 45 minutes (test with tooth-pick for doneness). After bread is removed from oven, pour glaze over it and allow to sit for 4 to 6 hours in the loaf pan. Wrap the bread in foil and allow to ripen over-night before serving. Lemon verbena may be substituted for lemon balm.

Glaze:

juice of 1 lemon
1/2 c. sugar
1/2 c. hot water
1/4 c. lemon balm
  leaves, finely
  chopped

Mix all ingredients together.

Friend Annie's No-Knead French Bread   *Judy Hand*
(Alias: Simon and Garfunkel Bread)

My friend always adds parsley, sage, rosemary and thyme...and, of course, we just had to name it "Simon and Garfunkel Bread" from the lyrics of the song. It is bound to become a family favorite!! I often like to make round loaves (I think they are more attractive) by placing the dough in well buttered ovenware dishes (about 3" deep and approximately 6" in diameter).

4 c. white flour	1 T. sugar
1 pkg. yeast	1 t. salt
2 c. lukewarm water	herbs (optional)

Dissolve yeast and sugar in lukewarm water. Add other ingredients and beat well. Dough will be soft and sticky. Allow dough to rise in mixing bowl until it doubles in bulk. Stir down, divide dough evenly into two loaf pans and let rise again. Place in cold oven. Turn heat to 400 degrees and bake for 30 minutes. Bread is done when it is brown on top and when thumped, gives a hollow sound. If you want an herb bread (and who doesn't?), add herbs as you stir down the dough just before putting into pans. Hint: 1 tablespoon of herbs usually makes a mildly flavored loaf...add more if desired, to suit taste.

Carrot Bran Muffins   *Gretchen Georgiopoulos*

2 c. bran cereal	1/2 c. brown sugar, packed
1 1/4 c. milk	1/4 c. sugar
1/3 c. cooking oil	2 t. baking powder
2 eggs, beaten	1 t. baking soda
1 1/2 c. carrots, shredded	1 1/2 t. cinnamon
1 1/4 c. flour	1/2 t. salt

In a large bowl combine cereal, milk, oil, and eggs. Let stand 10 minutes. Stir in carrots. In another bowl combine flour, sugars, baking powder, baking soda, cinnamon, and salt. Add cereal mixture to flour mixture, stir until just combined. Grease muffin cups, or line with paper baking cups. Fill two-thirds full. Bake in a preheated oven at 375 degrees for 18 to 20 minutes, or until toothpick inserted near center comes out clean. Makes 12 muffins.

Blooming Breads

Morning Glory Muffins

Frances Guch

2 c. flour
1 1/4 c. sugar
2 t. baking soda
2 t. cinnamon
1 t. salt
2 c. carrot, grated
1 c. raisins

1 c. pecans, chopped
1/2 c. sweetened shredded coconut
1 apple (peeled, cored and grated)
3 large eggs
1 c. vegetable oil
2 t. vanilla

In a bowl sift together flour, sugar, baking soda, cinnamon and salt. Stir in grated carrot, raisins, pecans, coconut and apple. In a bowl, beat eggs with vegetable oil and vanilla. Stir mixture into flour mixture until the batter is just combined. Spoon the batter into well-greased muffin pan cups, filling them to the top. Bake muffins in preheated oven at 350 degrees for 30 to 35 minutes, or until they are springy to the touch. Let the muffins cool in the tins on a rack for 5 minutes. Turn out onto rack and let cool completely. Makes about 15 muffins.

Blueberry-Lemon Muffins

Glenda Nations

1 3/4 c. all-purpose flour
1/2 c. plus 2 T. sugar
2 1/2 t. baking powder
3/4 t. salt
1 egg, beaten

3/4 c. milk
1/3 c. cooking oil or melted
   shortening
3/4 to 1 c. fresh blueberries
1 t. lemon peel, grated

Stir together flour, sugar, baking powder and salt. Make a well in center. Combine egg, milk and oil. Add all at once to dry ingredients, stirring just until moistened. Fold in blueberries and lemon peel. Fill greased or paper baking cup-lined muffin pans two-thirds full. Bake at 375 degrees for 18 to 20 minutes.
Dip tops, while warm, in melted butter or margarine, then in sugar. Makes 12 muffins. If using frozen blueberries, thaw and drain before adding to mixture.

Oatmeal Apple Muffins

Kathleen Griffin

1 c. quick oats (not cooked)
3/4 c. milk
1 1/4 c. all-purpose flour
2 t. baking powder
1/2 t. salt
1/2 c. raisins (optional)

1 egg
1/2 c. brown sugar, packed
1/4 c. oil
1/2 t. cinnamon
1/2 c. apple, chopped

In a small bowl combine oats and milk and let set. Core and peel 1 to 2 apples. Soak the raisins in a little hot water to "plump" them, then drain. Combine in a medium bowl flour, baking powder, salt and cinnamon; mix well. Beat egg and add brown sugar and oil; beat until blended. Stir in oats and milk and add to dry ingredients. Blend in apple and raisins. Stir together until blended. Grease and fill muffin pan three-fourths full. Bake at 400 degrees for 15 to 20 minutes.

Garden-Angel Biscuits

Rebecca Welsh

Regular-size biscuits are nice for breakfast or brunch, or mini-size for savory bites on the tea tray.

1 pkg. active dry yeast	**1/2 c. shortening or lard**
2 1/2 c. all-purpose flour	**1/4 c. carrot, finely shredded**
1 T. sugar	**2 T. snipped parsley**
1 1/2 t. baking powder	**2 T. green onion, finely**
1/2 t. baking soda	**chopped**
1/4 t. salt	**1 c. buttermilk**

In a small mixing bowl dissolve yeast in 2 tablespoons warm water (105 to 115 degrees). Meanwhile, in a large mixing bowl stir together flour, sugar, baking powder, baking soda and salt. Using a pastry blender, cut in shortening or lard until mixture resembles coarse crumbs. Stir in carrot, parsley and green onion. Make a well in center of flour mixture, add softened yeast and buttermilk all at once. Using a fork, stir until just moistened. On a well-floured surface, knead dough for 6 to 8 strokes, or until nearly smooth. Pat or lightly roll into 1/2" thickness. Cut with a cutter of desired size, dipping the cutter into flour between cuts. Place biscuits on an ungreased baking sheet. Bake in a 450 degree oven for 10 to 12 minutes or until golden. Serve warm. Makes 12 to 14 regular-sized biscuits, or 24 to 28 minis.

Croutons

Peggy Gerch

Be frugal and make your own croutons using your stale bread and rolls! Cut bread in small pieces and place in a large mixing bowl. Melt butter or margarine and add herbs to it (oregano, onion, garlic or whatever herb you choose). Pour over bread cubes, stir and spread on a cookie sheet. Preheat oven to 300 degrees. Bake 15 minutes, turn, then bake 15 minutes more. I make large batches and store in the freezer. For a variety, try a mixture of cinnamon and sugar or parmesan cheese instead of herbs. Herbed croutons are delicious on those fresh garden veggies of lettuce, tomatoes, cukes and peppers.

Bagel Crisps

Peggy Gerch

6 T. margarine
8 bagels (approx. 4 to 5 slices per bagel)
3 t. dried oregano leaves or 1 1/2 t. garlic powder

Bagels are easier to cut when slightly frozen. Take the slightly frozen bagels and slice 1/4" thick. Lightly butter and sprinkle with herb of your choice. Bake in 250 degree oven until crisp. Usually 15 to 25 minutes, depending on how crisp you like them.

Herb Bread Blends

Mary Murray

Add one tablespoon of any combination of herbs to each loaf of homemade bread dough, or add one tablespoon of any herb mixture to 1/4 pound of butter and spread on a sliced loaf. Wrap in foil and reheat in the oven until warm. Here are some combination ideas:

With Beef or Stew:

2 c. summer savory   **1/2 c. marjoram**
1 c. parsley   **1/2 c. chives, finely chopped**
1/2 c. thyme

With Chicken, Ham or Pork:

equal parts of sage and parmesan cheese

With Spaghetti, Lasagna, Tortellini, Fettuccini:

equal parts of oregano, dried garlic chips
    and parmesan cheese

French Bread Topping

Delores Berg

Great for a brunch, Christmas Eve supper or with spaghetti.

1/4 c. onion, chopped   **dash of worcestershire sauce**
1/2 c. parmesan cheese   **1 c. mayonnaise**

Mix all ingredients together with electric mixer. Spread over bread slices and broil about 2 minutes or until lightly browned. Smells wonderful while broiling. Serves 4 to 6.

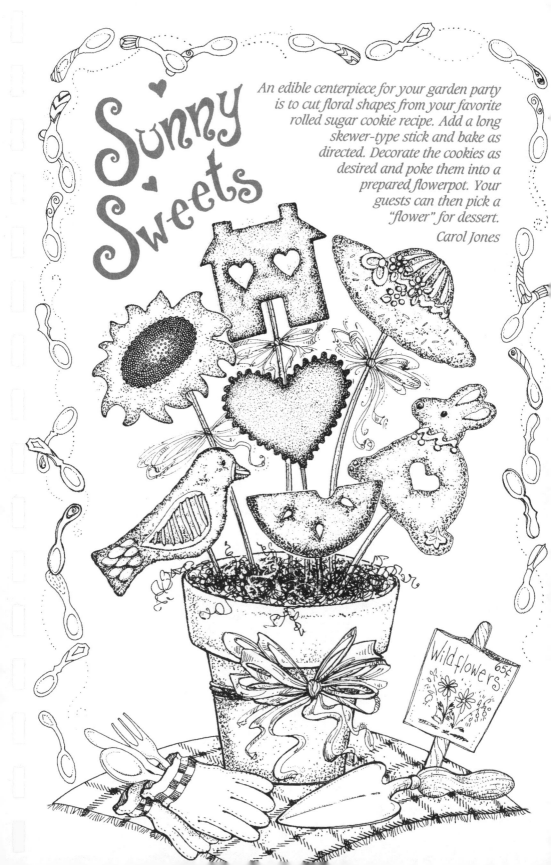

Sunny Sweets

An edible centerpiece for your garden party is to cut floral shapes from your favorite rolled sugar cookie recipe. Add a long skewer-type stick and bake as directed. Decorate the cookies as desired and poke them into a prepared flowerpot. Your guests can then pick a "flower" for dessert.

Carol Jones

Wildflowers 65¢

Rose Geranium Cake

Judy Hand

There are two preparations that must be done the night before making this cake and frosting...wrapping sticks of butter with leaves AND making the rose geranium sugar for the frosting.

Prepare the night before:

24 rose geranium leaves
1 c. butter or margarine (use sticks)

Rinse leaves and wrap 5 or 6 leaves around each stick of butter. Wrap butter in foil or plastic wrap, refrigerate overnight.

Next day:

1 3/4 c. sugar
6 egg whites
3 c. cake flour, sifted
4 t. baking powder

1/2 t. salt
3/4 c. milk
1/2 c. water
1 t. vanilla

Remove leaves from butter (save for further use); gradually add sugar, creaming until light and fluffy. Add egg whites two at a time, beating well after each addition. Sift together flour, baking powder and salt. Combine milk, water and vanilla. Alternately add dry ingredients and milk mixture to creamed mixture, beginning and ending with dry ingredients; beat smooth after each new addition. Grease and flour two 9" round or 8" round layer cake pans. Arrange 10 to 12 rose geranium leaves (including those saved from the butter) on bottom of each pan. Spoon batter over leaves and bake in 350 degree oven for 30 to 35 minutes or until done. Cool in pans for 10 minutes. Remove layers from pans and let cool on racks. Gently remove rose geranium leaves from bottom and discard.

Rose Geranium Frosting (prepare the night before):

1 1/2 c. sugar, divided
3 or 4 fresh rose geranium leaves

Use a container with a tightly fitted lid and pour 3/4 cup sugar into container. Wash rose geranium leaves, add to sugar container. Cover with another 3/4 cup sugar. Cover container and let stand overnight. Remove leaves before using sugar.

Next day:

1 1/2 c. rose geranium sugar
2 egg whites
1/3 c. cold water

1/4 t. cream of tartar
dash of salt

Place rose geranium sugar (that you have prepared the day before), egg whites, water, cream of tartar and salt in top of double boiler (do not over heat). Beat 1 minute with electric beater. Place over, but not touching boiling water. Cook, beating constantly until frosting forms stiff peaks (about 7 minutes). Remove from boiling water, beat until spreading consistency (about 2 minutes). Frost between layers and spread frosting to cover sides and top of 2-layer cake. Garnish frosted cake with candied rose geranium leaves made by rolling dampened leaves in sugar.

Hint: If the above recipe is too time consuming, but you want a special cake...just cover the bottom of a cake pan with rose geranium leaves and pour batter for a pound cake, or even a plain white cake, over leaves. Bake and remove leaves from bottom after baking. Imparts a wonderful flavor to cake!

 Add a windowbox to your garden gate and fill with your favorite herbs or flowers!

Vanilla Chip Fruit Tart

Lisa Richard

A delicious summer fruit dessert. Use the season's freshest fruits.

Crust:

3/4 c. butter, softened   **1/2 c. confectioner's sugar**
1 1/2 c. flour

Heat oven to 300 degrees. Beat butter and sugar until light and fluffy, blend in flour. Press mixture onto bottom and side of 12" round pizza pan. Bake 25 to 30 minutes or until lightly browned. Cool completely.

Filling:

10 oz. bag vanilla chips   **8 oz. cream cheese**
1/4 c. whipping cream

In microwave-safe bowl, microwave vanilla chips and whipping cream at high for 1 1/2 minutes or until chips are melted and mixture is smooth when stirred. Beat in cream cheese. Spread on cooled crust.

Fruit layer:

Select summer's great fruits like blueberries, strawberries, kiwi, peaches, nectarines. Slice and arrange over filling.

Fruit topping:

1/2 c. granulated sugar
2 T. cornstarch
1 c. orange juice
1 t. lemon juice

In small saucepan, combine sugar and cornstarch. Stir in juices. Cook over medium heat, stirring constantly until thickened. Cool completely. Pour over fruit layer. Serves 8 to 10.

Chocolate Fruit Dip

Amy Schueddig

Stir up this creamy dip in a hurry and serve with the best fruits of the season.

8 oz. pkg. light cream cheese, softened
1 c. powdered sugar
1/4 c. unsweetened cocoa
1/4 c. skim milk
1/4 t. orange extract (optional)
assorted fresh fruit for dipping

In a small mixer bowl, beat cream cheese until fluffy. Blend in powdered sugar, cocoa, milk and orange extract. Beat at medium speed until smooth. Cover. Refrigerate several hours or overnight for flavors to blend. Just before serving, rinse and dry fruit (bananas, kiwi fruit, strawberries), cut into serving size pieces if necessary. Brush bananas with lemon juice to prevent browning. Arrange fruit on serving platter with dip in center. Serve dip well chilled. Refrigerate leftovers. Makes about 2 cups.

White Chocolate and Mint Mousse

Susan Mroz

Delightful and delicious!

4 oz. good quality white chocolate
1/2 c. heavy cream
a bunch of mint leaves

4 eggs, separated
fresh mint sprigs or frosted mint leaves to decorate

Carefully melt the chocolate in the top of a double boiler or in a heat-proof bowl set over simmering water. Meanwhile, warm the cream in a small saucepan with 8 mint leaves. Remove the cream from the heat and leave to infuse for a few minutes. Beat the egg yolks into the melted chocolate. Beat the egg whites until stiff. Remove the mint leaves from the cream and add the cream to the chocolate mixture. Stir well, then fold in the egg whites. Spoon the mousse into small, individual, stemmed glasses and chill for 2 to 3 hours. Decorate each serving with a sprig of fresh mint or frosted mint. Serve with crisp wafers or cookies.

Rhubarb Batter Cake

Yvonne Bendler

This recipe was on the reverse side of a chicken recipe I cut from our newspaper years ago. Only recently did fate have me turn it over to discover this dessert (much better than the chicken). At first I thought the directions had to be wrong but I went ahead and the results were great. I've changed a few things and added others and it's wonderful. A sauce forms on the bottom while a light cake layer floats on top with a crusty cinnamon/sugar surface. Guild the lily and add a scoop of vanilla ice cream to this warm treat. Thin sliced apples, fresh sliced peaches or blueberries or raspberries work equally well. It goes together quickly too. Enjoy!

2 c. fresh rhubarb, diced or
   half strawberries
2 T. lemon juice
1 1/2 c. sugar, divided
1 c. flour
1 t. baking powder
1/2 t. salt

3 T. butter, cold
1 t. vanilla
1/2 c. milk
1 T. cornstarch
1/2 t. cinnamon
1 c. boiling water

Preheat oven to 350 degrees. Butter 9" pan and set aside. Sprinkle rhubarb over bottom of dish and sprinkle on lemon juice. In mixing bowl combine 3/4 cup sugar, flour, baking powder, salt and butter (cut into 6 pieces). Mix until butter is in rough small pieces. Combine milk and vanilla and mix in. Mix just enough so you can still see little butter pieces. Pour batter over rhubarb. Combine remaining 3/4 cup sugar, cornstarch and cinnamon. Mix well to blend. Sprinkle over batter. Put cake in oven and now carefully pour boiling water over cake. THIS WILL WORK! Bake 45 to 55 minutes or until you see that the sauce has thickened and is bubbling around the edges. Serve warm.

Family Favorite Wild Blackberry Pie   *Lora Past*

After two years in college studying to be a high school math teacher, I took this summer off. It was only then that I noticed that logging around our house has resulted in a regrowth of wild blackberries. These sweet, small berries are ripe in late June and July, and picking them can be more difficult than a calculus quiz! But the foxglove and other wildflowers that bloom all around the berry bushes make the task almost enjoyable. Although I've been making pies for my husband and son for 10 years, this was an immediate favorite.

Pie Crust:

2 scant c. flour*   **1/4 c. water**
1/3 c. plus 2 T. shortening   **dash of salt (optional)**
**   (I like butter-flavored)**

Using a pastry blender mix shortening, flour and salt. Add water and knead together until just blended. Divide into two equal portions. Put 1/2 cup flour on rolling surface and spread around. Take one portion and shape into round circle, pressing down on dough. Pick up, redistribute flour on rolling surface, then turn dough with floured side up and roll into circle. Makes 2 crusts.

*Or "finger" approximately 1 tablespoon out of each cup

Filling for a 9" pie:

5 c. berries   **1/3 c. flour**
1 1/3 c. sugar   **1/4 t. vanilla (optional)**
2 t. margarine

Combine all ingredients except margarine in a bowl. Place in prepared pastry shell. Dot margarine over top of berry mixture and place top crust. Cut holes in top pastry. For a golden brown crust, lightly brush water on top crust and sprinkle with sugar. Bake at 425 degrees for 35 to 45 minutes. To keep crust edges from over browning, place foil over edges and remove 15 minutes before pie is to be removed from oven.

Fried Apple Pies

Alma Law

dried apples
cinnamon, or apple pie spice
cooking oil

sugar, to taste
pastry dough

Cook dried apples with water until soft. Add sugar to sweeten, and cinnamon or apple pie spice. Let cool. Make up regular pastry and roll as for pie crust into circles 6 or 7 inches in diameter. Put a layer of sweetened apples about 1/2" thick on one half of the pastry. Fold over the other half (into shape of half moon) and cut away excess pastry. Crimp edges together with floured fork. Slip gently into iron skillet which contains about 1/2" hot cooking oil. Fry until brown on side. Turn gently and fry on the other side. Serve hot or cold.

Fruit-Filled Burritos

Linda Cuellar

6 flour tortillas
1 can fruit pie filling of your choice

Dip tortillas in hot oil, briefly. Remove and spoon filling onto tortilla. Sprinkle a little sugar and flour on top of fruit filling. Roll up burrito style and place on greased cookie sheet. Sprinkle butter, sugar and cinnamon on top. Bake at 400 degrees for 10 to 12 minutes or until crispy. Delicious served warm with vanilla ice cream. Serves 6 generously. Not recommended for those watching your calories!

Blackberry Cobbler (Sonker) *Annabelle Whitaker*

This is an all-time favorite in North Carolina, where we have a sonker festival.

8 c. fresh blackberries **2 c. sugar**
1/3 c. all-purpose flour **1 c. water**
1/2 c. butter or margarine, melted

Dredge blackberries in flour, add sugar and water; mix well. Set aside. Roll three-fourths of pastry to 1/8" thickness on a lightly floured surface. Place into a 13"x9"x2" baking dish then bake pastry at 400 degrees until dry looking but not completely baked. Spoon in blackberry mixture. Roll remaining pastry out to 1/4" thickness on a lightly floured surface and cut into 1/2" strips. Arrange in lattice fashion over blackberries. Brush strips with melted margarine and sprinkle with sugar. Bake at 350 degrees for 1 hour.

Pastry:

4 c. flour
1 c. shortening,
    heaping
1 egg
1 t. vinegar
1 t. salt
10 T. cold water

Mix with pastry blender.

Dip:

3/4 c. sugar
2 T. flour
2 c. milk

Heat until a little thick (just a little bit). Pour over pie as it is being served.

Easy Fresh Peach Cobbler

Pat Akers

My grandpa always used to say, "I don't have a foot for dancin' but I sure have a mouth for pie!"

1 1/2 c. fresh peaches,
   thinly sliced
1 c. sugar, divided
1/4 c. water
1 egg
1 T. shortening

1 T. milk
1/2 c. all-purpose flour
1/2 t. baking powder
1/4 t. salt
light cream or ice
   cream

About 1 hour before serving, preheat oven to 375 degrees. Grease 11"x7" glass baking dish. In medium-size saucepan, combine peaches, 1/2 cup of sugar and water. Bring to a boil, stirring frequently, keep the peach mixture hot. Meanwhile, with a spoon beat egg, 1/2 cup sugar and shortening until fluffy. Add milk, stir in flour, baking powder and salt. Spread batter in prepared baking dish, pour hot peaches over all. Bake 25 to 30 minutes, or until tender. Serve warm, with cream or ice cream. Makes 6 servings. You can use fresh blueberries, blackberries or apples instead of peaches.

Freeze-Ahead Peach Pie Filling

Sue Meyer

When peaches are abundant, make this filling!

1 qt. peaches, peeled and sliced
1 c. sugar
3 T. tapioca

1/8 t. salt
1 T. lemon juice

Line pie pan with foil. Pour in filling. Freeze then remove from pan and place in large plastic bag in freezer. When the snow flies...defrost filling, place in crust-lined pie pan. Add top crust, cut slits in top. Bake at 350 degrees 35 to 40 minutes or until crust is browned and filling bubbles. Taste summer again!

Lemon-Glazed Pound Cake

Susan Mroz

2 T. warm water
1/2 t. vanilla
fresh lemon verbena leaves
lemon twists

1 c. confectioner's sugar
1/4 t. lemon zest, grated
a pound cake

Night before, combine water and vanilla and place a few of the lemon verbena leaves in mixture. Soak overnight. The next day, remove the lemon verbena leaves. Stir in the confectioner's sugar and lemon zest into the flavored water to form a glaze. Pour the glaze over your favorite pound cake, letting the glaze drip down the sides. Garnish with lemon twist and more lemon verbena leaves.

Lemon Basil Cookies

Elizabeth Timmins
Gooseberry Patch Artisan

1/4 c. butter
8 oz. pkg. cream cheese
1 egg yolk
1 t. lemon juice
1 T. dried basil

1/2 t. lemon rind, grated
18.25 oz. box lemon cake mix
1/4 c. coconut, shredded
1/4 c. walnuts, chopped

Cream butter and cheese. Add egg yolk and lemon juice until blended. Blend in dry cake mix one-third at a time, last portion by hand. Stir in the coconut, nuts, lemon peel and basil. Drop by teaspoon onto a greased cookie sheet. Bake at 350 degrees for 10 to 15 minutes or until golden in color.

Lemon Snowflakes

Helene Hamilton

The name makes me feel cool on a hot summer day!

1 c. butter, softened
1/2 c. sugar
3/4 c. cornstarch

1 1/2 c. flour
1 c. pecans, finely chopped
glaze

Cream together butter and sugar. Sift together cornstarch and flour. Gradually add cornstarch and flour mixture. Chill dough at least 1 hour. Shape dough into 48 small balls. Scatter finely chopped pecans on waxed paper. Drop each dough ball on nuts and flatten with bottom of glass dipped in flour. Place nut side up on buttered cookie sheet. Bake at 350 degrees for 13 minutes. Cool.

Glaze:

1 c. powdered sugar
2 T. butter, melted

2 to 3 lemon balm leaves, finely chopped
T. fresh lemon juice

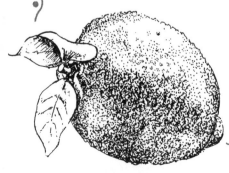

Mix all ingredients together until smooth. Swirl on top of each cookie. Let set before serving. Yields 4 dozen.

A Bucket of Sand

Renee Hobler

2 c. milk
4 oz. pkg. vanilla or banana-flavored instant pudding
12 oz. pkg. vanilla wafer cookies, crushed
8 oz. container whipped topping, thawed

Blend milk and pudding in a large bowl by beating with wire whisk for 1 to 2 minutes; refrigerate for 1/2 hour. Stir in 1/2 of the cookies and the whipped topping. In the bottom of a plastic sand bucket (one that you'd normally take to the beach), sprinkle enough cookies to cover the bottom. Pour 1/2 of the pudding mixture into the bucket, then add a layer of cookies (1/2 of remaining). Finish off with the remaining pudding mixture, topped by remaining cookies. Refrigerate until ready to serve. Decorate with gummy shells and stars, add party umbrellas, and dish it up with your plastic shovel. Individual sand cups can be made simply by using 8 to 10 clear plastic cups instead of the bucket.

There's no prettier sight than a rose-covered cottage!

Watermelon Cookies

Sue Meyer

My grandchildren love to help with these cookies.

1/3 c. margarine
1/3 c. shortening
3/4 c. sugar
1 large egg
1/2 t. salt
chocolate mini morsels

1 T. milk
1 t. vanilla
2 c. flour
1 1/2 t. baking powder
red paste food coloring

Beat in a large mixing bowl margarine and shortening. Add sugar, egg, milk and vanilla. Mix in flour, baking powder and salt. Add a small amount of red paste food coloring. Shape into a ball, cover and chill at least 3 hours. Roll dough to 1/4" thickness, cut out with 3" round cutter. Cut circles in half. Place on ungreased cookie sheet. Press several chocolate mini morsels in each cookie. Bake at 375 degrees for 8 to 10 minutes, do not brown. Cool on racks.

Frosting:

1 1/2 c. powdered sugar
small amount of green paste food coloring
2 T. water

Combine powdered sugar, water and a small amount of green paste food coloring. Dip round edge of cookie in green frosting. Place on wax paper until frosting is firm. Makes about 3 dozen.

Lavender Cookies

Karen Jackson

Dried lavender may be found in health food stores or natural food markets. Be sure to buy the type that is processed as a food product and not for crafts to avoid poisons and preservatives.

3 1/2 T. dried lavender
1 c. butter or margarine
3 eggs
2 t. baking powder
1 t. vanilla

2 c. sugar
1/2 c. milk
3 1/2 c. flour
1/2 t. soda

Grind lavender and sugar into powder in food processor. Cream butter, add sugar and lavender then the beaten eggs. Add vanilla. Into one cup of flour sift soda and baking powder. Add this sugar mixture. Alternate remaining flour with milk to make a soft dough. Bake at 350 degrees for 8 to 10 minutes.

Chocolate Zucchini Cake

Barb McFaden

A great way to use the overgrown zucchini in your garden. A great tasting cake and so easy to make!

1/2 c. butter or margarine
1/2 c. oil
1 3/4 c. sugar
2 eggs
1 T. vanilla
1/2 c. buttermilk
2 to 3 c. zucchini, grated

2 1/2 c. flour
1/2 t. salt
4 T. cocoa
1 t. baking soda
1/2 t. cinnamon
1/2 c. nuts
2 c. chocolate chips

Mix all the ingredients (except chocolate chips) in a mixing bowl. Add 1 cup of the chocolate chips to the mixture. Pour into pan and sprinkle the other cup of chips on the top. Bake 325 degrees for 45 minutes or until knife when inserted comes clean. Delicious and very moist.

Place a drop of lavender or rose oil on a light bulb.
Your rooms will be filled with warm memories of summer.

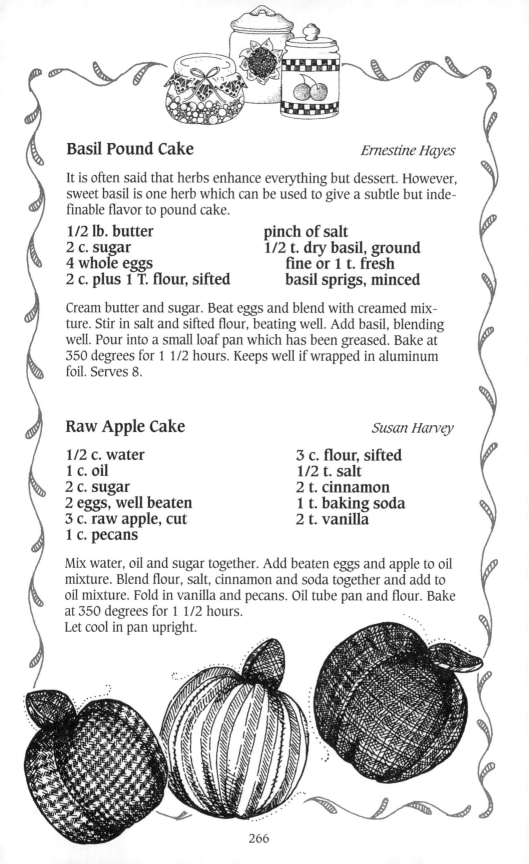

Basil Pound Cake

Ernestine Hayes

It is often said that herbs enhance everything but dessert. However, sweet basil is one herb which can be used to give a subtle but indefinable flavor to pound cake.

1/2 lb. butter	pinch of salt
2 c. sugar	1/2 t. dry basil, ground
4 whole eggs	fine or 1 t. fresh
2 c. plus 1 T. flour, sifted	basil sprigs, minced

Cream butter and sugar. Beat eggs and blend with creamed mixture. Stir in salt and sifted flour, beating well. Add basil, blending well. Pour into a small loaf pan which has been greased. Bake at 350 degrees for 1 1/2 hours. Keeps well if wrapped in aluminum foil. Serves 8.

Raw Apple Cake

Susan Harvey

1/2 c. water	3 c. flour, sifted
1 c. oil	1/2 t. salt
2 c. sugar	2 t. cinnamon
2 eggs, well beaten	1 t. baking soda
3 c. raw apple, cut	2 t. vanilla
1 c. pecans	

Mix water, oil and sugar together. Add beaten eggs and apple to oil mixture. Blend flour, salt, cinnamon and soda together and add to oil mixture. Fold in vanilla and pecans. Oil tube pan and flour. Bake at 350 degrees for 1 1/2 hours.
Let cool in pan upright.

Cinnamon Roll-Ups
Vi Mitchell

This is a nice addition to a brunch buffet. Every time I serve these to a new group, I have requests for the recipe.

1 large loaf sandwich bread, sliced	1 1/2 c. plus
8 oz. cream cheese	1/4 c. sugar
2 sticks butter, melted	3 t. cinnamon
1 egg yolk	

Trim crusts off bread and roll flat with a rolling pin. Beat egg yolk, cream cheese and 1/4 cup sugar. Spread each slice of bread. Roll each slice tightly and dip in melted butter. Mix 1 1/2 cups sugar and cinnamon; roll each buttered roll in it. Freeze on cookie sheet, seam side down overnight. Bake as needed in 400 degree oven for 15 minutes. Special for a coffee break too. Makes about 2 dozen roll-ups.

Picnic Chocolate Cake
Delores Berg

2 c. flour	1 c. water
2 c. sugar	2 eggs
1/2 t. salt	1 t. soda
2 sticks margarine	1 t. vanilla
4 T. cocoa	1/2 c. buttermilk

In a large bowl mix together flour, sugar and salt. In a small saucepan heat margarine, cocoa and water. Stir chocolate mixture into flour mixture until smooth. Add eggs, soda, vanilla and buttermilk. Mix until smooth and then pour into a 13"x9" pan. Bake at 375 degrees for 15 to 20 minutes. Let cake stand for 5 minutes before frosting; frost while still warm.

Frosting:

1 lb. powdered sugar	4 T. cocoa
1 stick margarine	6 T. buttermilk

Put powdered sugar in a large bowl. In a saucepan melt (do not boil) margarine, cocoa and buttermilk. Add to powdered sugar and mix well.

Raspberry Hazelnut Chocolate Torte

Cheryl Berry

This is an easy but elegant dessert that would be lovely for an afternoon tea. It looks, sounds and tastes delicious, and is not terribly high in fat...just use a light cake mix and egg whites!

18.25 oz. box chocolate cake mix (can use light mix)
1 c. hazelnuts, chopped
1 jar all-fruit raspberry spread
powdered sugar, sifted very fine

Toast hazelnuts on a baking sheet at 300 degrees until lightly browned (don't over toast). Set aside. Prepare chocolate cake mix according to directions. Pour into two 9" round cake pans. Bake according to mix directions. Cool completely. Melt raspberry spread in small saucepan. Cool. To assemble torte, slice the two 9" layers in two to make four thin layers. Place one layer on cake plate. Spread with 1/3 melted raspberry spread and sprinkle 1/3 cup nuts. Top with another cake layer and continue with raspberry spread and nuts. Top layer of chocolate cake should have no spread or nuts. Sprinkle or stencil powdered sugar on top using a paper doily. If powdered sugar is used to garnish the top layer, the torte should be served fairly soon, otherwise the sugar tends to melt into the cake and you lose your lacy design from the doily. Serves 8 to 10.

Nectarine and Raspberry Crisp
Kara Kimerline

A yummy summertime treat!

2 large nectarines,
   halved and pitted
1/3 c. apricot preserves
1 t. vanilla
2 c. fresh raspberries
1/2 c. all-purpose flour
1/3 c. brown sugar, packed
1/2 t. ground cinnamon
1/4 t. ground nutmeg
1/3 c. butter or margarine
1 c. granola
1/4 c. toasted slivered almonds, chopped coarsely
vanilla ice cream

Cut nectarines into 1/2" slices. In an 8"x8"x2" baking pan or dish or an 8"x1 1/2" round baking dish, stir together nectarines, preserves, and vanilla. Carefully fold in berries. In a bowl, combine flour, sugar, cinnamon and nutmeg. Cut in butter until mixture resembles coarse crumbs. Add granola and almonds. Toss with a fork until mixed. Sprinkle this mixture over the fruit in the baking pan. Bake at 375 degrees for 25 to 30 minutes or until topping is golden. Serve warm or at room temperature with ice cream. Enjoy! Makes about 6 servings.

Springtime Rhubarb Crunch
Linda Zell

This is a family favorite...and that is saying a lot from a family who collects rhubarb recipes.

1 c. brown sugar
3/4 c. oatmeal
1 c. flour
1/2 c. melted butter
1 t. vanilla
4 c. rhubarb, sliced
1 c. sugar
1/2 c. water
2 T. cornstarch

Combine brown sugar, flour, oatmeal and melted butter. Press 1/2 of the mixture on the bottom of a 8" or 9" square pan. Reserve the rest. In a large saucepan combine rhubarb, sugar, water and cornstarch; cook until clear. Add vanilla. Pour rhubarb mixture over crust. Cover with remaining crunch. Bake at 350 degrees for 40 to 45 minutes. Cool.

Raspberry Orange Cups
Jane Gossett

2 large oranges
4 mint leaves or fresh rose buds

1 pt. fresh raspberries

Slice oranges in half. Hollow out oranges (you can use meat of orange in your juice). Fill with fresh, clean raspberries. Garnish with a mint leaf or a small fresh rose bud.

Strawberry-Rhubarb Crunch Pie
Phyllis Ross

My family loves this combination of fruit. It's a great way to make use of the produce from our June garden.

pastry for 9" single pie crust
1 1/3 c. sugar
1/3 c. flour
2 c. fresh strawberries, sliced

2 c. fresh rhubarb,
   cut in 1/2" pieces
1/2 t. orange peel, grated
2 T. butter or margarine

Heat oven to 425 degrees. Prepare pastry. Stir together sugar, flour and orange peel. Combine rhubarb and strawberries in a large bowl. Mix the fruit mixture with the sugar mixture. Turn fruit into pastry-lined pie pan; dot with 2 tablespoons butter.

Crumb Topping:

1 c. unsifted all-purpose flour
1/3 c. sugar
1/2 t. cinnamon
1 t. water

1/4 t. salt
1/2 c. butter or margarine
1 T. confectioner's sugar

In medium-size bowl, make crumb topping. Combine flour, sugar, cinnamon and salt. Cut butter (or margarine) into this mixture with a pastry blender until it resembles coarse crumbs. Pat crumb topping all over pie. Cover edge with 2 to 3 inches of aluminum foil to prevent excessive browning; remove foil during last 15 minutes of baking. Bake 40 to 50 minutes or until crumb topping begins to brown. Remove from oven and cool. Before serving, combine confectioner's sugar and water to make glaze. Drizzle over pie.
Makes 8 servings. Enjoy!

Rhubarb Bread Pudding
Cheryl Ewer

I serve it warm and topped it with frozen whipped topping, ice cream or pour half & half over it.

1 1/2 c. milk	1 c. rhubarb, sliced
2 eggs, slightly beaten	1 c. sugar
4 slices of toast, cubed	1/2 t. cinnamon

Scald milk, add eggs and mix well. Add toast, rhubarb, sugar and cinnamon. Pour into buttered casserole. Bake at 350 degrees for 1 hour or until custard is set.

Karen's Fresh Fruit Freeze
Paula Griffen

Great for coffee parties, along with muffins!

6 oz. lemonade	1 or 2 bananas, sliced
6 oz. orange juice concentrate	20 oz. can tidbit pineapple
1/2 c. sugar	1 pt. fresh strawberries
3 c. water	6 to 8 oz. jar maraschino cherries
17 oz. can fruit cocktail	lemon-lime carbonated drink

Drain all fruits, use no juices. In a 13"x9" pan mix lemonade, orange juice, sugar and water. Add fruit cocktail, bananas, pineapple, and strawberries. Cut up cherries and lay on top. Freeze. Remove from freezer 20 minutes before serving. Pour lemon-lime drink over dessert. Put in sherbet dishes.

Frozen Raspberry Dessert

Sandi Stewart

I always get requests for this recipe whenever I take it to a function.
It's one of those "tastes like you fussed, but didn't" recipes that can
be made well in advance, since it's frozen and saves you from last-
minute preparation when you invite guests for dinner. I usually
double the recipe when I'm taking it to an outing so it makes one
large pan (13"x9") plus one deep dish pie size to keep in my freezer
for those times you have unexpected guests to entertain.

Crust:

1 c. sifted flour   **1/4 c. brown sugar**
1/2 c. walnuts, chopped   **1/2 c. margarine, melted**

Mix the flour, nuts, brown sugar and melted margarine together.
Press into a 2-quart oblong cake pan. Bake at 350 degrees for 15 to
20 minutes. Cool and process in food processor (half at a time) or
break into crumbs with a fork. Take out 1/3 of the crumbs and
spread the rest evenly in the pan.

Filling:

2 egg whites
3/4 c. sugar
2 T. lemon juice
2 c. fresh (or frozen) raspberries
   8 oz. container of frozen whipped topping

Beat the egg whites with mixer on high until
stiff. Then slowly add the sugar, lemon juice,
raspberries and whipped topping. Mix well.
Pour on top of crumbs. Sprinkle reserved
crumbs on top. Freeze at least 2 hours.

*Gardening all day in the hot sun
can dehydrate you...*

Independence Day Shortcake
Candy Hannigan

Since these are really just scones, you can serve leftovers with fresh jam and butter. Freeze well too!

2 c. flour
1 T. baking powder
1/2 t. salt
2 T. butter, melted
2 T. granulated sugar
1 egg
3/4 c. butter

1/2 c. plus 1 T. cream
1/4 c. sugar
strawberries and blueberries,
   about 3/4 c. per serving
whipped topping or sweetened
   whipped cream

Mix together flour, baking powder, salt and sugar. Cut in butter until fine crumbs. Mix egg and cream together. Blend into dry ingredients. Knead dough lightly on floured surface. Divide dough in half. Pat out each half to about 1/2" thick. Cut one-half with round biscuit cutter and place on greased cookie sheet. Cut other half with star cookie cutter and place on greased cookie sheet. Bake in preheated 400 degree oven for 8 to 10 minutes or until done. After 6 minutes, brush stars with melted butter and sprinkle with red tinted sugar. Continue baking until done. Wash and dry fruit, slice strawberries. Toss with 2 tablespoons sugar for each cup of fruit and chill for an hour or more. Assemble as follows (for each serving)...round scone, heaping spoon of topping or cream, 3/4 cup fruit, star scone, small blob of topping or cream, then top with a tiny American flag or whole berry. Serves 6 to 8.

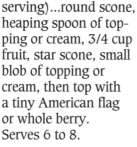

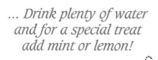
... Drink plenty of water and for a special treat add mint or lemon!

Sesame-Orange Scones

Pat Akers

What is more wonderful than a piping hot, butter-filled scone? I find these treats always a hit at brunches, bridal luncheons or baby showers. The room is always filled with ooh's and ahh's!

1/3 c. sesame seeds	1 T. baking powder
3 T. orange rind, grated	3/4 t. salt
3 c. all-purpose flour, unsifted	3/4 c. vegetable
3 T. light brown sugar	shortening
3 T. granulated sugar	1 c. orange juice

Heat oven to 425 degrees. Grease a baking sheet. Set aside 1 tablespoon sesame seeds and 1 teaspoon orange rind. In a large bowl, combine flour, remaining sesame seeds and orange rind, brown sugar, baking powder and salt. With a pastry blender or 2 knives, cut in shortening until mixture resembles coarse crumbs. Reserve 1 tablespoon orange juice. Add remaining orange juice to dry ingredients, mix lightly with fork until mixture clings together and forms a soft dough. Turn dough out onto lightly floured surface and knead gently 5 or 6 times. With lightly floured rolling pin, roll dough into a 7" round. Cut into 4 wedges. Place scones 1" apart on greased baking sheet. Pierce tops with tines of fork. In a small saucepan heat reserved orange juice and granulated sugar to boiling, stir in reserved orange rind and brush over top of scones. Sprinkle with remaining sesame seeds. Bake 15 to 18 minutes or until golden brown. Brush again with orange glaze. Serve warm. Good with orange-honey butter.

Cream Puff Cake

Sheri Berger

This is a light (but sweet) addition to the afternoon tea fare. Yummy!

8 oz. pkg. cream cheese, softened
8 oz. container frozen non-dairy
**   whipped topping, thawed**
3 (4-serving size) boxes instant
**   vanilla pudding mix**
1/2 c. (1 stick) butter

1 c. flour
4 c. milk
1 c. water
4 eggs
chocolate syrup

Pour water in saucepan and add butter. Bring to a boil. Add the flour and stir until well mixed. Remove from heat and let cool 2 minutes. Beat in eggs, one at a time, beating well after each addition. Spread mixture into a greased 13"x9" pan. Bake at 400 degrees for 30 to 35 minutes. Let cool. Combine pudding mix, cream cheese and milk and mix thoroughly. Pour into cooled crust. Cover with whipped topping and drizzle with chocolate syrup. Keep refrigerated. Yields 12 servings.

Ice Cream Cone Cupcakes

Ildiko Mulligan

These "ice cream" cones are great summer picnic or birthday treats for children, and you don't have to worry about them melting!

18.25 oz. pkg. cake mix (any flavor)
30 ice cream cones, with flat bottoms
1 can each of vanilla and chocolate frosting
red food coloring
sprinkles

Prepare cake mix batter according to directions on package. Stand cones up in a large rectangular cake pan. Fill each cone half way with batter and bake according to cupcake directions on package. Cool completely. Tint half of the vanilla frosting with red food coloring to make it pink. Cut the corner off a plastic bag and fill it with frosting. Frost the cupcakes with a swirling motion to make them look like cones filled with vanilla, chocolate, and strawberry ice cream. Decorate with sprinkles. Makes 30 delicious ice cream cone cupcakes.

Rose Petal Sorbet *Peggy Baker*

This makes a wonderful light summer dessert. You can also use 12 sprigs of lavender, 4 scented geranium leaves or a cup of violet blossoms to change the flavor. I garnish it with a blossom of the flavor I make.

1 large cup rose petals　　**scant 2 c. water**
1/2 c. fine sugar　　**zest and juice of one lemon**
1 egg white

Dissolve the sugar in water and add lemon zest. Bring to a boil stirring continuously, then simmer for 6 minutes. Add rose petals, remove from heat and cool. Strain the mixture and add the lemon juice. Freeze 2 or 3 hours until mushy, add the stiffly beaten egg white and continue to beat. A food processor works well for this. Freeze again until firm. Serves 6.

Sherbet Watermelon *Laurinda Dawson/Courtney Dawson*

This is a favorite at kids' parties! Nice to have a piece of sherbet watermelon and fresh strawberries on a hot afternoon or after a barbecue!

1/2 gal. lime sherbet　　**12 oz. pkg. semi-sweet**
1/2 gal. raspberry sherbet　　**chocolate chips**

Soften the lime sherbet and make a layer 1" thick on the bottom and sides of a medium mixing bowl. Return to freezer for 1 hour or until firm. Soften the raspberry sherbet, and stir in the chocolate chips gently. Spoon into the bowl with lime sherbet lining. Fill; smooth the top; return to the freezer. Chill 6 to 8 hours or overnight. To unmold, let the bowl sit at room temperature for 10 to 15 minutes. Loosen sides with a knife or spatula. Turn upside down onto a plate. Serve immediately. Slice pieces with a wet knife. Serves 6 to 8.

Watermelon Sorbet

Janet Mitrovich

A great tasting cool treat!

1 c. sugar
3/4 c. water
2 to 4 c. watermelon pulp,
** chopped and seeded**

1/3 c. lemon juice
a rose geranium leaf
** (or 1 t. rose water)**

Boil the water and sugar gently for 4 minutes; cool. Put pureed fruit into a stainless bowl along with cooled water mixture, lemon juice and rose geranium. Cover and freeze 4 hours. Process with whisk, freeze until mushy, about an hour. Beat again and freeze until firm. Serve.

Peppermint Ice Cream

Lauren Pineda

several sprigs of peppermint plant
vanilla ice cream
few drops of peppermint extract
smashed peppermint candies

First, get peppermint leaves. Chop the peppermint sprigs up very fine. Mix the peppermint in with the vanilla ice cream. Add a few drops of peppermint extract. Take the smashed candies and stir them in. Put the bowl in the freezer for about 1 hour.

Flowerpot Pudding

Lori Webb

This dessert gets lots of attention and is very attractive on the table. In spring you may want to use tulips; in summer, sunflowers; in fall, mums and in winter, poinsettias.

2 large pkgs. instant vanilla pudding
6 c. milk
8 oz. cream cheese*
1 c. powdered sugar
1 stick margarine
16 oz. container frozen whipped topping, thawed*
1 1/4 lb. chocolate with vanilla cream sandwich
    cookies, crushed

Prepare vanilla pudding according to instructions on box and chill. Blend cream cheese, powdered sugar and margarine with a mixer until creamy. Stir the creamed mixture into the pudding. Fold in the whipped topping. Layer crushed cookies and pudding in flowerpot, making sure you leave enough cookies to cover the top of the pudding mixture. Chill overnight. Next day, insert long stemmed silk flowers into pudding mixture along with a few (gummy worms) peeking through the "dirt" if desired. Use a hand spade for serving, after removing the flowers.

*For a lighter dessert use light cream cheese and whipped topping.

Peach Delite

Sonia Bracamonte

1 3/4 c. vanilla ice cream
2 fresh peaches, pitted and
    quartered
2 eggs (1 will work fine, but two
    eggs make it richer)

Combine the above and blend in blender at medium to high speed until smooth. Pour into 2 parfait or ice cream soda glasses.

Garden Gatherings

Start now canning jams, vinegars and drying herbs. You'll be all set and ready to give wonderful homemade gifts at Christmas!

Deb Damari-Tull

Barbecue Sauce

Mary Dechamplain

1/4 c. vinegar
1/2 c. water
2 T. brown sugar
1 T. prepared mustard
1/2 t. salt
1/4 t. cayenne pepper

1 thick slice of lemon
1 onion, peeled and sliced
1/4 c. margarine
1/2 c. ketchup
2 T. worcestershire sauce
1 1/2 t. liquid smoke

In a saucepan mix together vinegar, water, brown sugar, mustard, salt, cayenne pepper, lemon slice, onion, and margarine; simmer, uncovered, for 20 minutes. Add ketchup, worcestershire sauce and liquid smoke; bring to a boil. Makes 1 3/4 cups.

Pickled Zucchini

Pat Husek

4 medium zucchini, unpeeled
    and thinly sliced
1/2 c. onion, chopped
1/2 c. green pepper, chopped
1/2 to 3/4 c. celery, chopped
2/3 c. cider vinegar
1/2 c. sugar

1/4 c. wine rose or
    burgundy (optional)
1/4 c. salad oil
2 t. red wine vinegar
1 t. salt
1/4 t. or more pepper

Combine zucchini, onion, green pepper and celery in a bowl. Mix together the cider vinegar, sugar, oil, red wine vinegar, salt, pepper and wine. Stir well, but gently; pour over vegetables. Refrigerate. Will keep for at least two weeks in covered container.

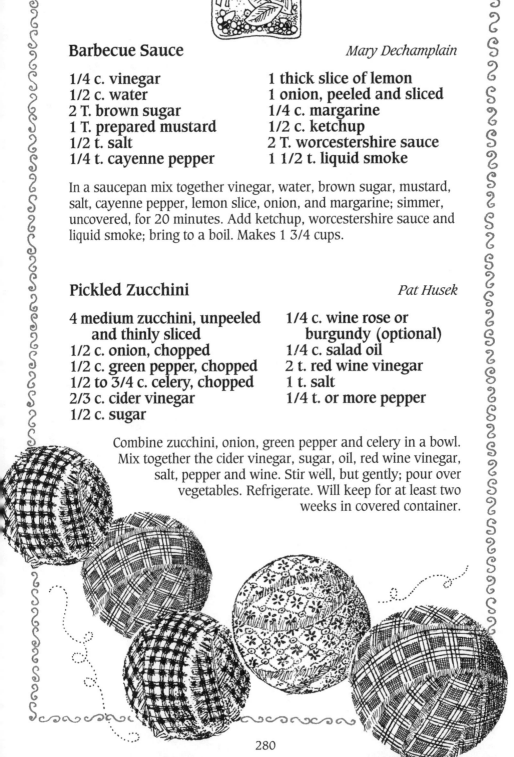

Garden Gatherings

Grandma's Piccalilli

Laurie Micarelli

A great accompaniment to pork, lamb and pot roast, or great on sandwiches with leftover meat.

22 medium-sized green tomatoes, quartered
6 red peppers, seeded and cut
6 green peppers, seeded and cut
1 pt. small yellow onions
1 1/2 qt. apple cider vinegar
3 1/2 c. sugar
1/4 c. salt
1 1/2 t. ground allspice
1 1/2 t. ground cinnamon
4 t. celery seeds
1/2 c. mustard seeds

Wash all vegetables, chop medium to fine in food processor. Drain and discard juices. Place veggies in a large kettle. Add 1 quart of vinegar. Boil 30 minutes, stirring frequently. Drain and discard liquid. Return veggies to kettle. Add remaining vinegar and sugar, salt, allspice, cinnamon, celery seed and mustard seed. Simmer 3 minutes. Continue simmering while packing into hot sterile jars (one at a time). Fill to 1/8" from top and seal. Makes 6 to 7 pints.

Olive Pesto

Jeannine English

Great on focaccia (flat, sweet pizza-type bread). Also a delicious side accompaniment with baked halibut or swordfish steaks.

3/4 c. black nicoise olives, pitted
1/2 c. fresh flat leaf parsley sprigs
1/4 c. fresh basil leaves
2 shallots
2 garlic cloves, peeled and crushed
3 T. extra-virgin olive oil
1/4 c. parmesan cheese, freshly grated

In a blender or food processor place the olives, parsley, basil, shallots and garlic. Process until finely minced. Add oil and cheese, process until blended. Transfer to a small bowl and cover. Refrigerate. Makes 1 cup.

Pesto

Pegi Stengel

Fresh jersey tomatoes and basil picked right from the garden...two reasons to wait, however impatiently, for summer! Serve this wonderful pesto over pasta, add a salad of sliced tomatoes and fresh mozzarella and a loaf of crusty French bread. What a feast!

1 c. fresh basil leaves   **1/4 c. butter, melted (microwave)**
1 big clove garlic   **1/4 c. olive oil**
1/4 c. pine nuts   **1/2 c. parmesan cheese,**
1/2 t. salt   **freshly grated**

Combine all ingredients in a food processor, whirl until combined. Will be quite thick, no need to heat, just stir it into hot pasta. Will keep, covered in the fridge, for several weeks. A great source for pine nuts is your local health food store. Take your own measuring cup and buy only what you need. Much cheaper, no waste. To toast pine nuts: put nuts in a single layer in pan in 350 degree oven. After 10 minutes, shake, then toast for 5 minutes more. Watch closely...they burn in a flash! Serves 4.

Garden Gatherings

Summer Pesto With Pecans
Eleanor Moore

2 c. fresh basil leaves, washed
   and patted dry
6 garlic cloves
1 c. parmesan cheese

1 c. pecans
1 c. olive oil
salt and pepper
   to taste

Combine in processor. Toss with cheese and tortellini (cooked, drained and cooled), green beans, or red potatoes.

Lemon Balm Pesto
Susan Mroz

2 c. fresh lemon balm
3 to 4 cloves garlic

1/2 c. olive oil

Chop and blend together lemon balm, olive oil and garlic cloves. Use as a baste for broiled or grilled fish and meats. Can be floated in hot soup; added to dressings for salad, sauces, gravies and onto all varieties of pasta. Suggested herbs for herb bastes are basil, chervil, cilantro, dill, fennel, coriander, marjoram, mints, parsley, rosemary, sage, savory and tarragon.

Make it an herbal Christmas... garlands, topiaries, live trees, fragrant wreaths, spicy pomanders, bundles of herbs, berries, dried apples, oranges, red roses, potpourris, and rich oil. Rosemary and bay are popular Christmas herbs.

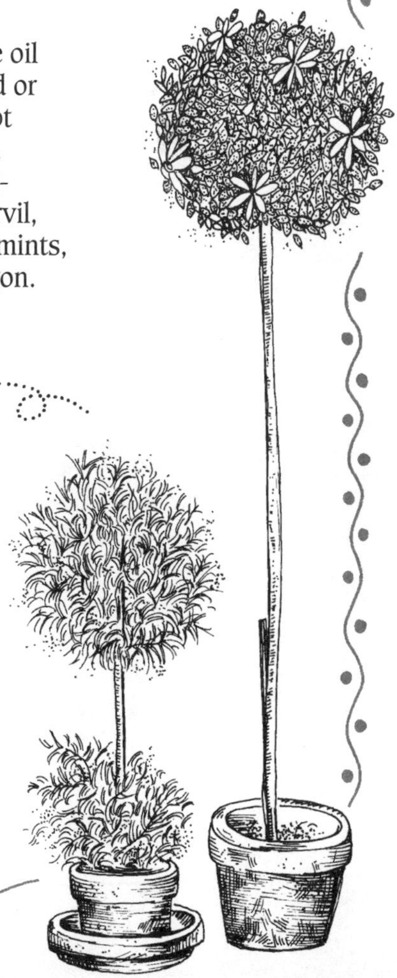

Can't Wait for
Three Days Salsa

Mary Alice Feucht-Foster

My home town, Reynoldsburg, Ohio, is the "Birthplace of the Tomato," so this recipe more or less honors it. This salsa is not for the timid. It is a very flavorable HOT salsa, and I guarantee you that it is the best you will ever eat. I have named it "Can't Wait for Three Days Salsa," as I have never yet been able to wait for three days before I started dipping in and enjoying it!

4 lb. ripe, roma tomatoes	2 T. ground cumin
2 large onions, chopped	2 T. dried parsley
2 cloves garlic, cleaned and minced	1 T. salt
8 oz. jar jalapeno peppers	1 T. vegetable oil
2 T. dried cilantro	1 T. cider vinegar
1 t. black pepper	

Tomatoes should be scalded, peeled and chunked. Chop jalapeno peppers, remove seeds and stems. Mix all ingredients together. Place in a stainless steel, or glass bowl and cover. Refrigerate for three days so flavors will blend. Be sure to use roma tomatoes, as they are less juicy. You do not cook this salsa.

Fresh Berry Syrup

Laura Hodges

Fresh berries from the garden (or supermarket) make a wonderful syrup for pancakes, waffles, or French toast. I discovered this recipe, one morning when my husband was complaining about the seeds in raspberries hurting his sensitive teeth. Now he enjoys the taste he loves, without the seeds.

1 c. raspberries or blackberries	1/4 c. sugar*
2 c. water	

Place all ingredients in a small saucepan and bring to a boil, simmer for about 5 minutes, stirring often. Pour through a strainer directly onto pancakes or whatever you like. This tastes wonderful and is quick and easy. Remaining syrup can be kept in the refrigerator for several weeks. Enjoy!

*Or more depending on the tartness of the berries.

Herbal Dressing

Marlene Wetzel-Dellagatta

1/2 t. black pepper, freshly ground
1/2 t. fresh chives, finely chopped
1/2 t. fresh parsley, finely chopped
1/2 t. fresh tarragon, finely chopped
1 clove garlic, finely minced (optional)

10 T. olive oil
3 T. wine vinegar
1 t. dijon mustard
1/2 t. salt

Place all ingredients together. Blend with wire whisk.

Green Tomato Relish

Betzie Smith

15 to 20 medium green tomatoes
24 onions
salt
2 T. turmeric
6 T. mustard seed
12 green peppers

12 red peppers
white vinegar
2 T. allspice

Slice tomatoes. Cover with salt. Allow to stand over-night. Grind onions, green peppers and red peppers. Drain salt off tomatoes. Pour cold water over them. Dip tomatoes out of water using a strainer. Add to onions and peppers. Barely cover with white vinegar. Add turmeric, all-spice and mustard seed. Cook 20 min-utes. Pack in hot sterilized jars.

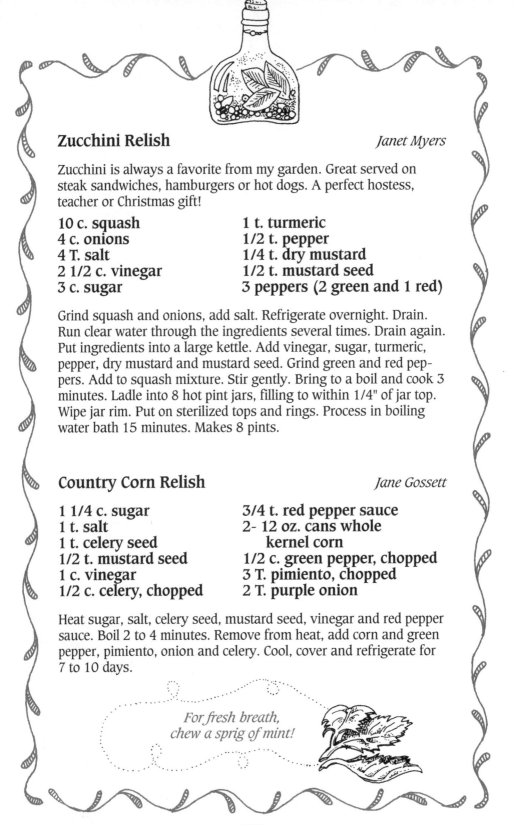

Zucchini Relish

Janet Myers

Zucchini is always a favorite from my garden. Great served on steak sandwiches, hamburgers or hot dogs. A perfect hostess, teacher or Christmas gift!

10 c. squash	1 t. turmeric
4 c. onions	1/2 t. pepper
4 T. salt	1/4 t. dry mustard
2 1/2 c. vinegar	1/2 t. mustard seed
3 c. sugar	3 peppers (2 green and 1 red)

Grind squash and onions, add salt. Refrigerate overnight. Drain. Run clear water through the ingredients several times. Drain again. Put ingredients into a large kettle. Add vinegar, sugar, turmeric, pepper, dry mustard and mustard seed. Grind green and red peppers. Add to squash mixture. Stir gently. Bring to a boil and cook 3 minutes. Ladle into 8 hot pint jars, filling to within 1/4" of jar top. Wipe jar rim. Put on sterilized tops and rings. Process in boiling water bath 15 minutes. Makes 8 pints.

Country Corn Relish

Jane Gossett

1 1/4 c. sugar	3/4 t. red pepper sauce
1 t. salt	2- 12 oz. cans whole
1 t. celery seed	kernel corn
1/2 t. mustard seed	1/2 c. green pepper, chopped
1 c. vinegar	3 T. pimiento, chopped
1/2 c. celery, chopped	2 T. purple onion

Heat sugar, salt, celery seed, mustard seed, vinegar and red pepper sauce. Boil 2 to 4 minutes. Remove from heat, add corn and green pepper, pimiento, onion and celery. Cool, cover and refrigerate for 7 to 10 days.

*For fresh breath,
chew a sprig of mint!*

Sun-Dried Tomatoes

Erin Clary

Make great gifts. Great served over rice with steamed peppers and sausages, or over spaghetti or cold pasta salad.

tomatoes
olive oil

rosemary

Slice tomatoes approximately 1/4" thick; place in a dehydrator to dry. After the drying process is complete, place in a well-sealed, decorative jar (stuffed full) and fill with olive oil and sprigs of rosemary.

Fresh Tomato Salsa

Karen Wald

Delicious, tastes like summer!

1/2 c. green bell pepper, chopped
1/2 c. fresh cilantro, chopped
2 medium tomatoes, seeded, chopped (2 c.)
1 jalapeno pepper, seeded, chopped (2 T.)
1/2 c. onion, chopped
1 T. lime juice
2 T. lemon juice

In small non-metal bowl, combine all ingredients; mix well. Cover, refrigerate 1 to 2 hours to blend flavors. Store covered in refrigerator up to 5 days. Serve tortilla chips.

Chili Sauce

Mickey Johnson

For all gardeners who have an abundance of tomatoes. Makes a great Christmas gift!

20 ripe tomatoes	**2 c. vinegar**
3 large onions	**3 T. salt**
2 green peppers	**1 t. allspice**
1 c. sugar	**1 t. cloves**
1 t. cinnamon	

Put tomatoes, onions and peppers through food chopper, using coarse blade. Add sugar, vinegar, salt, allspice, cloves and cinnamon and simmer slowly for an hour. Pour into sterilized jars and seal. (To sterilize jars and jar lids, put in water and boil for 10 minutes.) Yields 5 to 6 pints or about 3 quarts. Always let the jars cool and make sure lids have popped down.

Dilly Beans

Judy Hand

These beans are so good that friends have often sat and munched on them as a late evening snack. A nice garnish for sandwiches too!

2 lb. fresh, tender green beans	**2 t. mustard seed**
cayenne pepper	**2 1/2 c. white vinegar**
4 cloves garlic, peeled	**2 1/2 c. water**
4 heads fresh dill or 2 t. dill weed	**1/4 c. canning salt**

Wash tender beans, string if not using stringless variety. Leave beans whole, trimming to fit jar, if necessary; pack lengthwise into hot sterilized pint jars. In each pint jar, add one dash cayenne pepper, one clove garlic, one head dill, and 1/2 teaspoon mustard seed. Combine the vinegar, water and salt in a saucepan; bring to a boil. Pour this over the beans, filling to within 1/2" of the top. Seal immediately. Process in hot water bath for 10 minutes. Beans should stand in sealed jars at least 2 weeks before serving.

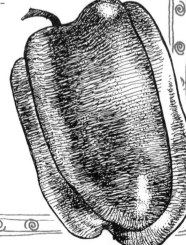

Garden Gatherings

Pumpkin Seeds
Tori Jones

pumpkin seeds **1 T. oil**

Whenever you clean out a pumpkin, remove the seeds and wash them thoroughly. Let them dry for about a day on paper towels. Pour oil in a bowl, add the dried seeds and toss until well coated. Spread them out on an ungreased cookie sheet and bake at 350 degrees for 1/2 to 1 hour. Stir every 10 to 15 minutes while baking. If desired, lightly salt.

Sunflower Seeds
Geraldine Knatz

sunflower seeds **1 t. salt**
1 qt. water

After sunflowers die, put a plastic bag loosely over the flower (so birds don't get the seeds). When seeds are brown, cut head off plant. Extract seeds and soak in saltwater for 30 minutes. Dry seeds on paper towels and spread on cookie sheet. Bake at 225 degrees for 30 minutes, then at 350 degrees for 15 minutes. Cool and store in a tightly covered container. Ideal for snacking!

Pickled Beets
Mickey Johnson

A great addition to your Thanksgiving or Christmas dinners. Also makes a great Christmas gift.

2 qt. beets, prepared as directed **2 c. vinegar**
2 c. sugar **2 t. salt, if desired**
2 c. water

Boil beets until tender, dip into cold water, peel and slice. Combine sugar, water, vinegar, salt and bring to boil. Add beets and bring to boil again, about 5 minutes. Fill sterilized jars and seal. (To sterilize jars and jar lids, put in water and boil for 10 minutes). Yields 5 to 6 pints or 3 quarts.

Bread & Butter Pickles

Pat Husek

1 gal. cucumbers, sliced
8 medium onions, sliced
2 lb. sweet peppers, strips
1/2 c. coarse salt
5 c. sugar

5 c. vinegar
2 T. mustard seed
1 t. turmeric
1 t. whole cloves

Slice cucumbers thin leaving peel on. Slice onions into thin slices and peppers into strips. Dissolve salt in water and pour over sliced vegetables to cover. Pour extra ice on top of cucumbers. Let stand 2 to 3 hours. Drain. Combine vinegar, sugar and spices and bring to boil. Add drained vegetables and heat to boiling point (do not boil). Seal in sterilized jars.

Melon with Lavender Syrup

Maureen Sanchirico

Delicious in morning as well as after dinner.

1/2 c. sugar
1/2 c. water
1/4 c. sweet dessert
 wine
2 T. orange juice
1/4 c. lavender flowers,
 fresh or dried
1 large ripe melon,
 cut into cubes

Bring water, sugar, wine and orange juice to a boil. Reduce heat and simmer 5 minutes, stirring to dissolve sugar. Add flowers. Cover and steep 1 hour. Strain flowers. To serve, pour syrup over melon. Garnish with mint leaves. Serves 4.

Rose Geranium Jelly
Tamara Gruber

2 1/8 c. of white Zinfandel wine
10 to 12 large rose
   geranium leaves
3 oz. liquid fruit pectin

3 T. lemon juice,
   freshly squeezed
3 c. sugar
2 T. rose water

Remove stems from UNSPRAYED geranium leaves. Place wine and roses in a sterilized quart jar. Cover jar with plastic wrap and top with lid. Refrigerate for several days until wine has captured the delightful rose geranium flavor. Strain leaves from wine, discarding spent leaves. Measure 2 cups wine. Any leftover wine becomes the cook's treat!

Place wine in a 3 to 4 quart non-reactive saucepan with 3 cups sugar and 3 tablespoons freshly squeezed lemon juice. Stir to dissolve sugar. Bring mixture to a boil over medium heat stirring constantly until mixture reaches a full rolling boil that cannot be stirred down. Remove pan briefly from heat and add 3 ounces liquid fruit pectin (there are two 3 oz. packets of liquid pectin in each box, use only 1).

Return to heat and when mixture comes back to a full rolling boil, boil hard for 1 minute stirring constantly. A few seconds before minute is up, add 2 generous tablespoons of rose water. Remove from heat and stir and skim if necessary for about 5 minutes. Place 1 washed and dried rose geranium leaf in each of four 8-ounce canning jars that have been sterilized according to safe canning directions. Jars should be very hot and dry.

Pour in jelly to about 1/4" from top of jar. Use a sterilized non-reactive table knife to release air bubbles. Wipe tops of jars clean and put on clean sterilized tops and rings. Screw lids down and process jars in a boiling water bath for 10 minutes. Check with your County Extension agent before making jelly, or consult a canning and preserving manual if this is your first try. Remove jars from boiling bath to racks to cool. Check the next day to be sure jars are properly sealed. Makes four 1/2-pint jars.

Earth laughs in flowers.
Ralph Waldo Emerson

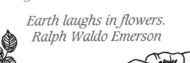

Rose Geranium Honey

Tamara Gruber

Heat a jar (your choice of size) of honey by pouring honey into a non-reactive saucepan. A mild clover honey works best. Add as many clean dry geranium rose leaves as mixture will comfortably hold and place pan over medium heat. When mixture starts to bubble, turn down heat and allow mixture to cook gently (no boiling) for a half hour or so. Pour mixture into a large sterile jar that will just hold leaves and honey. Set aside for a week or two. Taste!

Violet Jelly

Cora Baker

I really love this jelly. It tastes wonderful and looks like a little jewel on a plate with muffins or scones. It is a beautiful violet color. I put it in pretty little jars and give it as gifts.

1 qt. violet blossoms　　　**1 3/4 oz. pkg. fruit pectin**
boiling water　　　　　　**4 c. sugar**
juice of one lemon　　　　**1/2 t. margarine or butter**

Fill a quart jar with violet blossoms and cover with boiling water. Steep for 24 hours; strain. To 2 cups of this strained liquid, add the juice of one lemon and the fruit pectin. Bring to a boil. Add sugar and the margarine or butter (this will keep it from boiling over and will eliminate foaming on top). Bring to a full rolling boil and boil for 1 minute. Ladle into sterilized jars and seal with paraffin or freeze. Makes 5 cups.

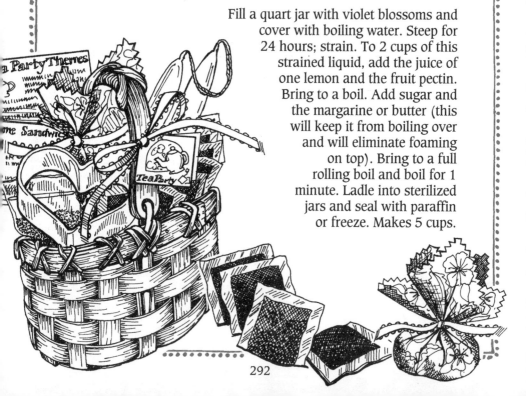

Rose-Petal Honey

Edwina Gadsby

This is absolutely delightful spread on fresh hot scones and served with afternoon tea. When you take a taste of this rose-petal honey, you won't believe how simple it is to prepare. It makes a lovely gift.

**1/4 c. fragrant rose petals, pesticide-free, of course
1 c. mild-flavored honey**

Carefully wash rose petals and let dry. Place them in an 8-ounce sterilized glass jelly jar. Gently heat honey until warm; pour over the rose petals. Seal jars. Delicately shake jar to distribute the rose petals. Keep in a cool, dark place for at least 48 hours to give the rose petals time to permeate the honey. Makes 1 cup.

Fresh Basil Dressing

Joan Brochu

Bottle and don't refrigerate. Excellent on fresh garden tomatoes or tossed salad.

**1/2 c. wine vinegar
1 1/4 t. sugar
salt**

**pepper
1 c. olive oil
6 T. fresh basil leaves, minced**

Citrus-Spice Marinade

Lisa Prichard

Marinate a 1 1/2 pound flank steak in this citrus-spice marinade and grill with your veggies.

**1 c. orange juice
1/3 c. lemon juice
1/4 c. cooking oil
3 T. worcestershire sauce
1/2 t. pepper**

**3 cloves garlic, minced
1 t. ground cumin
3/4 t. onion powder
1/2 t. salt**

Walk barefoot through your garden!

Hot Peach Jam

Sonia Bracamonte

Delicious on crackers with creamed cheese, as an ice cream topping and glaze for baked ham!

1 1/2 c. cider vinegar	6 c. sugar
1/4 c. jalapeno pepper, quartered*	1 t. allspice
9 fresh peaches, finely chopped (approx. 5 c.)	2 pouches (6 oz.) liquid pectin
1 t. celery seed	

Combine vinegar and pepper in blender. Process in stop-and-go fashion to desired fineness. Combine with peaches, sugar, celery seed and allspice in large pot (not aluminum) and bring to a boil. Reduce heat and simmer 50 minutes, stirring often. Let cool 2 minutes, then add pectin. Ladle into jars, leaving 1/2" space at top of jar. Adjust caps and process 15 minutes in boiling water bath. Cool.

*Or other fresh green chili pepper

Zucchini Jam

Sheryl Esau

My sister and I have a craft and bake sale every year. This jam has become a hit! It is always sold out within the first hour of the sale.

6 c. raw zucchini, peeled and ground
6 c. sugar
1/2 c. lemon juice (can use reconstituted)
1 c. crushed pineapple and juice
6 oz. pkg. orange gelatin

Drain zucchini; then boil until clear (6 minutes). Add sugar, lemon juice, pineapple and juice. Boil 6 minutes. Remove from heat and add orange gelatin. Stir until dissolved. Seal in clean jars. This a good way to use up any zucchini and the jam is a favorite.

*A man of words and not of deeds
Is like a garden full of weeds.
Anonymous*

Rhubarb-Blueberry Jam

Cheryl Ewer

6 c. rhubarb, cut up
3/4 c. water
4 c. sugar

1 large can blueberry pie filling
2- 3 oz. pkgs. raspberry gelatin

Cook rhubarb in boiling water until tender. Add sugar and boil about 5 minutes. Add blueberry pie filling. Cook for 5 to 8 minutes longer. Stir in 2 packages gelatin and cook about 5 minutes longer. Put in clean, dry jars and seal. Makes approximately four 1/2-pints. Works well with cherry pie filling also.

Layered Jam

Yvonne Bendler

You CAN have your cake and eat it too! You can also have two kinds of jam layered in the same jar. Make sure that you put this jam in clear glass containers so that you can see the layers. It's a pretty gift from your kitchen for the holidays. Use different fruits. Strawberry and kiwi looks very Christmasy. When making jam from kiwis you may have to add a few drops of green food coloring as the kiwi loses color when it's cooked. You can freeze whole strawberries and skinned sliced peaches on a foil-covered baking sheet. When frozen just pop them into a freezer bag. They will not stick together and you have the ability to remove the amount needed.

Radish Jelly

Marie Alana Gardner

Serve with cream cheese and crackers.

2 c. radishes, finely chopped
2 1/2 c. granulated sugar
2 t. prepared horseradish

3/4 c. water
1 3/4 oz. pkg. pectin

In a large stock pot combine radishes, sugar and water over medium-high heat, stir constantly until sugar dissolves. Bring to a rolling boil. Add pectin; stir until dissolved. Bring to a rolling boil again and boil 1 minute longer. Remove from heat and skim off foam. Stir in horseradish. Pour into sterilized jars and seal. Store in refrigerator. Yields about 2 pints.

Red Pepper Jam

Janet Myers

A nice hostess gift at Christmas time. A jar of red pepper jam will make an unusual, festive and delicious Christmas hors d'oeuvre! Just spoon some of the jam (never the whole jar) over an 8-ounce package of cream cheese and serve with crackers or melba toast. I make it during the summer months and have it on hand for Christmas giving.

12 red peppers
1 T. salt
slices of onion

2 c. white vinegar
3 c. sugar

Remove seeds and membranes from peppers. Put peppers and onion through food grinder. Sprinkle with salt and let stand 3 hours. Drain very well. Add vinegar and sugar and cook slowly (approximately 1 1/2 to 2 hours), until thickened as for jam. Pour mixture into clean, hot 1/2-pint jars and process for 10 to 15 minutes in boiling water canner. Makes six 1/2-pint jars.

*Plant thyme between stones in your walkway
and you'll smell a wonderful fragrance every time
you take a step or pass by.*

Garden Gatherings

Herbal Spiced Cider Mix

Jan Jacobson

1/4 t. cardamom seeds	1/2 T. dried lemon balm, chopped
1 t. whole allspice	3 T. dried orange mint, chopped
1 t. whole cloves	1 t. dried lemon verbena, chopped
1 stick cinnamon	2 t. dried lemon basil, chopped

Mix all together in a bowl. Place in a baggie and tie shut with a ribbon. Make a sticker with the directions of how to prepare, and attach to bag; or put directions on a little card, punch a hole in the corner of the card and tie on with the ribbon.

DIRECTIONS: Add contents to 1/2 gallon apple cider, cranberry juice or red wine. Bring to a simmer and let simmer for 10 minutes. Remove from heat, cover and steep 20 to 30 minutes. Strain and serve.

Vegetable Relish

Kim Burns
Gooseberry Patch

This makes a nice, quick Christmas gift. Everyone enjoys home-made goodies!

6 large onions (4 c.)	6 c. sugar
12 green peppers (5 c.)	2 T. mustard seed
1 medium head cabbage (4 c.)	1 T. celery seed
6 sweet red peppers (1 1/4 c.)	1 1/2 t. turmeric
10 green tomatoes (4 c.)	4 c. cider vinegar
1/2 c. granulated pickling salt	2 c. water

Wash onions, peppers, cabbage and tomatoes, and then grind using a coarse blade. Sprinkle with pickling salt and let stand overnight. Rinse and drain. Combine sugar, mustard seed, celery seed, turmeric, cider vinegar and water. Pour over vegetables. Bring to a boil, and let boil gently for 5 minutes. Fill hot jars within 1/2" of tops. Process in boiling water bath for 5 minutes. Start timing when water returns to a boil. Makes approximately 6 to 7 quarts.

Herb Bouquets
(for the cook)

Judy Hand

1/2 c. dried parsley flakes
2 T. dried rosemary leaves
1/4 c. dried thyme leaves
2 T. dried marjoram leaves
1/4 c. dried celery leaves
double-thickness cheesecloth
5 medium dried bay leaves, crushed

In a small bowl, stir herbs together until
well mixed. Cut 16- 4" squares of cheesecloth.
Place 1 level tablespoon of herbal mixture in
the center of each square. Bring corners together and tie with string to make a bag. Store in
airtight container in a cool, dark place. Use
the bouquet garnis or bundle of mixed
herbs to flavor stock for soups or
sauces. Use 1 herb bouquet bag
per quart of stock. After simmering desired time, remove
prior to serving.

Freezer Strawberry Preserves

Glenda Nations

This is a great spread on toast, homemade bread, or as an ice
cream topping!

2 1/2 c. fresh strawberries
3 c. sugar
4 t. lemon juice

1 3/4 oz. pkg.
powdered pectin
3/4 c. water

Add lemon juice and sugar to strawberries. Mix and let set 20 minutes, stirring occasionally to make certain all sugar is dissolved.
Mix water and pectin and boil for 1 minute, stirring constantly.
Slowly pour hot pectin into the berries, stirring all the while and
continue to stir for 2 or 3 minutes. Pour into containers. Cover and
allow to remain at room temperature until set. Store in freezer or
refrigerator. Makes 5 to 6 1/2-pint containers.

Herb Salt

Susan Mroz

A recipe for dried herbs. This herb salt is a concentrated melange of flavors and is good on any dish that requires several herbs.

1 c. sea salt	2 T. mint
2 T. rosemary	2 T. tarragon
2 T. thyme	2 T. dill weed
2 T. lemon balm	2 T. paprika
4 T. parsley	4 T. basil

Place ingredients in a medium-sized bowl and mix well. Blend in batches, in a blender or food processor. Store in a glass container or decorative shakers.

Whipped Herb Butter

Rhonda Harrison

This butter is wonderful brushed over hot corn-on-the-cob or grilled vegetables. Melt some in a skillet and sauté fresh shrimp for a speedy appetizer or light entree. Spread some on sliced bread, sprinkle with parmesan and broil for the best garlic toast imaginable. The possibilities are endless once you get started.

1 c. butter or margarine, softened	1/4 t. garlic powder
1 t. dried marjoram	1/4 t. sage
1 t. thyme leaves	1/4 t. basil
1 t. rosemary leaves	

Beat all ingredients together at high speed in a small mixer bowl until fluffy. Store covered in refrigerator.

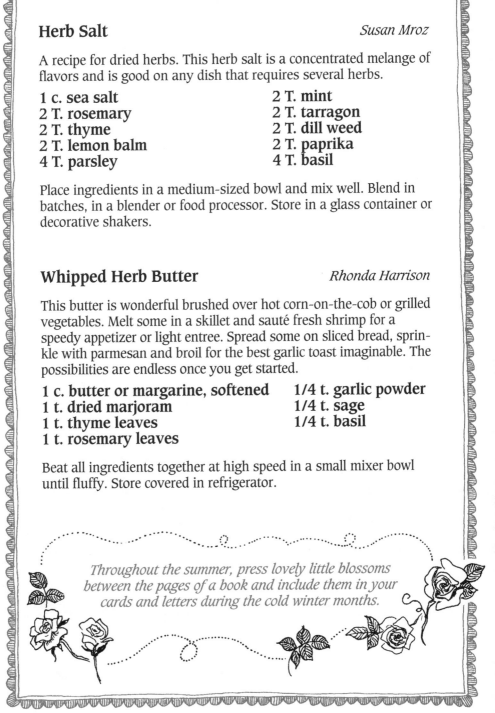

Throughout the summer, press lovely little blossoms between the pages of a book and include them in your cards and letters during the cold winter months.

Cheddar Herb Butter
Mary Ann Riehl

1/2 c. butter
1/2 c. sharp cheddar cheese
2 T. fresh chives, chopped

1/4 t. garlic powder or fresh
  garlic (adjust to taste)
3 dashes hot pepper sauce

Combine all ingredients. Let stand 1 to 2 hours. Use on baked potatoes and hot bread. Add other herbs if you wish.

Flower Butter
Tammy Anundson

Use flower butter as a spread, or as a substitute in your favorite sugar cookie or pound cake recipe.

1/2 c. edible flowers

1/2 lb. sweet unsalted butter

Finely chop flower petals and mix into soft butter. Put in a glass bowl and cover with plastic wrap. Let mixture sit at room temperature for several hours, then shape into mold and refrigerate for several days to bring out the flavor. Flower butter may be kept refrigerated for 2 weeks or frozen for up to 6 months.

Herb Salt Substitutes
Deborah Biondo

For those of us watching our salt intake, either of these recipes adds a zing that plain salt doesn't. Great on noodles, baked potatoes and toasted French bread.

Recipe 1:

5 t. onion powder
1 T. garlic powder
1 T. paprika
1 T. dry mustard

1 t. thyme
1/2 t. celery seed
1/2 t. cayenne pepper

Recipe 2:

1 T. garlic powder
5 t. onion powder
1 t. parsley

1 t. basil
1 t. oregano

Garden Gatherings

Herb Spread

Mary Ann Riehl

3/4 c. mayonnaise or lowfat yogurt
1/2 to 3/4 c. parmesan or
    asiago cheese
2 t. worcestershire sauce

2 T. fresh chives
1 T. fresh oregano
garlic to taste

Mix all ingredients together. You can spread on bread and bake.
It makes a wonderful topping. Use on baked potatoes. Sometimes
I vary the herbs. If I'm serving fish, I might use dill or fennel in-
stead of oregano, or I use rosemary if serving chicken.

Barbecue Brush-On Butters

Vicki Hockenberry

Brush on foods (red meats, fish, poultry and vegetables) before and
during cooking. Flavor 1/2 cup softened butter with one of the following. Makes 1/2 cup.

Cajun (serve on poultry):

1/2 t. oregano, crushed
1/8 t. thyme, crushed

1/4 t. cumin, ground
dash of red pepper

Lemon Basil (serve with veggies, fish or meat):

1/2 t. lemon peel, finely shredded
1/2 t. lemon juice

1/4 t. basil, crushed

Parmesan Butter (serve on veggies):

1 T. grated parmesan cheese
1 small clove garlic, minced

2 t. parsley

Garlic Butter (serve on veggies and red meat):

1 t. garlic powder

1/4 t. paprika

Tarragon-Onion (serve on veggies and red meat):

2 T. green onion, finely chopped
1/2 t. dried tarragon, crushed

2 T. snipped parsley

Lavender Cream

Elizabeth Timmins
Gooseberry Patch Artisan

Pour whipping cream over fresh cut lavender flowers and leave overnight. Next day remove lavender and whip cream...wonderful on fruit salad or use to frost a cake.

Candied Violets

Juanita Williams

Candied violets are great on top of chocolate cake. Can be used to decorate with for a garden party or summer wedding shower. These delicate edible confections can be used as decorations on cakes or simply put out for nibblers on a glass plate. Both scent and flavor are exotic.

1 egg white   **granulated sugar**
perfect violets and their leaves

Whip egg white until it is frothy but does not stand in peaks. Gather perfect violets and their leaves; wash them gently and quickly in cold water and drip dry. When dry, dip each violet or leaf in the egg white and roll it quickly in granulated sugar to coat evenly, taking care not to get the sugar too thick. Lay out on waxed paper to dry well separated. In several hours or a day, the blossoms will be quite crisp and can keep for several months without losing fragrance or flavor. Store in airtight tin, layered between waxed paper. Makes dozens.
Variation: You can make candied mint leaves using fresh mint and follow same procedure as above.

Lavender Sugar

Elizabeth Timmins
Gooseberry Patch Artisan

In a food processor finely chop 2 tablespoons dried lavender flowers. Add 1 cup of sugar. Blend. Store in an airtight container.
A nice addition to your next tea party.

Southwestern-Style Butter
Peggy King

3/4 c. fresh cilantro leaves,
    packed
1 1/2 T. fresh jalapeno pepper,
    chopped
1 T. lime juice
1 t. lime peel, grated
1 stick butter
1/4 t. salt
1/8 t. ground red pepper

Using a food processor, finely chop cilantro, jalapeno pepper and lime peel. Add butter, lime juice, salt and red pepper; combine well. Simmer in a saucepan for 2 minutes. Use as a baste.

Quick and Easy Fresh Fruit Butter
Dottie Dobbert

1 stick unsalted butter, room temperature
1 c. confectioner's sugar
1 to 2 c. fruit or berries, cut-up

In food processor, process butter and sugar until well blended. Add fruit and process until well blended. Wonderful served with pancakes, waffles, French toast, scones, etc. Keeps in refrigerator for about 1 week. Freezes well. Use margarine containers to freeze. If frozen, let stand at room temperature for 2 hours before serving.

Lemon-Basil Butter
Marie Alana Gardner

Serve with meat, poultry, fish or vegetables.

1/4 c. margarine or
    butter, softened
1/2 t. lemon peel,
    finely shredded
1/2 t. lemon juice
1/4 t. dried basil,
    crushed

Combine all ingredients.

Flower Sugar

Tammy Anundson

Flower sugar is an elegant topping, lightly sprinkled over fruit or sorbet.

2 c. granulated sugar   1 c. flower petals, minced

Pound sugar and minced petals in a mortar, or process them well in a food processor. Put into a clean glass jar, cover, and let stand for one week. Sift, if desired, and store in an airtight container. Makes 2 1/2 cups.

Rose Geranium Sugar

Diane Michaels

This sugar has a wonderful aroma and tastes lovely in tea.

small jar (4 to 6 oz.) with lid
white sugar
4 to 5 small to medium rose geranium leaves

Snip leaves and wash gently. Dry with paper towel. Rub each leaf to stir up rose scent. Place one leaf on bottom of jar, add a tablespoon of sugar. Repeat layering until jar is full. Let sugar stand 1 to 2 weeks.

Sugared Fruit, Flowers and Leaves

Tammy Anundson

Sugared fruits give an elegant and summery look to ice creams and sorbets.

1 egg white, beat lightly
1 c. super-fine sugar
whole fruits with stems, rinsed and dried
flowers or leaves, rinsed and dried

In a small bowl, using a fork lightly beat egg white until smooth and frothy. Holding by stem or inserting fork into fruit, dip fruit, flowers or leaves in egg whites. Or use a small brush to coat all surfaces evenly. Brush off excess. Coat evenly with sugar. Dry on a sugar surface for 30 minutes or until sugar forms a crisp, dry coating.

Herb Garden Mix

Elizabeth Timmins
Gooseberry Patch Artisan

1/2 c. parsley, dried
1 c. chervil, dried

1/2 c. chives, dried
1/2 c. tarragon, dried

Makes 3 cups. Store in an airtight container away from light.

Herb Butter

Elizabeth Timmins
Gooseberry Patch Artisan

1 lb. butter, softened
1 1/2 T. Herb Garden Mix (above)

Mix together until well-blended. Store in refrigerator overnight for flavors to blend. Great on hot vegetables or broiled fish, steak or poultry. Use fat-free margarine in place of butter for a fat-free spread.

Garden Cheese Spread

Elizabeth Timmins
Gooseberry Patch Artisan

1/2 c. butter, softened
16 oz. cream cheese, softened

3 T. Herb Garden Mix

Combine softened butter and cream cheese well. Add herbs and blend. Serve in crocks or lined clay pots with fresh herbs or edible flowers as a garnish. Great on crackers, with bread sticks or on raw veggies.

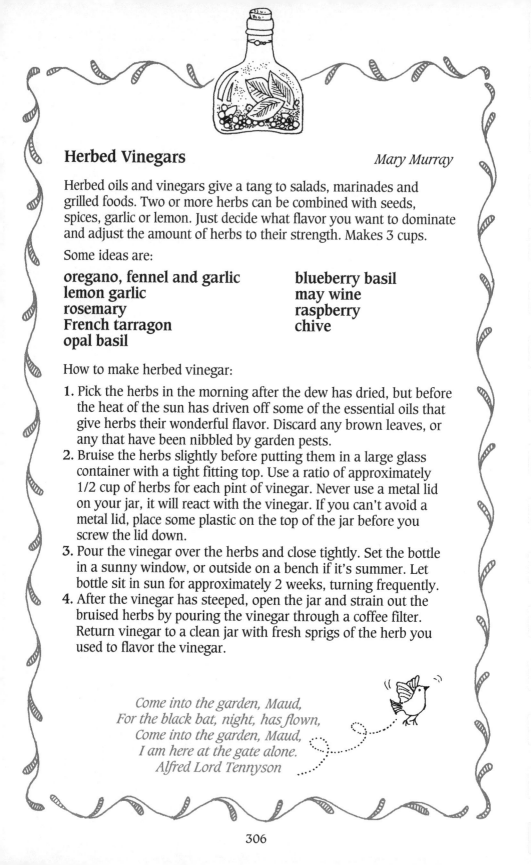

Herbed Vinegars

Mary Murray

Herbed oils and vinegars give a tang to salads, marinades and grilled foods. Two or more herbs can be combined with seeds, spices, garlic or lemon. Just decide what flavor you want to dominate and adjust the amount of herbs to their strength. Makes 3 cups.

Some ideas are:

oregano, fennel and garlic   **blueberry basil**
lemon garlic   **may wine**
rosemary   **raspberry**
French tarragon   **chive**
opal basil

How to make herbed vinegar:

1. Pick the herbs in the morning after the dew has dried, but before the heat of the sun has driven off some of the essential oils that give herbs their wonderful flavor. Discard any brown leaves, or any that have been nibbled by garden pests.
2. Bruise the herbs slightly before putting them in a large glass container with a tight fitting top. Use a ratio of approximately 1/2 cup of herbs for each pint of vinegar. Never use a metal lid on your jar, it will react with the vinegar. If you can't avoid a metal lid, place some plastic on the top of the jar before you screw the lid down.
3. Pour the vinegar over the herbs and close tightly. Set the bottle in a sunny window, or outside on a bench if it's summer. Let bottle sit in sun for approximately 2 weeks, turning frequently.
4. After the vinegar has steeped, open the jar and strain out the bruised herbs by pouring the vinegar through a coffee filter. Return vinegar to a clean jar with fresh sprigs of the herb you used to flavor the vinegar.

Come into the garden, Maud,
For the black bat, night, has flown,
Come into the garden, Maud,
I am here at the gate alone.
Alfred Lord Tennyson

Rose Petal Vinegar
Marlene Wetzel-Dellagatta

3 c. white wine vinegar
1 rose bud (to place in bottle)
5 c. rose petals, lightly crushed*

Add the vinegar to the crushed rose petals. Place in a glass jar or crock and cover. Place in cool place for 4 weeks. Taste occasionally to check the vinegar flavor. When ready, use a coffee filter or several layers of cheesecloth to strain the mixture. Place the rose bud into a bottle. Bottle and cork the rose-flavored vinegar, then store in a cool dark place. Makes 4 cups.

*Use roses free of any pesticide, do not use roses from florist.

Fruit Vinegar
Marlene Wetzel-Dellagatta

4 c. fruit, chopped   **2 c. vinegar**

Pour vinegar over the chopped fruit, that has been put into a glass jar or crock. Vinegar should cover the fruit, if not add more if needed. Place fruit mixture, covered, in a cool place or refrigerate 2 to 10 days. Taste occasionally to check the vinegar's flavor. When ready, use a coffee filter or several layers of cheesecloth to strain the mixture. Bottle and cork the flavored vinegar, then store in a cool dark place.

Fruits that can be used: Apricots, peaches, nectarines (remove pits); cover with apple cider vinegar.
Lemons, limes, oranges (use juice and zest of 5 fruits); cover with white wine vinegar.
Blackberry, raspberry, cranberry, blueberry; cover with white wine vinegar.

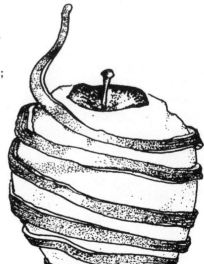

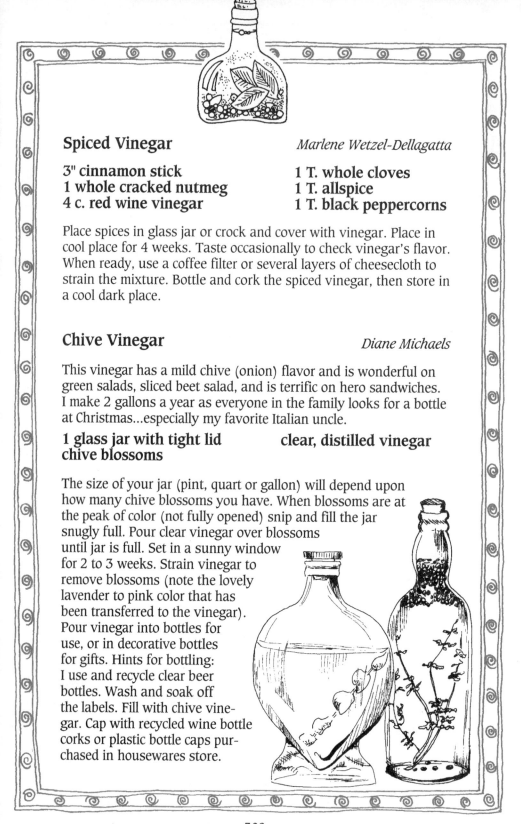

Spiced Vinegar

Marlene Wetzel-Dellagatta

3" cinnamon stick
1 whole cracked nutmeg
4 c. red wine vinegar

1 T. whole cloves
1 T. allspice
1 T. black peppercorns

Place spices in glass jar or crock and cover with vinegar. Place in cool place for 4 weeks. Taste occasionally to check vinegar's flavor. When ready, use a coffee filter or several layers of cheesecloth to strain the mixture. Bottle and cork the spiced vinegar, then store in a cool dark place.

Chive Vinegar

Diane Michaels

This vinegar has a mild chive (onion) flavor and is wonderful on green salads, sliced beet salad, and is terrific on hero sandwiches. I make 2 gallons a year as everyone in the family looks for a bottle at Christmas...especially my favorite Italian uncle.

1 glass jar with tight lid   **clear, distilled vinegar**
chive blossoms

The size of your jar (pint, quart or gallon) will depend upon how many chive blossoms you have. When blossoms are at the peak of color (not fully opened) snip and fill the jar snugly full. Pour clear vinegar over blossoms until jar is full. Set in a sunny window for 2 to 3 weeks. Strain vinegar to remove blossoms (note the lovely lavender to pink color that has been transferred to the vinegar). Pour vinegar into bottles for use, or in decorative bottles for gifts. Hints for bottling: I use and recycle clear beer bottles. Wash and soak off the labels. Fill with chive vinegar. Cap with recycled wine bottle corks or plastic bottle caps purchased in housewares store.

Herbed Oils

Mary Murray

These are less common than vinegars, but just as useful for gift giving. Try really spicing an oil up for use in your oriental wok, great for stir-fried foods. Another oil made with Mediterranean herbs like thyme and rosemary makes a quick pasta sauce. How about a barbecue oil made with garlic, chili, rosemary, and other herbs used to baste grilled meats, or as a marinade. Oil with peppermint, garlic, cumin, coriander, cloves, and fennel adds a Middle East flavor to your foods.

Here's how to make herbed oil:

Simply add the desired herbs and spices to the oil (olive oil is the best, but you can also use a good vegetable oil) and steep in a closed bottle or container in a warm, but not hot, place for a few weeks before using. Open the jar, strain out the bruised herbs by pouring through a coffee filter. Return oil to a clean bottle or container with fresh sprigs of the herb you used to flavor the oil.

Cucumber Dill Sauce

So chilly and fresh!

1 c. water
1 c. sugar
1 T. salt
1/3 c. white vinegar
cucumber, peeled, seeded and diced
1 c. sour cream
1 T. fresh dill, chopped

Combine water, sugar, salt and vinegar. When sugar and salt are dissolved, add cucumber. Refrigerate 1 hour before serving. When ready to serve, drain cucumber, fold into sour cream and add dill. Makes 4 servings.

INDEX

birdhouses · watering cans · clay pots · garden gloves · bumblebees · annuals · topiaries · herbal oils & vinegars · relax | wheelbarrows · herbal tea · farm · fresh memories · garden journal · perennials · flower boxes · posies · lemonade · edible flowers · wreaths · herbs · seeds · gardeny delights ·

Gooseberry Patch Originals

WELCOME HOME for the HOLIDAYS
your companion from ★ September through December

Welcome Home For The Holidays

~ from harvest through Christmas...a treasury of holiday recipes, decorating tips, traditions & easy-to-make gifts

Old-Fashioned Country Christmas

A holiday keepsake of recipes, traditions, homemade gifts, decorating ideas, & favorite childhood memories

OLD-FASHIONED COUNTRY COOKIES
hundreds of recipes, tips, & ideas

Old-Fashioned Country Cookies

Yummy recipes, tips, traditions, how-to's, and sweet memories...everything Cookies

OLD-FASHIONED COUNTRY CHRISTMAS
our all-time BEST SELLER!

GOOD FOR YOU!
recipes, fun ideas, heartwarming stories, good for body, mind, soul

For Bees & Me

FOR BEES & ME
garden-fresh recipes, backyard entertaining & gifts from the garden

A Bouquet of Garden-Fresh Recipes, Memories, Hints, Simple Pleasures, Herbal Beauty Do's and Backyard Entertainment & Easy-to-Make Gifts

Good For You!

A collection of good food, good fun, good stories for the body, mind & soul!

Gooseberry Patch Originals

Reserve your copies today!.....

HOMESPUN CHRISTMAS
A heartwarming collection of Christmas recipes, tips and ideas

Homespun Christmas
Treasured family recipes, memories, homemade decorations, heartfelt gifts & holiday traditions

Collect the WHOLE Set!

Celebrate Spring
A freshly gathered bouquet of tender recipes, brand new how-tos and tempting tips for the joyous days of springtime.

Celebrate Summer
A star-spangled collection of luscious recipes, carefree tips and easy how-to's for long, lazy summer days.

Celebrate Autumn
A bushel of fresh-picked fall recipes, tips & how-to's for the festive season of friends & family.

Celebrate Winter
A warmhearted collection of recipes for joyful holidays, sparkling celebrations & cozy fireside feasts.

birdhouses · watering cans · clay pots · garden gloves · bumblebees · annuals · topiaries · herbal oils & vinegars · relax (wheelbarrows · herbal tea · farm· fresh memories · garden journal · perennials · flower boxes · posies · lemonade · edible flowers · wreaths · herbs · seeds · gardeny delights ·

birdhouses · watering cans · clay pots · garden gloves · bumblebees · annuals · topiaries · herbal oils & vinegars · relax (wheelbarrows · herbal tea · farm-fresh memories · garden journal · perennials · flower boxes · posies · lemonade · edible flowers · wreaths · herbs · seeds · gardeny delights ·

birdhouses · watering cans · clay pots · garden gloves · bu

mblebees · annuals · topiaries · herbal oils & vinegars · relax { wheelbarrows · herbal tea · far

m- fresh memories · garden journal · perennials · flower bo

oxes · posies · lemonade · edible flowers · wreaths · herbs · seeds · gardeny delights ·

Gooseberry Patch
149 Johnson Drive
Department BOOK
Delaware, OH 43015

A Country Store In Your Mailbox

Please send me the following Gooseberry Patch books:

Book	Quantity	Price	Total
Old-Fashioned Country Christmas	————	$14.95	————
Welcome Home for the Holidays	————	$14.95	————
Old-Fashioned Country Cookies	————	$14.95	————
For Bees & Me	————	$17.95	————
Good For You!	————	$14.95	————
Homespun Christmas	————	$14.95	————
Celebrate Spring	————	$12.95	————
Celebrate Summer	————	$12.95	————
Celebrate Autumn	————	$12.95	————
Celebrate Winter	————	$12.95	————
Coming Home for Christmas	————	$14.95	————
Family Favorites	————	$14.95	————

Merchandise Total ————
Ohio Residents add 6 1/4% ————
Shipping & handling: Add $2.50 for each book. Call for special delivery prices. ————
Total ————

*Quantity discounts and special shipping prices available when purchasing
6 or more books. Call and ask! Wholesale inquiries invited.*

Name: ————————————————————————

Address: ——————————————————————

City: ———————————— State: ———— Zip: ——————

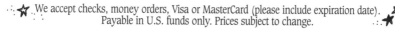

We accept checks, money orders, Visa or MasterCard (please include expiration date).
Payable in U.S. funds only. Prices subject to change.

birdhouses · watering cans · clay pots · garden gloves · bumblebees · annuals · topiaries · herbal oils & vinegars · relax · wheelbarrows · herbal tea · farm-fresh memories · garden journal · perennials · flower boxes · posies · lemonade · edible flowers · wreaths · herbs · seeds · gardeny delights ·